T0043286

Cameron Douglas

LONG WAY HOME

Cameron Douglas is an actor, writer, and filmmaker.
He lives in Los Angeles.

LONG WAY HOME

LONG WAY HOME

A Memoir of Fame, Family, and Redemption

Cameron Douglas

VINTAGE BOOKS
A Division of Penguin Random House LLC
New York

FIRST VINTAGE BOOKS EDITION, SEPTEMBER 2020

Copyright © 2019 by Cameron Douglas

All rights reserved. Published in the United States by Vintage Books,
a division of Penguin Random House LLC, New York, and distributed
in Canada by Penguin Random House Canada Limited, Toronto.
Originally published in hardcover in the United States by Alfred A. Knopf,
a division of Penguin Random House LLC, New York, in 2019.

Vintage and colophon are registered trademarks of Penguin Random House LLC.

Some names and identifying details have been changed
to protect the privacy of individuals.

The Library of Congress has cataloged the Knopf edition as follows:
Name: Douglas, Cameron, author.
Title: Long way home / Cameron Douglas.
Description: First Edition. | New York : Alfred A. Knopf, 2019.
Identifiers: LCCN 2019002253
Subjects: LCSH: Douglas, Cameron, 1978– | Douglas, Cameron, 1978—Family. |
Drug addicts–Biography.
Classification: LCC HV5805.D68 A3 2019 | DDC 362.29092 B —dc23
LC record available at https://lccn.loc.gov/2019002253

Vintage Books Trade Paperback ISBN: 978-0-525-56245-0
eBook ISBN: 978-0-525-52084-9

Book design by M. Kristen Bearse

www.vintagebooks.com

Printed in the United States of America
10   9   8   7   6   5   4   3   2   1

I dedicate this book to my mother and father, who never faltered in their love or gave up on me in the face of a relentless tide of nightmares. I can only now begin to imagine how difficult it must have been for you.

And to my loving family:
Pappy, Granny, Anne, Catherine, Viviane, Lua, Dylan, Carys, Hudson, Hawk, and Imara, thank you not just for affording me the opportunity to come back into your lives but for welcoming me back with open arms.
You all are my heart and soul and the force that drives me.

Contents

PART ONE

Caged

I am in a cage
Underwater
Only my neck and head above

I hear panic and bedlam
All around
Then I see . . .
Glistening onyx serpentine shapes
Gliding on the water
Such deadly enticing grace they possess
Leaving thy silver wake
Infinitely kissed by the Sun
Flick of the tongue
Now it is me
That is their intention
So close I can realize the cunning death in their eyes
"Calm yourself" I say as they
Swirl around me
Whispering into my ears
Serpentine tongue licking at my resolve
Searching for the scent

Then a splash
Warmth surges through my body
I sense acutely the water's caress
Streaming past me peacefully
A moment
And I can see
That most elegant onyx design
Melting into the distance.
Perhaps
The redolence they sought
Was naught
In me

I remain caged
Head
Just above the water's surface

U.S. Department of Justice
Federal Bureau of Prisons

70707-054

DOUGLAS
CAMERON
DOB: 12-13-1978   Eye: BL   Ht: 5'11"

Vending

INMATE

1

2004: "Don't Gaslight Me"

Ever since Mom and Dad's divorce, they've shared custody of S'Estaca, their cliffside property in Spain, on the northwest coast of the island of Mallorca. Mom has it July 15 to New Year's Day. Dad gets it the other half of the year.

On a breezy July day when I'm twenty-five, Dad, my friend Erin, and I are eating lunch on the veranda, which is shaded with a vine-covered trellis and overlooks the sea. The woman serving lunch comes over and tells Dad he has a phone call. He leaves to take it in the bar, a good twenty-five yards away. A minute later I hear a high-pitched sound, a keening moan that is human, but I can't tell who it is. "Oh no, oh no, oh no." I stand up and run toward the person, realizing finally that it is Dad. My heart drops into my stomach. I've never heard him make that sound. Something devastating must have happened. He puts down the phone and turns toward me. He's crying. "We've lost Eric," he says.

Eric is Uncle Eric, Dad's half brother. The call was from the New York City Police Department. Someone flagged down a cruiser after finding Eric in his apartment this morning. He had overdosed and, at the age of forty-six, is dead.

As long as I can remember, Eric was battling some pretty serious demons. He was often having conflict with Pappy, my grandfather, who's been amazing to me but is a tough guy and, as I understand it, could be hard on his children. Pappy is known to the world as Kirk Douglas, the international box-office star of the 1950s and '60s, a Hollywood legend nearly as famous for his conquests (Lana Turner, Ava Gardner, Rita Hayworth) as for his illustrious career acting in movies like *Champion, Lust for Life, Paths of Glory, The Bad and the Beautiful,* and *Spartacus.* He scored three Best Actor Academy Award nominations in the process, rebelled against the studio system by starting his own independent production company, and also broke the Hollywood blacklist, hiring Dalton Trumbo to write *Spartacus* under his own name. In the summer of 2004, Pappy is still vital at eighty-seven, and despite experiencing a stroke eight years ago, he has now outlived one of his sons.

We all knew that Eric was gay, but he wasn't out. It's something he clearly wrestled with, and I believe was tormented by. Although I think the family would have accepted his sexuality unreservedly, he may have feared otherwise, given that Douglas men tend toward a square-jawed breed of masculinity.

Eric tried on many hats, professionally. Beyond a handful of roles (like a made-for-TV movie in which he played the younger, flashback version of Pappy's character, and an episode of *Tales from the Crypt,* in which he played the son of Pappy's character), he got little traction as an actor.

In recent years, he'd been trying to make it as a comedian, and from what I've heard, he was pretty good at it. But he was angry, and most of his jokes made fun of Pappy and Dad, known to other people as Michael Douglas. From Eric's point of view, Dad, given the success he'd found, should have looked out for his brothers more. Dad had tried to be supportive, going to several of Eric's comedy shows, but then he had to sit there and listen to a series of jokes ridiculing him and Pappy and, most painfully, Eric himself: "There's Kirk, Michael, and me. Oscar winner, Oscar winner, and Oscar Mayer wiener."

Eric and I had a warm relationship, but he had a hair-trigger temper that could be frightening. I remember once, when I was a toddler, being with him at a convenience store, where he got into a fight and was beaten up in front of me. Dad and Mom would often say things to me like "You don't want to turn out like Eric." This disturbed me on several levels. Beyond sharing a famous last name and a drug dependency, a combination that made both of us newsworthy to tabloids, I didn't think I was anything like Eric. It bothered me that they thought I *might* be like him. Deep down, I suppose I was most upset by the fear that in some essential way I *was* like him.

I feel enormous pride in our family. It's with a mix of reverence and awe that I look at the careers of both Pappy and Dad. Eric's life, ruined by impossible expectations both real and imagined, was the more typical one for a star's son. Dad's success, equal to if not greater than his father's, is something that almost never happens in the second generation of Hollywood families. He has won Oscars as both a producer (Best Picture for *One Flew Over the Cuckoo's Nest*) and an actor (Best Actor for playing Gordon "Greed Is Good" Gekko in *Wall Street*), and has made enormous amounts of money in a career that has also included iconic films like *Romancing the Stone, Fatal Attraction,* and *Basic Instinct.* Fifty-nine and silver-haired when Eric dies, Dad remains a force in the industry.

I'm sure Eric felt that pride too, but I can also relate to the pressure he felt and his struggle being a Douglas. It's strange growing up seeing your father and grandfather as giants projected on screens and billboards. It's unnerving to walk into rooms full of people who know all kinds of things about you, or think they do, while you know nothing about them. It's diminishing to be perceived mainly as someone else's son or brother, and it's hard to develop a sense of yourself as a person intrinsically worthy of others' respect. How do you compete with Kirk Douglas? How do you live in Michael Douglas's shadow?

The NYPD called Dad first, and now it's his responsibility to tell Pappy and Anne, Pappy's wife of fifty years, that their son is dead. After he makes the call, I have never seen such utter panic and raw sadness in Dad. He arranges to fly to L.A., and I follow close behind. In the limousine that brings us all to the cemetery, everyone's quiet. Throughout the funeral service and burial at the cemetery in Westwood where Marilyn Monroe was buried, I feel physically queasy, with an anxiety I don't allow myself to pinpoint.

I cry only once, when Oma, as Anne likes her grandchildren to call her, almost passes out while she stands over Eric's grave throwing dirt onto the coffin. I don't feel the depth of emotion that I know I should, and it's not a huge mystery why. I'm a bona-fide liquid-cocaine addict. Drugs are my number one priority, and my most reliable friend. They're always there for me, in bad times and worse.

Afterward, there's a reception at Pappy's house in Beverly Hills. Pappy speaks. Oma tries to but is overcome by grief. They'd gone through so many struggles with Eric, and I believe they were recently in a tough-love phase, so on top of everything else they feel guilt. I feel guilty too, because toward the end of his life Eric reached out several times to get together, but I heeded Dad's advice to stay away from him. We spoke on the phone, and I told Eric I loved him, but I wish now that I had been there for him more. His life was so tortured. There was a tempest inside him that created a tempest around him.

For Dad, Eric's death hits even closer to home. Dad was in rehab for drinking and drugging in the early '90s. His brother Joel, my uncle Jojo, has struggled with both alcohol and drug abuse. And then

Uncle Eric.

there's me. I've been using and abusing drugs since I was thirteen. I've been in and out of trouble, and in and out of treatment. My current addiction is particularly nasty: I inject coke as often as three times an hour when I'm on a run. My once-promising career as a DJ has been destroyed by my irresponsibility. I've had opportunities to make a life in acting and squandered them. I've hardly been giving my family, or myself, reasons to feel proud. When Dad looks at me, recently, I don't see love; I see concern and sadness and frustration. When we talk, it's usually a tense interaction about money or the latest way I've disappointed him. Maybe I really am like Eric. But I don't want to die the way he did. And in the grip of a young man's sense of immortality, I'm not afraid that I will.

As soon as I can, I slip away. I tell myself that there's nothing for me to do here, no way to help, nothing for anyone to do now. The worst-case scenario has already happened.

Within days of the funeral, Erin and I return to Spain, which we're using as our base while I do some lingering DJ gigs around Europe.

When I met Erin, I had just broken up with Amanda, my girlfriend of five years. Our relationship had been tumultuous and off-key and had gone on way too long—to the point where, when it ended, I resolved not to get into another serious relationship.

Erin was a sub-promoter at Go, where I spun a midnight set on Thursdays, and my biggest fan. She had been premed at Villanova, then worked in the IVF clinic at New York-Cornell Hospital. After two of her roommates and best friends died on 9/11, and her long-time boyfriend had a psychological crisis and broke up with her, Erin turned away from her old life, deciding to live in the moment.

She was attractive and warm, and we started hanging out. Then she started working for me; with Amanda gone, I needed someone to keep me organized and on track with my commitments, and Erin traveled with me wherever I went for DJ gigs. We'd also sleep together. I told her, as I told any woman I became involved with after Amanda: *Buyer beware.* I wouldn't be her boyfriend, and she should know that up-front. So my relationship with Erin is more than just friendly, but she isn't my girlfriend. She accepts this arrangement, and our emotional connection is real: I have a lot of love to give, and when I am focused on her, I offer genuine affection. I consider her family. Like me, she is a drug addict.

Dad isn't here, and Mom isn't here, so we stay in the compound's main house, in the master bedroom. Erin, who speaks Spanish, goes to a pharmacy to get us needles, claiming she has diabetes. I drive forty-five minutes to score coke at a strip club in Palma. Eric's fate is already out of my head. My urge to get high is stronger than any fear his death should sensibly inspire. I take Old Bessie, an ancient Range Rover that belonged to my grandmother Pat, Mom's mother, who I called Nana. It's a big car, with a huge, metal ram bar in front, and on the way back, taking a narrow turn, I sideswipe a line of parked cars. I leave my phone number on one of the windshields but never hear from anyone about it.

Then Mom hears from her best friend, Luisa, who's known me since I was a kid, and who is also staying at S'Estaca. Luisa has observed that I stay inside all day and come out only at night. One morning, I pass her and notice her looking at my arms. They are ravaged, scabbed over with track marks. Usually I tie bandannas around them, but I wasn't expecting to run into her. Luisa immediately calls Mom, who tells Dad, who calls me and says they don't want us staying in the main house anymore. We can stay in a guest cottage. I feel like I have a contagious disease. Maybe I do.

In early September, back in New York, I run into Amanda at the 60 Thompson hotel in SoHo. I met Amanda when I was nineteen and she was twenty-three. She had nightclub contacts in Manhattan, and got me hired as a DJ. We became fast friends, and within a couple of months boyfriend and girlfriend. She was a balancing influence who gave me structure and stability, and she was instrumental in building my DJ career. I loved her, but she was a surrogate mother more than anything, which made it both hard to break up with her and hard for me to remain faithful to her. Nothing takes the romance out of a relationship like feeling that you're dating your mom. Instead of finding the courage to end things, I stayed in the relationship much longer than I should have, cheating on her, hating myself for it, and hating her, irrationally, for "making" me do something that made me hate myself. It was a volatile, tortured relationship.

Since finally breaking up, three years ago, we've remained dramatically entangled; Amanda is an unstable figure lurking on the fringes of my life, part angel of mercy, part agent of chaos. I genuinely love and respect her, and, when we're getting along, I enjoy being with her. But she is still *in love* with me. We want different things from the relationship, but neither of us has the wisdom or strength to accept that; so we never fully go our separate ways.

When I told her we should take a break, her response was to form an alliance with Mom, who took her on as her assistant and invited her to live with her, first in New York and now in Santa Barbara, where Amanda is living in my childhood bedroom. Their real bond is a shared preoccupation with my destructive choices, degenerate behavior, and relationship with Erin, who they blame for my downward spiral.

Before Amanda left New York, she had basically become a spy for Mom and Dad, and she'd sometimes show up at the apartment where I live with Erin and a few friends and cause a scene. It's a fifth-floor two-bedroom in Greenwich Village that I'm paying for, and which is dominated by a Balinese opium bed in the living room. We're a makeshift little family of addicts.

At the Thompson, Amanda's eyes flick to the sweatband covering my elbow.

"You have track marks."

"What the fuck are you talking about, Amanda?"

"Don't gaslight me. I can see the track marks on your elbow."

"You're a fucking lying psycho bitch. I'm not doing anything. Stop telling my parents I'm doing this stuff. 'Cause I'm not."

I'm not trying to scare her—she's tough, and not really scareable—but I'm tired of her meddling and need to make her understand that she needs to stop talking about me. This is wishful thinking, but it feels good to vent. I know she's going to call Dad, so I beat her to it.

He seems to believe my story that I'm being harassed by my crazy ex-girlfriend. I have become a fluent liar.

The next day, Amanda storms into the apartment and finds me in the closet off my bedroom. I spend most of my time there now—shooting coke, wearing outlandish clothes, and imagining imminent police raids. When Amanda shows up, I have a needle in my arm. She berates me, slaps me, grabs my box of hypodermics, and leaves in a huff as I shout after her. Then I find Erin, who's on the couch in the living room grinding her jaw, and yell at her for leaving the door to the apartment open.

I'm sure Amanda has already called Mom to say I'm out of control. I know Amanda's staying with her friend Jackie on the Upper East Side, and I cab up there to tell her to leave me the fuck alone. Amanda refuses to buzz me in, and Erin and I get into a fight on the corner of Seventy-Fifth and Madison, while a large man nearby watches a little too intently.

I know I'm out of control: I'm an addict; I'm not crazy.

Dad calls. I haven't seen him since Eric's funeral. Our lives couldn't be more different. He lives on an estate overlooking Hamilton Harbour in Bermuda, where Granny grew up. He's now married to Catherine Zeta-Jones, and the two of them, paparazzi magnets with two young children to raise, moved there for privacy a couple of years ago.

I know he's been in New York for the past two weeks, staying at his apartment on the Upper West Side, but I wasn't expecting to hear from him after our short conversation yesterday. "Hey, Cam," he says, "I'm going out of town tomorrow, but I'd really like to spend some time with you before I go, just to talk and see where everything's at."

This makes me feel great, and I say, "Absolutely, I'd love that." For the man I respect most in my life to call me in this precarious moment feels something like divine intervention. I'm excited that I'm going to see Dad, and optimistic about mending our relationship.

With Dad at a Red Cross benefit.

The next day, he comes to the Village, and I go downstairs to meet him in front of the building. I bring Junior, my chocolate Lab, along, so he can get a walk in. Friends often tell me that Junior is me in dog form, which makes me so proud, because Junior is an exceptional animal: loyal, smart, and sweet, with an adorable habit of licking Erin's hamster. Dad and I stroll down University Place to Washington Square Park and find a bench.

As we sit there, he talks about what happened to Eric, the pain his addictions caused for him and his family, and Dad's fear of something similar happening to me.

"Cameron, you're fucked up."

Being compared to Eric again is hard to hear, but I can't argue. What I say next is actually the truth.

"You're right, Dad, I am fucked up. I do want to make some changes. I really appreciate you coming down to talk to me like this." For a long time, my relationships with him and Mom have been shadowed by my drug use and their frustrated responses to it. There's not a lot of trust on either side.

Dad talks about Erin, saying she's an enabler. He talks about my roommate Jay, my closest friend since childhood. When we were growing up, Jay was easygoing, everyone liked him, and he was a good sidekick, always down for whatever. We were both distant from our families. His father lived somewhere else, his mother was religious to the point of not acknowledging Jay's issues, and his stepfather was an asshole. We found love and support in each other and said we were brothers. We each have a tattoo of the other's initials on the back of our left arm. People always ask, "Where's Cameron and Jay?" Dad thinks Jay is the worst thing that ever happened to me. Jay doesn't have a job, or any of the other traits a parent looks for in a friend of their child's. He's a freeloader. He got me into shooting coke. Normally I'm defensive about my friends. This time I say, "I hear you."

For the next half hour, I open up to Dad. I agree that it's time for me to straighten up and get my life figured out. I've been making good money touring as a DJ in Europe, but it doesn't cover the cost of supporting myself and my friends and our drug habits. The bookings are dwindling, and I'm embarrassed that I still have to ask Dad for help. He listens. He doesn't judge me. He says to quit DJing. Relocate to California. "Get away from your drug family, Cam." I'm moved and happy. We've had a meaningful, productive conversation.

He's flying to Scotland tonight, on a golf vacation, and says he'd better get going. As we head back toward my building, Dad pans his head, like he's searching for something. Then he says, "Junior's a really great dog, he's so obedient; do you mind if I walk him?"

"Absolutely," I say, handing over the leash.

As we reach my block, Dad's looking around again. This time I follow his gaze, and notice a big guy stealthily walking behind us. Dad starts to speed-walk away from me, pulling Junior with him. Now I see that, in addition to the guy behind us, who is quickening his pace, there are two more hulking dudes barreling out of a van parked by the curb and coming swiftly toward me. One of them is the guy who I saw on the Upper East Side a few days ago, watching me and Erin fight. Dad is now on the far side of the sidewalk, and as the three guys surround me, I go into fight-or-flight mode.

"Fuck you, Dad!"

"You need help, Cameron."

The goons start trying to reason with me. I say, "I don't know what the fuck you think is going to happen right now, but I can promise you it's not going to turn out well." I'm a cornered animal, and they can see that.

They look at Dad and shake their heads, like: *We're calling it off.*

I grab Junior's leash from Dad.

"You're a fucking pussy," I say. "All you had to do was ask me to get in that car, and I'd have gone."

I am furious and really hurt. The fact that Dad is motivated by concern doesn't matter to me. I feel crushed and betrayed. I know that Dad, with some justification, firmly believes that I'm full of shit when I say I would have gotten into that car if only he'd asked me to. But after our talk, I felt a connection with him that I hadn't felt in a long time. Doesn't he know how much I love him and look up to him and want to do right by him? Can't he have some faith in me?

I stop answering his calls. For a few more months, I continue traveling for gigs. But things feel like they've gotten as bad as they can get. The coke has chewed my life to pieces, and I want so badly to be off it. I have nothing going for me. I have no money of my own. I really do want to get away from the club scene. I decide to focus on acting. It's something I know, it's in my blood, and in October I move to L.A., hoping to reset my life.

2

Mom

Mom was nineteen when she married Dad in 1977, and twenty when she had me. Later, she'd say we grew up together.

At first we lived on Tower Grove Drive, in Beverly Hills. Then Dad bought a place in Santa Barbara, and we started spending more time there.

In my earliest memories, Mom is young and beautiful and full of music. She was finishing college at UCLA and would do her homework while I played on the floor. Together we'd drive around Los Angeles in her silver Ferrari, Mom belting out Hall & Oates and other '80s hits, fully committing to each song, as if she were auditioning for something. At home, we'd dance to my favorite record by the Talking Heads—who I called the Talking Potatoes—boinging around the living room, which looked out onto a lawn and pool and the city below. At night, when Mom put me to bed, we'd pretend we were radio DJs and do a little jazz routine, taking turns on the different instruments. "Okay, Cameron, take it away." I'd do a high-hat hiss. Mom would play sax. I'd switch to trumpet. She'd go to drums. As I fell asleep, she'd give me "softies," gently stroking my back.

With Dad away working eight, ten months of the year, and Mom left to raise me on her own, when I was five Dad agreed to move us all to

New York. Mom had friends there, and she seemed to find her footing as a model, working for Eileen Ford and appearing on the cover of the first issue of *Mirabella*. She raised money for the Red Cross and became a producer of documentaries for the Metropolitan Museum of Art's film and television division. Some nights, after the museum closed for the day, Mom and I would wander through the Temple of Dendur and the galleries of medieval knights' armor.

Mom had an affinity for unusual pets. When I was a toddler in California, I had a large, floppy-eared rabbit who would sit on my high chair nibbling carrots while I stuffed SpaghettiOs in my mouth. In New York, I got a ferret named Tiki. He liked to nip hands, so I'd go into Mom's closet and take her long, leather evening gloves, which protected my hands but were destroyed in the process.

Mom's own animals were another level of exotic. In Manhattan, she got a serval—a small, leopard-like wildcat native to the sub-Saharan savanna and illegal to own in about half of the fifty states. Ours, which Mom named Sangral, was a baby when we got him but quickly showed his hunting instincts. I'd walk into the kitchen in the morning, and Sangral would assume a defensive crouch and hiss at me. Sometimes, in the middle of the night, I'd wake up with him on my chest, licking his chops. On other occasions, he climbed out the window onto a narrow ledge that ringed the Kenilworth, our building on Central Park West. I'm sure people on the street were wondering what a zoo animal was doing there. I had the feeling that Dad secretly hoped Sangral would fall off. We'd lure him back inside with dog food, his favorite—but he would eat anything. We were always rushing him to the veterinarian, who'd pull oddities out of his stomach: a glove, a piece of rubber, kitchen refuse.

One of Sangral's favorite stalking games was sneaking up on you and pouncing. Once, Dad was in the sitting room at the apartment, having tea with Janie Wenner, Jann's wife, when Sangral leaped, landing on Dad's head. Dad wrestled with him as I giggled and Janie sat there in shock.

"Michael, what's going on?"

Dad finally threw the cat off and said, "Don't worry, that's Diandra's pet."

"You're bleeding."

Dad had a gash on his eyebrow.

"It's all right."

"It's not all right, Michael, it's pretty crazy."

We took Sangral with us when we moved back to Santa Barbara, where Mom had a zoo-like enclosure built for him, but eventually she realized he should be in something closer to his natural habitat and gave him away.

With Dad still traveling for months at a time, Mom young and unhappy and isolated, and me her only child, I became her confidant—her receiver of rants and soother of bruised feelings. I learned that Dad's prolonged absences weren't the only marital hardship Mom had to endure. When I was seven and we were in Aspen, she held up a little plastic bag with what looked like the dried flowers she used to make the bathroom smell nice. But these plants were the color of moss and a lot smellier.

"Do you know what this is, Cameron? This is a *drug*. Your father is using *drugs*."

Because of this and other evidence she presented to me, I said, "We've got to pack our stuff and get out of here before he comes home and finds out."

I proudly saw myself as her rescuing knight.

Mom began looking elsewhere for her fulfillment, and she took to going away on her own adventures, sometimes for weeks at a time. I'd ask her, when she put me to bed, "Are you going out tonight?"

"I don't think so."

"So you aren't?"

"No."

I'd wake up in the middle of the night, go to my door, look down the hall, and see her door open, with the light on. I'd run down there and find her bed empty and undisturbed.

Some people are born with a sense of rhythm. Mom was born with innate style. Dad was practical and unconcerned with how he looked; he got away with a lot, fashionwise, because he was a movie star. Mom had a huge closet filled with priceless dresses and jewelry, and she had a visionary gift for design. Under her exacting direction, our homes were impeccably rehabbed, decorated, and made over.

Our house in Montecito, on Hot Springs Road, had big wrought-iron gates, and a long driveway bisecting the property on its way to the house. Mom turned a huge untamed area of rough bushes at the bottom of the estate into a beautiful Japanese meditation garden with koi and a teahouse. She put in a tennis court, fountains, a den, and quarters for the help. She regraded the hill that sloped down to the pool, creating an enfilade effect. She trucked in palm trees. She called the property by its original name, La Quinta.

Mom was born in Washington, D.C., where her naval officer father, Robert Luker, worked for the Defense Department, running a project exploring the use of nuclear explosions to propel spacecraft, but she grew up largely on Mallorca. Her mother, Pat, or Patricia, was supposedly from a shipping family; she had studied at the Sorbonne, where she met her future husband, then stationed in Paris.

Mom's parents split up when she was six, and she had a lonely childhood. Pat was a beautiful, fascinating woman—an adventuress, a pilot, an archaeologist, and a writer. She would bring her daughter, Dia, along on her digs, or with her to Venice, where Pat sometimes spent summers studying at a monastery library on one of the city's islands. But Pat already had brain tumors that wouldn't be diagnosed until years later, and she was hardly a roaring hearth of maternal warmth. She enjoyed her freedom and male company, and she rarely spoke about her own family history. She always said she was of mixed

English and Spanish ancestry, that she was a cousin of the Spanish king, Juan Carlos de Borbón, and that her maiden name was de Morrell—the middle name she gave Mom—but Pat's wedding announcement in a 1945 newspaper gave her name as Patricia Portland, and said she was from Australia.

Mom knew even less about her father. He'd been injured at Pearl Harbor and become an alcoholic, and after Mom was sent off to Ecolint, a boarding school in Geneva, when she was seven, she stopped seeing him. A few years later, when she was walking with a friend in the town square, Mom saw her father walking toward her. As he approached, she was about to say hello, but he just kept walking. He hadn't seen her in so long that he didn't recognize her. He died from heart disease when she was fourteen.

The house in Montecito.

During summer breaks, Mom went back to Mallorca and stayed with Pat at Miramar, a house near Valldemossa, on the northwest coast, which had belonged to the Habsburg archduke Luis Salvador. It had no electricity. Tanks of compressed gas powered the refrigerator, a record player, and other appliances. Whatever her parents' shortcomings, Mom grew up in a culturally and intellectually rich environment, surrounded by writers and artists like Joan Miró and Kenneth Noland. Robert Graves came over for tea every afternoon at four. Mom rode Andalusian horses and became skilled at dressage.

Starting when I was seven, we spent every summer in Mallorca. At first we stayed at a hotel in Deià, the beautiful little town populated by expatriate artists who'd visited and never left. When I was twelve, shortly after Dad won his Best Actor Oscar, he and Mom decided to buy their own place, and the three of us spent days hiking across beautiful fincas, looking for the perfect property. Once, we went for ice cream, and I can still picture Mom taking a bite from a cone and then Dad taking a bite from the ice cream in her mouth. It's a moment that has stuck with me, a rare memory of when things were still good between them. Maybe because those were the years before their marriage curdled, and maybe because it was a time before I grew angry and detached and got into drugs, Mallorca holds wholesome, innocent associations for me.

They ended up buying a piece of land next to Miramar. S'Estaca, the name given to the site centuries earlier by a Moorish conqueror, was magical. Two hundred and forty-seven cliffside acres of pine and olive and orange and almond trees plunged down to the ultramarine sea. The whitewashed stone house at the center of the property dated to the nineteenth century, when it had belonged to the Habsburg archduke. Mom was even more ambitious for S'Estaca than for the house in Montecito. She began a grand restoration, which was a precarious undertaking. The house was off the road to Puerto de Valldemossa, a long, steep, corkscrewing ribbon of asphalt wide enough for only one car, and with a sheer drop-off on one side. Visitors would be terrified by the time they got to our gate, and then would have to navigate the dirt driveway—which was equally thin and treacherous, and went on for three quarters of a mile before it reached the house.

In the beginning, there were huge trenches along the route, and the workmen stretched boards over them so their trucks could get through. The whole project took many years. Once the main construction was out of the way, adding the details and accoutrements was a massive undertaking in itself.

Eventually the house became a compound, with seven different buildings, a cobbled driveway, grassy terraces stepping down to the Mediterranean, a Moroccan-themed guesthouse and an Italian one, and star-lights cut into the concrete base of the pool, which was directly above the kitchen. Long before "sustainability" was a buzz-word, Mom designed S'Estaca to be self-sufficient, with generators, organic vegetable gardens, preserves, organic wine, spring water, fish from the port, and forest deadwood for the fireplace. S'Estaca was Mom's masterpiece.

At the house, I'd tag along everywhere with Juán, the caretaker. Deià, which was nearby, had an arty, commune-like vibe. Many of the residents were foreigners, and my friends were their children. S'Estaca was always fun and filled with people. Dad would swim out into the bay of the Cala Deià, and I would follow him with Shirk, our giant schnauzer, paddling behind me. Eventually I'd turn back, but Shirk would follow Dad all the way out and then, when they were both tired, back in to the beach.

S'Estaca was also where Puma, a capuchin monkey Mom got after Sangral, lived year-round. Puma was a baby when we got her. At night she slept next to me, in a bed I made for her in a shoebox, and I fed her with a dropper. During the day, she'd attach herself to me while I walked around, hugging my wrist or ankle. Monkeys show affection by grooming each other, and she'd act like I had thick fur, weeding through it and pretending she'd found a bug and was putting it in her mouth. Then I'd do the same to her.

As Puma got older, she became more aggressive. She liked to collect things, and guests lying around the pool at S'Estaca would catch her grabbing a set of keys with one hand, a wallet with the other, and a pack of cigarettes with one foot. If you wanted to light your cigarette and approached her to reclaim your Zippo, Puma would start rapidly puffing her cheeks in and out, like she was hyperventilating. If you reached for your property, she might drop it, jump on you, and bite you. People started refusing to come to the house if she was going to be outside, so Puma spent increasing amounts of time in her cage, which only made her behavior more erratic, until it became difficult to let her out if guests were around.

Eventually, Mom would get a miniature baby owl named Merline.

With Mom and Dad in Spain.

——

When I was a kid, I chafed at Mom's tendency toward grandeur. Before every plane trip, she'd dress me up in a suit and tie, like Little Lord Fauntleroy, over my scowling objections. I'd buck at her efforts to keep my hair a certain length. Later, Mom went through a period where she put together Sunday high teas, with finger sandwiches and scones, which I'd smirk my way through but must admit I found extremely tasty. When Mom was around her European or society friends, our dog Pumpkin would suddenly be named Luna, and Mom's voice would acquire a vaguely Continental accent. I was always hyperaware of how she seemed able to turn it on and off at will.

But over time, I came to admire her ease in gliding among different worlds. When she later had a series of assistants, young girls who looked up to her, she became their mentor, changing their lives by teaching them grace and style. Her sense of aesthetics rubbed off on me, as well. I started taking care in how I dressed. It definitely wasn't the clothing Mom would have selected for me, but it was my style, with its own flair.

3

Dad

I don't remember when I first became aware that the man I called Daddy, then Dad, then Pop, wasn't like other fathers, that he didn't belong only to me. When I was a few months old, my godfather, Jann Wenner, put me on the cover of *Rolling Stone,* a naked infant slung over Dad's shoulder and mooning America. As I grew up, there were always people nervously/aggressively/amiably approaching Dad for his autograph. We lived at posh addresses: the house with a view in Beverly Hills, the spacious apartment on Central Park West, the seven-acre estate in Montecito, the compound on Mallorca.

Sometimes I saw him on a screen like everyone else. One time I saw him on a screen and he was talking only to me. When he accepted the Oscar for Best Actor in 1988 for *Wall Street,* I was nine years old and three thousand miles away, at home in New York City, watching as he stood on the stage of the Shrine Auditorium in Los Angeles, looked into the camera, and said, "Good night, Cameron, I love you." If he did this now, I'd feel flattered and proud. At the time, in my kid's mind, it didn't seem like anything special. This was my dad, and he was getting a big award for the thing he'd been doing as far back as I could remember, and he was saying good night to me, and that he loved me. I loved him, too.

In more innocent days, with Dad
at a Rolling Stone *cover shoot.*

At home, Dad was a regular father. He'd read the newspaper over breakfast. He enjoyed simple food. He liked to watch sports. He wasn't focused on how he looked. I was confused about our relationship. I wanted to impress him. I wanted him to be my friend. I felt good when he'd come to my sports games.

When he was away, which was much of the time, he'd call nearly every day at bedtime to say good night. Our relationship was a series of jump cuts, vivid bursts when we were together punctuating longer stretches when we were apart. Each of our times together, and every one of his sporadic gifts to me, felt especially precious.

He'd fly me to see him on set. When I was ten, and he was making *Black Rain* in Japan, I spent a few days in Osaka, where Ridley Scott was shooting the film in a huge steel mill amid gigantic industrial machinery and lots of hot metal and flying sparks. I was really into video games, and Andy Garcia, Dad's costar, was kind, shepherding me around to several of the country's amazing arcades.

Other times, Dad organized bonding trips. Once, just the two of us went on a whitewater rafting trip through the Grand Canyon. Another time, when I was sixteen, he rented a houseboat on Lake Shasta and took me, Uncle Jojo, and my friends John and Jesse.

Later, when I was in and out of juvenile hall, Dad was liberal with me. He let me smoke cigarettes around the house. It made me feel so good, like we were buddies, even though Dad would regularly tell me, "I'm your father, not your friend, Cameron."

When I was seven and we were living in Manhattan, I went to Jeremy Kaplan's birthday party at a studio in midtown, where we watched a magician levitate his assistant and pass a ring around her. Afterward, I was expecting Joaquín, my caretaker, to pick me up, but Dad arrived instead. I hadn't seen him in months and didn't even know he was back in town. He was holding a present, which I thought might be for the birthday boy, because I hadn't brought one. But then Dad said it was for me.

It was a skateboard with a bow tied around it. It had a wood deck, topped with diamond-dust grip tape cut out in the middle to reveal a blue graphic. The underside was an orange-and-black checkerboard. The wheels were a clear, gummy green. It was as tall as me, and I didn't know how to stand on it. I knelt on it with one knee, using the other leg to kick myself forward. It was a chilly day in late fall, but Dad and I walked home that way, me scooting ahead, Dad strolling behind me. The same year, Dad gave me a Yamaha 80 dirt bike. I couldn't believe my good fortune, and I decided then that seven was my lucky number.

Later, after we moved back to Montecito, I'd borrow Dad's Handycam and make short movies. Once, my friend John and I were working on a film starring us, and shot by us, so we handed the camera back and forth to film each other. We shot a motorcycle ride. We filmed in the gym at my house, where Dad worked out when he was getting in shape for a part. The story built to a climactic fistfight between two bodybuilders—us, with not very built bodies, since we were only ten—and we weren't sure how we were going to get the take, since we both needed to be in the shot. We were standing next to the pool. Mom was on a chair, sunbathing, and we considered getting her to hold the camera, but we were skeptical of her cinematography skills.

"Hey, Dad." He was in the Jacuzzi. "Can you help us out?"

He walked over, dripping, and we explained our movie.

Dad went into director mode.

"This just jumped in production value," John said. He was a precocious kid.

We thought we were only going to get one take from Dad, but as he filmed he continued giving directions. We had to rewind the tape and start over.

"That punch is weak, by the way," Dad said.

We looked at him.

"Put your hand by your face." He showed what he meant. I put my right hand on the left side of my face. Dad swung and hit it, and it made a realistic fist-hitting-face sound, without hurting me.

He said, "Do it to me." I did, and the same thing happened, but he also turned his face, recoiling as if he'd just received a serious blow to the head.

"That's how you make a punch look real," he said.

We reshot the scene while Dad filmed. His technique revolutionized our preteen filmmaking.

Dad's relationship with Pappy had its own tensions. Pappy and Diana, Dad's mother, divorced when he was seven years old, and Dad and Jojo spent most of their childhood on the East Coast, where they were raised in Connecticut by Diana, whom I'd know as Granny, and her second husband, Bill Darrid. Bill, my uncle Billy, was Dad's real father figure, and Dad loved him. Pappy, born Issur Danielovitch, had grown up in upstate New York as one of seven children in a Yiddish-speaking home. He later changed his name to Izzy Demsky and then to Kirk Douglas, and he was obsessed with his career. Dad only saw him during holiday breaks, visiting him on set or at his home in Palm Springs, where Burt Lancaster and Tony Curtis were regular guests.

Dad struggled with having a father who loomed so large. "He could do anything," Dad would say later. "He was a fast gun-drawer, he could jump on horses, he could juggle, he could walk the oars of a ship." Pappy was guilt-stricken about his disengagement and wrote letters in which he could be hypercritical. Dad grew up determined to prove he was more than "Little Kirk" and "Little Spartacus," as he was sometimes called as a kid.

Pappy eventually tried to make up for his earlier shortcomings, and he supported Dad's acting and producing ambitions. He attended every one of Dad's stage productions at UC Santa Barbara. He bought the film rights to the Broadway play *Summertree* and made it into a movie, casting Dad in the lead. He starred in the Broadway production of *One Flew Over the Cuckoo's Nest* and later, unable to secure financing for a film version, gave the rights to Dad. That Dad then cast Jack Nicholson rather than Pappy in the lead role, and that both Dad and Jack won Oscars for it, resulted in a long-running beef between Pappy and Dad.

After *Romancing the Stone* became a box-office success and established Dad as a leading man in 1984, his career sped up. Then, between 1987 and 1992, it went to the moon. With *Fatal Attraction, Wall Street,* and *Basic Instinct,* Dad became one of the world's top movie stars. He won that Oscar for *Wall Street.* And between his roles in *Fatal Attraction* and *Basic Instinct,* and the unending tabloid coverage of various affairs he was alleged to be having, he became identified with a certain kind of edgy, sexual, imperfect man. He'd tell me, "Listen, because of my profession, people are really interested in me, and people like to make up stories. You can't believe everything you read or hear." With his late-career success, his net worth ballooned, and during this period he added to our collection of homes, buying S'Estaca in Mallorca and Wildcat Ranch in Aspen. He also became even busier and more stressed. I revered Dad. Every son admires his own father, but everyone in the world admired mine.

My last name was something I was aware of mainly through other kids' reactions to it. When I went to basketball camp at Westmont College in Santa Barbara one summer when I was around ten, and kids from other schools found out who my father was, a pack of them came up to me and asked about him, and I got defensive. Another time, I was at Blockbuster with my friend John, and a clerk scolded us for running around. John said, "Do you know who his father is?" I turned to him and said, "Don't do that. I don't like it." I wanted to be Cameron, not Cameron Douglas.

Every now and then, something would happen that put my family in the news. In 1991, when I was twelve, I remember Dad getting a call about Pappy being in a helicopter crash. The helicopter had plummeted forty feet. Dad was really worried and scared, and I was upset. We watched the TV news and learned that two people had died in the crash. Pappy was bruised from the neck down, black and blue but, miraculously, fine. Since we heard right away that he was okay, I felt almost immediate relief, though I was sad about the people who died. The fact that Pappy didn't even break a bone only added to his aura of being an indestructible champion, a soldier—although, as we'd later find out, he was haunted by survivor guilt.

After the crash, and later a stroke, Pappy changed. He became a better husband, reembraced Judaism, and focused on writing books. Dad's own success, too, healed some of the old wounds. Maybe Dad's repeating of his father's foibles—seemingly putting career before family, and other women before wives—allowed him to empathize with the old man. They became much closer.

When Pappy asked Dad whether he'd been a good father, Dad paused before answering: "Ultimately." Pappy told Dad: "I had it much easier than you. I came from abject poverty, so there was no place to go but up."

Me on the Jewel of the Nile *set.*

I didn't know it then, but Dad was partying heavily through the 1980s. When we still lived in Beverly Hills, every now and then he'd take me out for breakfast on the roof of a hotel on Sunset Boulevard by the 405 exit. In hindsight, it's obvious to me that those were mornings-after, when he'd been out all night.

Dad's temper, when he and Mom were still together, scared me. At the dinner table, if I reached for the salt and accidentally knocked over my glass, he'd explode with anger or else brood silently, his jaw clenched, every pore of his body emitting the unmistakable message: *This fucking fuck-up kid.* When he was around, I walked on eggshells, feeling a persistent low-grade anxiety about provoking his wrath. I developed a tic where I'd put a finger in my hair and keep working it into corkscrews; my hair would become matted. Mom called it the curly-wurlies.

On our Lake Shasta trip, a couple of Jet Skis came with the houseboat, and John and Jesse and I wanted to take them out. "Don't get lost," Dad said. "The boat's going to be moving. Don't lose sight of it."

"Yeah, yeah, yeah," we said. "Sure, sure, sure."

Then we took off on the Jet Skis and couldn't find our way back to the boat. The lake had dozens of finger inlets that all looked the same. It got dark, and when we finally found the boat, hours later, Dad was irate. His arms were raised, his voice high-pitched. John later compared Dad, in that moment, to his angriest scenes in *Basic Instinct* and *Fatal Attraction*. Dad held on to things, and the incident became one of the exhibits he'd trot out to illustrate my knuckleheadedness. I'm sure there was no shortage of those.

With Mom at a costume party.

4

2004: A Consummate Host

L.A. is supposed to be my fresh start, my geographic cure, as such aspirational moves are called in 12-step meetings. I am putting three thousand miles between me and the nightclubs and DJ world that are inextricable from my cocaine use. I am leaving behind my drug family. Jay, whose favorite drug is crystal meth, is moving in with a dealer named Rob, to shoot ketamine and crystal and pornos. Under pressure from my friend Curtis, who I'm moving in with, I've sent Erin back to her family in Pennsylvania. It's probably good for both of us to be apart. I have some royalties coming in from *It Runs in the Family*, a movie I made with Dad and Pappy. I'm in a straight-to-video *National Lampoon* comedy coming out next year. I'm going to pursue an acting career and try to live a healthier life. This is my hope.

Acting appeals to me for both the right and the wrong reasons. I have some experience with it and, I'm told, some talent. It seems to come naturally to me. Unlike DJing, which indulges my most self-destructive appetites, acting offers a path where being an artist and achieving success aren't incompatible with living in a healthy way. It seems like something I have a real shot at. But I don't appreciate the art of it, not really. Or the work it takes to build a career. Or the extraordinary, door-opening advantages of being a Douglas.

Erin comes to visit a couple of weeks later and stays, moving in with me and Curtis in our apartment in Koreatown. Curtis just shakes his head, exasperated, but I guess my resolve to get clean isn't as strong as my attraction to injecting cocaine and the life that goes along with that. What I want and what I need are at odds with each other, not for the first or last time in my life. I'm just not willing to let the drugs, or Erin, go.

I haven't found a regular dealer here yet, but coke isn't hard to come by. Needles are. In New York, we bought packs of insulin syringes over the counter at Duane Reade, but when I send Erin to a pharmacy on Wilshire Boulevard to get more, she returns empty-handed: "They said in California you need a prescription."

"Fuck," I say. "Okay, let's find a needle exchange." There's one in Echo Park, and I wait in the car while Erin goes in and says she is from out of town and has diabetes. They give her a couple of points, which we keep using until the tip breaks off one and the other gets clogged. Then Erin finds a medical supply company online and e-mails them pretending to be in the phlebotomy field, and after that we just order them by the case, ten packs of ten in each one. We get two sizes, shorter and thinner for surface veins, longer and thicker for deeper injections. I've already destroyed the veins in my arms and am quickly tearing my way through the good ones in my legs.

At the apartment in Koreatown, I have my second seizure (my first was back in New York). One moment, Erin is shooting me up. The next thing I know, the doorbell is chiming. "I called an ambulance," Erin says. She has a fat lip from giving me CPR, and I have one too. My chest hurts from the compressions. My face stings where she's slapped me trying to wake me up. I am pissed, and not because Erin has resuscitated me. I am fine, but now, because of medical protocol, I will have to go with the paramedics to the hospital and get checked out.

It's hard to convey the degree to which a serious drug habit muffles emotion, choking off natural feelings and expressing them only in relation to the addiction. The closest I come to feeling any fear for my health or life is when, occasionally, I do a big shot and feel the signs of a possible overdose coming on. My legs get shaky, and I can't stand up. When this happens, I tell Erin to stay with me until the feeling passes, which it usually does after about thirty seconds. Then I tell Erin she can go.

Having seizured, I should feel more afraid, and there's no logical reason why I don't, but the reality is that my only fear is that the O.D. is going to cause me some kind of inconvenience. Either there's going to be a legal issue, or it's going to get in the way of what I want *right now*, which is simply to keep doing what I've been doing, even as I know how destructive it is. Years past my teens, I still have a teenager's delusions of invincibility, made all the more delusional by my reckless, incessant, intravenous coke habit. Even after what happened to Eric, I feel a bedrock conviction that the same thing won't happen to me. Mainly I'm just embarrassed and annoyed at the attention focused on my drug use. Now Erin and Curtis are going to be fearful and risk-averse and a drag.

In the car back to the apartment from the hospital, Erin seems shaken.

"New rule, Erin," I say. "If I overdose, don't even think about calling a fucking ambulance. You start giving me CPR and mouth-to-mouth immediately."

"Baby—"

"By the time an ambulance arrives I'll either be fine, or I'll have irreparable brain damage."

"Cameron—"

"I'm serious. People panic and call an ambulance and wait for it to arrive, but it makes no sense either way. You need to start getting oxygen to the brain right away."

Erin doesn't say anything.

As soon as we enter the apartment, I grab a paper bindle of blow and tap some out into a spoon. I don't lessen the dose. What's so dangerous about shooting coke is that the feeling you're going for is obtained only just sub-overdose. People call it a "bell ringer," because you literally hear bells ringing in your head, like you're in a French restaurant at lunchtime and hear only the clinking of silverware. It's intense. You chase that feeling and keep shooting up in pursuit of it. I squeeze a few drops of water over the powder. This coke is good enough that it dissolves into a clear solution without any heat, and I draw it into a syringe, which I plunge into my left thigh.

Shooting coke takes me to another planet. What's wrong with the one I'm on? At this point, I couldn't tell you. I'm not living an examined life. I don't know why I don't want to face reality. I'm not sure why I don't want to challenge myself. Am I afraid of success? Am I afraid of discovering my limitations?

I don't want to sell short the visceral and immediate rewards. I know what I'm going to get from coke every time, and it's always there for me. The ups and downs of life are unknowable and unnerving. The ups and downs of drug addiction are entirely predictable. There's a comfort in that. And I like the instant gratification. I want to do what I want to do *right now*. I want to feel good *right now*. The only thing I know of in life that can do that is drugs. I don't want to work for it, or expend the effort, or wait for who-knows-how-long for who-knows-what-result.

If the seizure has any chastening impact, it is to make an incremental contribution to my overall feeling that this can't last, a creeping, ominous desperation that has started to darken my days.

Everyone who meets Junior recognizes that he's a special dog. In Aspen, I'll huck a golf ball out into a snowdrift. Junior will pounce in and disappear, but you can see him moving under the snow, displacing it like a tunneling worm, and he brings that ball up every time. He's amazingly adaptable. Sometimes I sleep for eighteen hours, after being up for seven days straight, and Junior crashes with me.

I do love dogs. I've grown up with them my whole life and always had one. I enjoy their company. I've always felt that I understand them. I get their thinking. I know how to raise good ones. When people compliment me on how well-behaved Junior is, I tell them: It's not a secret or mystery. You treat them well, give them time and attention, and train them to be obedient, and that's what you get. You get out of a dog what you put in. Some dogs are smarter than others, but you're never going to get passive-aggressive behavior, or a lie, from a dog.

In Bermuda, Dad has a blond Labrador named Lola, and he asks if he can borrow Junior to sire a litter of puppies with her. I've had Junior since he was a puppy, and I'm proud that Dad thinks I've done such a good job of raising him. In our lopsided relationship, it feels good to have something that I can do for Dad.

I've learned that when it comes to Lab coloring, blond is recessive and black is dominant, so I think: *Great, I'll take one puppy from the litter and have another Junior.* I send Junior to Bermuda, where he does what he's supposed to and fathers eleven puppies—all black, all beautiful.

When Dad calls to tell me the news, I remind him I'd like one of the puppies.

"I don't think so," he says.

"Dad, I gave you Junior with the understanding I'd get one of the puppies."

"Maybe you can have one, but it would have to live here. Actually, I think Junior should stay here too."

"Come again?"

"I just don't think you're in the best place to take care of a dog, Cam. Don't take this the wrong way, but you can barely take care of yourself."

"How do you think Junior got to be such a good dog? Keep the fucking puppies, but you're going to send him back to me."

"Nah, I think he should stay down here."

"Either put him on a plane tomorrow to come back to me, or I'm going to come there and get him, and that's not going to be a good scene for anybody."

He sends Junior back, keeps a couple of the litter, and gives the rest away, none of them to me. I'm insulted. Now I'm not fit to take care of a puppy? I'm sure Dad's not trying to be mean. Maybe he's trying to drive home a point. But one thing I take pride in, even now, is that even if I've neglected myself, I've never neglected my animals, just like I've never neglected my friends. It's offensive to me that he thinks I'm so far gone. It stings even more because this whole breeding episode

With Dad at the Sherry-Netherland hotel in New York.

started out as a seemingly nice interaction with Dad. Also because, on some level, I know that my life has jumped the rails.

Fuck it. I'll breed my own litter of puppies and keep one of them. I start researching breeds, looking for a good physical match for Junior that's also strong in traits and characteristics he's weaker in.

By now, I'm going three, four, five days without sleeping. I feel like everyone's out to get me. Friends. Police. Am I just paranoid? Not necessarily. I'm hanging out with shady people doing shady shit, and everyone's fucked up on drugs, not thinking properly. There's a lot of jealousy in all directions. Jay, my best friend, is never really acting the way I feel he should toward me. When I'm not around, he talks me down. Add all that to the cocaine-induced reality distortion, and the paranoia keeps me on a constant edge, burning me out.

I'll be at home with friends and suddenly get the feeling that cops are going to come barging through the door. "Everybody be quiet!"

I say. "Be quiet!" Then I spend hours looking under the door to the hallway, scanning for shadows, and out the window, studying people and cars for signs of a threat.

I come back from a trip to New York to find Erin wearing a long-sleeve T-shirt that says ROGAN on the back. Rogan is her grandfather's name, and we've joked about naming a kid after him.

"Are you fucking Jay?" I say.

"What?"

"You're going to have a kid together and name him Rogan?"

"Cameron, what are you talking about?"

"Have you ever been to Las Vegas, Erin?"

"What?"

"You heard me," I say. "Have you ever been to Las Vegas?"

"Um, I went there once when I was in college. We were on a biology trip and did some experiments in the desert, and we stopped in Vegas for maybe an hour?"

"And you haven't been there any other time?"

"No."

"So you're saying you didn't go there this weekend and get married to Jay?"

"What the fuck are you talking about? No."

"I know you're lying," I say.

"Baby, you're being insane. You're not making any sense."

I ask why she's being so defensive.

Another time, we're with my friend Ryan at the Roosevelt Hotel downtown, and Erin goes to use the bathroom. A few minutes later, Ryan says he needs to hit the head. While he's gone, Erin comes back.

That night, I say, "I know you had sex with Ryan."

"What? The only reason you imagine these things is because it's what you'd do."

The next day, I find Erin on her laptop, researching people who can come to the house and give her a lie-detector test.

One night, we decide to road-trip to Lake Havasu in Arizona, where the original London Bridge is. We leave in the middle of the night, me and Erin and Curtis and Maria, a very attractive girl who, like me, spent some time in a tough-love boarding school and is now a drug addict and sometime DJ. There are hardly any other cars on the road. One passes us, going what must be 140 miles per hour.

I want to see if I can keep up, so I lead-foot it. Instinctively, I've always felt like it's my job to be a consummate host. I'm like Dad in that way. When he has people to stay with him, he works full-time, around the clock, planning and organizing and taking care of his guests. Our circumstances are different. Our guests are different. But I always want to make sure everyone with me is having the best possible time. If they're not, I feel like it's my fault. Right now, that means rocketing down the highway at an ungodly speed.

A cop on the side of the road sees us zoom past, turns on his lights and siren, and chases us, indicating for us to pull over. I keep the accelerator floored, the speedometer needle pinned. Everyone else in the car is freaking out. "What the fuck are you doing, Cameron? Stop!" I'm scared too, but there are syringes and drugs in the car. It won't be good if we get pulled over. Finally we catch up with a cluster of cars. I pull in front of one in the middle of the pack and rapidly decelerate. We wait for what feels like an eternity for the cop cars (there's now more than one) to catch up. I see them in the rearview mirror, then I hear them, then I feel the adrenaline in my stomach. The cops don't see us, and fly past. I feel vindicated.

I've felt distant from Mom for many years. Her recent chumminess with Amanda is just one more addition to my pile of grievances against her. I'm also not someone she particularly wants around right now. Until last year, Mom was engaged to Zack Hampton Bacon III, a hedge fund manager in New York. She and Zack made plans to have a child via surrogate. I visited Mom in San Diego, where she was staying during the pregnancy, but otherwise steered clear of the situation. "A child" turned out to be twin boys—Hawk and Hudson. But Mom was also determined to have a daughter, and adopted Imara.

I think Mom is scared of growing old and being lonely, and she knows that she can't count on me to be there for her. Like Dad, with his young kids, I think she wants a do-over, a chance to make different choices than she made with me. I'm ashamed that they feel so poorly about me, and how I've turned out, that they want another crack at parenting. But it seems they are doing a better job this time; they're much more present and hands-on.

Mom and Zack stopped getting along, broke up, and are now in a nasty custody fight over the twins. An unemployed drug-addict son isn't necessarily going to be a helpful credential for Mom. But she still likes to keep tabs on me, mainly through Amanda, who keeps riling her up. The gist of her reports to Mom: my life is falling apart without Amanda.

When Erin and I have our act together, we hide our drugs and works in a kitchen cupboard, at the bottom of a box of peanut butter Puffins. But increasingly we're careless, and when Amanda stops by, supposedly to say hello, she'll see needles or other signs of what I'm doing, then leave and immediately call Mom and tell her.

Amanda and I are at her friend Pia's house in Topanga Canyon one day. It has a big bay window with a view, and tons of sunlight pouring in. I don't know what gets into me, but I whip out a needle I've already loaded up with coke.

"Cameron, what are you doing? What the fuck are you doing?"

"I'm addicted to heroin, Amanda."

No one feels sorry for cokeheads. Everyone feels bad for junkies.

I dig around for a vein.

"This is insane. Why are you doing this?"

I start crying.

"Because I have AIDS," I say, pressing the plunger. "So what does it matter?"

Why the fuck did I say that? It's not true. Maybe I think it is? Maybe I'm desperate for sympathy. Maybe I just want to freak her out.

"What?!"

I sink into the couch, fading away, as Amanda's meltdown begins.

———

Another day, when I'm out, Amanda and Mom show up at my apartment together. For some reason the door's open, and they walk right in. When I get home later, Curtis says they went straight into my bedroom and found a bunch of points and some bloody Kleenex in the sink. "Dude," Curtis says. "Your Mom immediately jumped on the phone and called your Dad. She was pacing around the living room. She's like, 'Michael, I'm here right now, I just went through his bedroom, there's needles everywhere, and bloody rags! We've got to do something! We're going to lose our son!'

"Then I get a phone call from your Dad. He's like, 'Curtis, I just got a call from Diandra, I know what she found in the bedroom. It sounds like he's still doing drugs.'

"I say, 'Yeah, he is, Michael.'

"He says, 'Curtis, where's he getting the money to get the drugs?'

"I say, 'Well, I do recall this check showing up in the mail the other day, and it was from the studio, and Cameron opened it up and got a big old smile and said, "Royalties, baby, gotta love 'em." '

"He says, 'Son of a bitch, I told those motherfuckers not to send him checks anymore.' He starts wigging out, dude. Your mom's going apeshit in the apartment, your dad's wigging out on the phone."

Soon after, I'm supposed to fly to Germany to play my DJ friend Sebbo's birthday party. Just a few years ago, I was traveling the world for gigs. I spun at a festival in Turkey. I DJed the *Vanity Fair* Oscars Party, alongside EDM giant Paul Oakenfold. I DJed a Mercedes-Benz event in Milan where Christina Aguilera also performed. I got a booking agent in Germany who started getting me a lot of work in Europe. At the height of my career, I was making between $3,000 and $6,000 for a nightclub set, and between $15,000 and $60,000 for a two- to five-hour corporate gig. It was like a dream to me. For the first time, I had a life and an identity of my own. Mom and Dad, who'd seen Mark Ronson blow up, began to think maybe this DJ thing could work out for me after all. But these days I rarely work, and I'm grateful for Sebbo's invitation to spin at his party.

The day before my departure, Dad calls and asks me to swing by his house. He's renting Dan Aykroyd's house in the Hills, north of Mulholland. I don't know whether Dad is aware that Aykroyd considers the house haunted, possibly by the ghost of former owner Mama Cass, according to the Internet.

A couple of months have passed since Dad's concern-fueled kidnapping attempt. I still feel betrayed. He seems to have crossed the threshold between desperate and numb. During our rare phone conversations, he sounds increasingly detached, but now he's saying that he wants to see me.

I want to be left alone. I'm not interested in a plan to get me sober. I'm ashamed, and frustrated by my inability to get my act together. The only thing I seem able to do is cause a commotion. All of which just makes me want to stay far away from the people who bring up those feelings. I go to see Dad anyway.

When I get there, he's with Amanda and a woman I've never met. This can't be good. Dad speaks first.

"This is Candy Finnigan, she works with drug addicts."

"Okay."

"Amanda said you told her you have AIDS. Do you?"

"What? No! I never said that."

I turn on Amanda. "I never said that. You're making that up. You're so full of shit."

Dad seems to be wavering, unsure whether to believe me. Candy looks unmoved. She has the no-bullshit, been-there-done-that attitude of a recovering alcoholic with her own reality show on A&E, *Intervention,* and a forty-year marriage to the keyboardist from Big Brother and the Holding Company. She gives Amanda a reassuring look.

"Why would I say that? Where did I say that?"

"Where?" Amanda says. "Cameron, you said that at Pia's house, right before shooting yourself up in front of me. I believed you. Either you were telling the truth, and you need help, or you weren't, which is really fucked up, and you need help."

Candy talks about Suboxone, a methadone-like opiate that is

increasingly being used to wean addicts off of heroin. Dad speaks from the heart. He knows my flight to Germany has a stopover in Amsterdam, and he knows I'm not going to use it to tour windmills. He implores me not to go. "Please, Cam, have Thanksgiving with us. Please."

I call Curtis to come and pick me up. When he arrives, he can tell that I'm utterly defeated. "What's wrong?"

I say, "Well, it doesn't look like I'm going to be going to Germany."

The DJ gig wouldn't be a huge payday—plane tickets, a few nights at a good hotel, maybe a couple thousand dollars—but Sebbo's my friend, and I'd been looking forward to going. I tell Curtis what happened and that I'm going to stick around.

"Right on," Curtis says. "That's a good choice. It's the holidays, it's Thanksgiving, your family wants you around. You're making a good decision."

When I arrive for Thanksgiving, though, I find Dad in the living room with Mom sitting next to him. This is definitely not good. The last time the two of them were in a room together was more than ten years ago. Mom looks like she's been crying. Dad says, "Have a seat, Cam." They've arranged for a private rehab in Santa Monica, Dad explains, and he is going to drive me straight there after dinner.

I could just not go, but I'm an ambivalent addict, so I take the passive route. I'm not happy with my life, and I want to make Dad happy, and things have gotten so bad that I feel like I owe it to my parents to give rehab a shot. I'd love to wake up and be rid of my addiction, which is another way of saying that I don't actually want to quit coke, not really, or else I'd be willing to do whatever it takes to get clean. I'm stubborn, and I don't believe rehab will work or that I even want it to work.

I walk out the back door and call Curtis, who's at the apartment. "Hey," I say. "I'm not going to be coming home."

"What the fuck do you mean?"

"I'm going to detox. I'll be gone for a week."

"Okay."

"I need you to do me a favor. I need you to pack me a bag of clothes. Get my duffel bag from my bedroom and throw in some CIRCA T-shirts, shorts, and some shoes, and bring it to my dad's house. They don't want me to leave."

"Okay."

"And I need you to do me a bigger favor. When you pull up, I want you to have some fat lines already racked up on a CD. I'm going to walk out into the driveway and grab my shit."

"Okay. All right."

When Curtis arrives at the gate and calls me, I tell Dad, "Curtis has my clothes, I'm just going to grab them real quick."

Before he can react, I go outside to Curtis's car and get in. He hands me a rolled-up bill, and I snort half a gram of coke in ten seconds.

"Holy shit," Curtis says. "This is really happening."

"Oh yeah," I say, "it's going down. But don't worry, I'll see you in a week."

I have no memory of going back inside the house. Apparently I tell Dad that Curtis forgot some of my clothes and we need to stop by my apartment on the way to Santa Monica. Apparently, when we do, Erin says, "Are you okay, baby? You look really fucked up."

It's unusually cold for L.A. this year, and I am checked into a bungalow at the Fairmont under an alias. I have a bedroom, and there is a decent-sized living room. For the next week, I'll be under twenty-four-hour supervision by two caretakers who alternate shifts, while nurses and doctors periodically check in on me. I can walk around, but I can't go outside without an escort. I'm bored out of my skull.

I text Curtis and ask him to bring me the remote for my Sony PlayStation.

"Okay."

And some coke.

"Absolutely not."

Like me, Curtis is good at making fine, questionably existent distinctions. Bringing me coke before was a last hurrah. Bringing it to me now would be nuts.

When Curtis arrives, the caretaker searches him, patting his pockets and riffling through the bag he's brought with him. Curtis pulls some Gatorade and snacks out of it. Then we go into the bedroom, where he reaches into his tighty-whities and fishes out a mini-bottle of vodka. I should probably feel guilty, but the only thing I feel is an addict's edict to get high. My blinkered pursuit of that goal blots out any possibility of reflection upon what I'm doing.

The real problem is that the detox team thinks—because Dad thinks, because I use needles—that I am addicted to heroin. And I let them keep thinking it, even though I really do want to be free of the coke (or *wish* to, at least, since I've made no effort to make it happen). I feel there's a dark glamour to heroin, and that a heroin habit somehow puts me in a more sympathetic light—that its fabled addictiveness makes me seem less responsible for failing to wean myself off it. And so the treatment, which is for an opiate dependency I don't have, does nothing to cure me of my very real and destructive coke problem. On the upside, the narcotic they give me is strong stuff, and I get extremely high off it.

I feel endless turmoil. How did I let things get to this point? I don't like what my life has become, and at the same time I alone am responsible for it. I feel powerless to do anything, but only I can change it. But I don't, so I just hate myself and keep doing the thing that I hate, and keep spiraling perversely, desperately, into more extreme behaviors.

5

1983: What About This Guy?

Some of my fondest memories from when I was a young kid are of Christmas. It would be just the three of us—me, Mom, and Dad—at the house in Montecito. I'd come downstairs in the morning, and Dad had made a fire, and Mom had made everything beautiful, down to the last detail, with bulging stockings hanging from the mantel. Or else we'd go to Snowmass, near Aspen, where we rented a condo until Dad bought Wildcat Ranch, and he'd set up a tree, and it would be just our little family, cozy and warm and surrounded by snow.

I think Mom and Dad tried hard not to fight in front of me, and to the extent that I was aware of the tension between them, I didn't connect it to any likely long-term consequences. Instead, I remember happy times snowmobiling with Dad, or dirt biking together. Anything with an engine that went fast, we both loved. There was no inkling yet of the troubles that lay ahead, for Dad and for Mom and for me.

With Dad working so much of the time, and Mom often preoccupied, a village of other people helped raise me. Once a week, when we were in California, I'd go over to Pappy and Oma's in Beverly Hills, and they'd feed me spaghetti with butter and Parmesan for dinner. I felt loved by them. Pappy was big and good-looking and had real presence. He was a tough, virile guy, but he was always sweet and loving to me, and I never felt intimidated by him. Every time I'd see him, he'd stoop as if to retrieve something from the ground and say, "What's this?" Then he'd stand up holding a $50 bill, which he'd hand to me. In California and New York, Pappy would take me on great little outings to shows like Cirque du Soleil and the Big Apple Circus, which featured grizzly bears in diapers. "I don't think those bears like that very much," I said. "Nah, I don't think so either," Pappy said.

Other times, I'd be left at Granny's house in Sherman Oaks. I didn't realize then that these extended visits often coincided with periods when Mom and Dad were separated or going through a particularly rough patch in their marriage. Granny was an actress who often performed on the stage. From growing up in Bermuda, where her father

Me, Pappy, and Dad.

was attorney general, she had a slight British accent. I loved spending time with Granny and felt a deep connection to her. She taught me to play chess, and since she was a big golfer I'd tag along with her to the driving range. Then we'd go to Hamburger Hamlet for a bite. Years later, when I was DJing and taking a stab at acting, she'd be my champion, always believing in me and my abilities. I loved her so much.

I also loved Uncle Billy, her second husband, who'd raised Dad and Jojo. He was what I imagined Ernest Hemingway to have been like. He was a man's man, always smoking his pipe, a very sharp guy with zero tolerance for bullshit, and a gentleman who carried himself with grace.

When I was five, and we made the move to New York—driven east by Mom's unhappiness with California and show business—we lived on the Upper West Side, surrounded by friends. We spent a lot of time with the Wenners, who had a town house on Seventieth Street, a few blocks away. We'd sometimes spend the weekend at their place in Southampton. They had an amazing collection of movies, and I saw *The Breakfast Club* there for the first time. Sometimes if Dad wasn't around, Jann, being my godfather, stepped in. I remember him grounding me once; for exactly what, I don't recall. The Ronsons lived next door to us in the San Remo. I had a crush on Charlotte, was pals with Samantha, and looked up to Mark, who was a few years older than me and already playing around with turntables.

Sometimes Mom and Dad would drop me off to play with Sean Lennon, who was three years older than me, at the Dakota on Seventy-Second Street. I don't know if I already knew the details of his father's death, but I always had the distinct feeling that the building was haunted. Sean was quiet. Sometimes Yoko was there, but we mostly hung out in Sean's room, which had an egg chair hanging from the ceiling, listening to music or playing board games. One Sunday, Mom and Dad and I went over to Strawberry Fields with Sean and Yoko and linked hands for Hands Across America, the follow-up event to USA for Africa's "We Are the World." The idea was to forge a continuous human chain across the country to raise money to fight hunger and homelessness. I was vaguely aware that it was for a higher cause, but I was in my gym sweats from school and just felt like a little kid doing a sing-along with his parents.

Occasionally Mom would have her driver, Lawrence, a tall, distinguished gentleman, drop me off in Montclair, New Jersey, at the home of Patsy and Jimmy Webb and their six kids, for what seemed like weeks at a time.

Jimmy was a successful songwriter. He'd written "By the Time I Get to Phoenix," which was a Glen Campbell hit, and "The Highwayman," a number one country hit for the Highwaymen, a supergroup that included Johnny Cash and Willie Nelson. Patsy was the daughter of the actor Barry Sullivan, who'd starred opposite Pappy in *The Bad and the Beautiful,* and had met Jimmy when she was twelve. Dad met her around the same time, when he starred opposite her father in a *CBS Playhouse* episode called "The Experiment." When I stayed with the Webbs, Jimmy never left his den except to go into a side room where he built model battleships. He'd call me in, and he'd sit there in his bathrobe drinking whiskey while we watched movies, such as *Innerspace.*

I was closest to their son James, who was my age. We'd go up to his brother's room in the attic and play *The King of Chicago,* a 1930s mobster game, on his brother's Amiga computer, or we'd get Patsy to take us to an arcade at the Willowbrook Mall. She was a terrible driver, and I always felt that my life hung in the balance when I got in a car with her. James's older brothers had a pretty good band, and we'd hang around when they threw house parties and performed. We'd play ninjas with James's friend Ian and also take part in Mini V—Vietnam War reenactment for kids—which was basically an excuse to wear bandanna headbands and act like Rambo.

When I turned eight and we were living in New York, Mom and Dad threw my birthday party in the evening, at the Manhattan nightclub Regine's.

That summer, Dad decided I needed a more constant male influence in my life, someone to stand in his place when he was away. One day, he and Mom were having lunch at the Ivy in Beverly Hills, talking about their need for a nanny and someone to manage the house in Montecito. Dad was taken with the Hispanic busboy, who had Indian features and a knowledgeable smile and was very attentive. Dad said, "What about this guy? He seems very capable. He could be a house-man or something like that." Mom spoke to him in Spanish. His name was Joaquín, and he was from El Salvador. They got his number. Soon, Joaquín was living with us. He took care of me from the moment I woke up to the moment I went to sleep.

Joaquín came with us when we moved back to New York in the fall. He didn't speak English, so he and I spoke Spanish. His three favorite things in the world were *Three's Company,* the Argentine soccer player Diego Maradona, and hunting for dinosaur bones, which he would take me to do in Central Park while dressed in one of his sizable col-lection of safari suits, all in different colors, which he had spent a lot of money on. I don't think he actually thought we were going to find T. rex vertebrae in Sheep Meadow, but he was a dreamer. He was so passionate about dinosaur fossils, and Central Park was the closest thing to wilderness in New York City. Joaquín got especially serious about the bone-hunting when we went to Snowmass at Christmas; he'd grab perforated serving spoons from a kitchen drawer, and we'd head out to a hillside and start digging together.

In New York, Joaquín would pick me up at the elementary school I went to on the Upper East Side, Birch Wathen, where I had to wear a coat and tie, and we'd walk home across the park, turning our rou-tine into a mission where we'd climb over walls and shimmy up trees. Along the way, I'd pocket rocks that glinted with mica, and I amassed a large pile of them under my bed. I liked to hold on to things I thought were special.

Joaquín showed his love by feeding me. He'd cook me huge break-fasts of rice and beans and steak and eggs and grilled onions on a massive plate. He'd say: "Eat, eat, eat!" Dad thought I seemed unhappy, and when I started getting chubby, he investigated and found out Joaquín had been taking me to White Castle for bags of twenty-seven-cent burgers.

Sometimes I'd get Joaquín to take me to Chinatown, where I had my earliest exposure to the underworld and its dealings. A street hawker would take us down into a basement and pull bags out of the ceiling, with illegal fireworks inside. I loved fat, red M-80s with green wicks, which were packed with explosive flash powder; pineapples, which were twice as big; and Roman candles. My friends from Birch Wathen and I would have Roman candle wars in Central Park; and upstate, at our weekend rental in Pound Ridge, I'd bury a pineapple in a hole and set it off, or else use it to blow up someone's mailbox. Even then, I felt a thrill at my brush with the illicit.

This was during the time when Dad was becoming a huge movie star and traveling even more than usual, and Mom was bitter and not around much either, for all intents and purposes. Joaquín was the one who was always there for me. He woke me up, took me to school, picked me up, played with me, bought me Nintendo games, made me dinner. I spent more time with Joaquín than with my parents, and I often told him that I loved him more than them. Everything seemed so cut and dried in my young mind.

I was always in capable hands, and loved and cared for, just not necessarily by my parents. By now, I was starting to build some resentment toward Mom. As I saw it then, Dad had a legitimate excuse for his absence, and I was used to his comings and goings. Mom was supposed to be taking care of me, and for a while had done so, but increasingly she wasn't. She was still very young, and I think the issues between her and Dad were building, and she was in constant turmoil.

Right after we moved back to Santa Barbara, when I was ten, Joaquín, who'd brought his girlfriend and her daughter west to help around the house, came to me and told me he was leaving. He was crying. I was crying. His girlfriend and her daughter were crying. It was heart-

Rafting the Grand Canyon with Dad.

wrenching. He told me he was going back to his country to fight for his people's freedom. I'd later learn that Mom had found vodka bottles under Joaquín's bed and asked him to stop drinking. I'd seen the bottles there, and just thought of them as being like the pile of rocks I kept under my bed. We were so close, and I was devastated, and that moment is burned into my memory. I've always felt like we're going to cross paths again. Sometimes, on the street, I think I see Joaquín, and try to make eye contact, but after so many years, I know it's wishful thinking. Maybe he's not even alive anymore.

After Joaquín, I got a new caretaker, Geoff Akers, who was twenty-seven. He was from the Hamptons originally, but his mom lived in Santa Barbara. He lived with us, cooked for me, took me to school, picked me up, and played with me. We had a blast together. I'd ride my dirt bike, he'd be on his bicycle, and we'd chase each other around the grounds of our house in Montecito. Friday nights, we'd go to high school football games, and I'd run around with my friends while Geoff hung out with a girl he later married.

It was around that time, right after we moved back to Santa Barbara, that I really began to find comfort in my friends. I had a little crew—me and Jay and David, who I called my brothers—and we named ourselves the Sewer Rats, because we'd all wear long-sleeved blue shirts and chase each other through the pitch-black darkness of the giant cement water pipes that run beneath the town of Carpinteria, where Jay and David both lived.

I joined a Youth Football League team called the Cowboys. We'd do a drill where everyone lined up facing in one direction, and the kid at the top of the line, who'd have the ball, would start sprinting down the line. Then the coach would call out a name, and that kid would have to jump out from the line and tackle the oncoming ballcarrier. If you were the tackler, you'd want to get as much momentum as you could before making contact, because whoever had more momentum would hit harder and steamroll the other kid.

I was chubby, and picked-on, and I kept getting knocked on my ass. One day I asked my friend John, who I carpooled with, why I didn't tackle as well as other kids did. He said, " 'Cause you're afraid to hit. You're pulling up, and putting your hands up in front of you, right before you hit." Something clicked: if I was the sprinter, I'd still get tackled, but if I was at top speed, it would be the tackler who really got hurt. That day, I laid a kid out flat. From then on, I was a hitter. In one of our games, I sacked the quarterback, and he had to be carried off the field. I was thrilled, and I heard Dad boasting about my hits to his friends. "My son," he'd say, beaming. "He's a tough little kid." I loved hearing him say that.

I started to become slightly more mischievous than the average kid. Once, my friend Sean and I called a 1-900 sex hotline and kept getting put on hold or transferred, never reaching a live woman. Mom and Dad grilled me about the $400 charge on their phone bill. I don't remember exactly what the fallout was, but probably they grounded me.

S'Estaca, besides being a place of wonder for me, was also where I had some of my earliest brushes with adulthood. There were a lot of parties at the house, and Dad's friends who'd regularly come to visit included Jack Nicholson, Pat Riley, Oliver Stone, Danny DeVito, and Mansour Ojjeh, who owned the McLaren race team, and his wife, Kathy.

Even as a really young kid, I remember running joints back and forth between Dad and Jojo. Dad would say, "Hey, bring this over to your uncle," and I would, not realizing until years later what it had been. As I got older, I would creep from house to house on the compound, climbing balconies and seeing more than I was supposed to: beautiful grown-ups doing the things that beautiful grown-ups living lives of excess do.

When the guests were out of their rooms during the day, my friend Taylor and I would comb their rooms, riffling through their bags in search of whatever was responsible for their good times the night before. We agreed that if anyone asked what we were looking for, we'd say "Snickers." I was only twelve and didn't really have a handle yet on stash spots, or know exactly what we were looking for. We just knew there was something secret awaiting discovery, and that was enough to make our hunts exciting. It was activity I wasn't engaging in yet, but I was right at the brink, just about to start trying to smoke cigarettes.

6

1991: Thirteen

When I was in sixth grade, Dad announced that I'd be going to boarding school for junior high. He and Mom were fighting more than ever; he says now that he thought I should be away from their acrimony. At the time, he sold it as a great experience he'd had and that I should have too. He'd gone to Eaglebrook, where he roomed with Henry Kravis, the future buyout king, and loved it. I felt differently. I was tired of bouncing around, wanted to attend the same local public junior high school my friends were going to in Santa Barbara, and was staunchly against the idea of being shipped off to Massachusetts. Mom didn't want me to go, either. She hadn't liked her boarding school experience, and she says she enjoyed having me around. But she deferred to Dad, who insisted, saying he thought that I should be in a structured environment with other boys. In the face of my tears, he asked me to give it a chance. He was sure I'd have a good time, but if I didn't like it after a year, I could come home.

I'd barely started at Eaglebrook when Dad went into rehab for what was reported and distorted around the world as "sex addiction." As far as I could tell, he was there mainly for his drinking and to placate Mom. She had caught him in bed with another woman, given him an ultimatum that he had to deal with his drug and alcohol intake, and two weeks later he checked into Sierra Tucson, a clinic in Arizona, under the alias Mike Morrell (my and Mom's middle name). Part of the 30-day program at Sierra Tucson was a "family week," and I was pulled out of school to go to Arizona, where I mostly sat in group sessions with the kids of other patients, talking about our familial woes. I felt like a passenger in someone else's car. Mom and Dad had issues to work out, and I was just a kid along for the ride. I was more confused than anything, unsure what it would mean for me, and telling myself that I didn't care. Then I went back to school.

Boarding school in New England was a culture shock. I was thirteen. I had to wear a coat and tie to classes, and the school had its own ski slope. It was at Eaglebrook that I smoked pot for the first time. It was a joint rolled from a dirty dollar bill by Russell, one of the school's token black kids. He was outgoing and popular and a great athlete, and we had a lot in common: we both wrestled and played football, were into snowboarding, liked rap and hip-hop, and soon shared a taste for weed, too.

We were behind a dorm named Halsted House, at the foot of one of the ski trails. We'd only taken a couple of hits when we heard someone coming, and we panicked and snuffed the joint out. I'm sure the high felt good—before long, I'd be a pothead—but what comes back to me is the pleasure I felt in getting to tag along with Russell, who I wanted to be friends with. Drugs for me were, among other things, a path out of loneliness. But as I'd also learn, my drug friendships would tend to be based on little else, and if I took the drugs away, the bonds would dissolve.

I was still chunky. This was my first all-boys environment, and Matt, an older, bigger, good-looking kid in my dorm, singled me out for torture. Russell was Matt's best friend, and Matt seemed jealous that I was horning in on their bromance. I'd be walking down the hall in Macy, the dorm where we both lived, when I'd hear "Hey, Down syndrome," or sometimes just "Hey, Down." Matt would say this, as he lumbered toward me, in the speech-impeded voice of a person with a cognitive disability.

Basic Instinct had just come out, providing him with easy fodder. If Matt had an audience, he'd announce, with mock sympathy: "Leave Cameron alone; his dad's a sex addict." I experimented with various comebacks until landing on two subjects that seemed to get under Matt's skin: the way he ran—slowly, legs girlishly akimbo—and his puppy-like adoration of Russell. I knew I'd hit a nerve whenever Matt grabbed me by the throat. I was terrified of him, and I'd never been in any fights, and I didn't want to fight him.

If Matt was going to treat me like that, I was going to pay it forward. My roommate, J.D., was the nicest kid in the world, but I made him play Bloody Knuckles. Even after both our hands were swollen and bleeding, and he said he wanted to stop, I forced him to keep playing, saying, "No, it's your turn. *No, it's your turn.*" There was another kid in my class whose life was Guns N' Roses. I remember his face clearly, but not his name. He played guitar and had stacks of GNR T-shirts. I'd go into his room, mock his devotion to Axl Rose, and start whaling on him. One time, I overdid it. I felt terrible and apologized, and it was the last time I bullied anyone.

I was developing a taste for combat, though. I wrestled in the 126-pound weight class and was regularly lifted into the air and slammed to the mat. One time, I broke my thumb and dislocated it. But Pappy had wrestled when he was younger, and he was proud of me for doing it too, and his pride made me feel good. Dad told Pappy I was becoming an athlete, and whenever I saw Pappy he'd check out my body, having me show him my biceps and checking my strength with some arm wrestling.

I really just wanted to be back in California, living at home and hanging out with friends, and I convinced my friend John, from Monte-

Wrestling at Eaglebrook.

Me, as number 55, playing football at Eaglebrook.

cito, to join me at Eaglebrook for the second semester. He persuaded his mother to send him, but he hated it more than I did.

Dear Mom,

you are the greatest mom in the world. I love you and Dad more than anything in the world

You have been so kind to me and loving

You have made Life so Good For me EXCEPT

Sending me here.

Which I Hope was only a one year experience.

I Love you so much, and Hope to see you

SOON.

Always be safe and carful.

Happy Mothers Day.

Much

Love,

Cam

Dear Dad,

Sorry I haven't been writing to you much but I've been working hard. Your new movie sounds really funny, I can't wait to see it. I am starting right middy in Lax. We're having a game this Wednesday against Williston Northampton. It should be pretty tough. But our LAX Team is looking good. I can't wait to get home in the summer and see you and Mom. We're going to have a great summer. I was wondering if after school ends I can go home for a week or so. I hope you'll be finished with the movie so we can all spend time together. I'm starting to catch some more flack from Basic Instinct. But I'm dealing with it. Sometimes it really gets me down especially when I'm homesick, but that's ok I guess. Ned and John are being good friends to me and helping me out. Russell and I are becoming much better friends it looks like, at least I hope so. I'm doing much better in school I think. I got a B and an A+ on the last two math tests I took. I just took a Colonial Test and I think (or hope) I did

well. I hope everything is going good for you in the movie. I love
you a lot, and be careful. Write back if you get a chance.
   Sincerely, Cameron Douglas
   xoxoxoxoxo

P.S. Love you lots

At the end of the school year, John and I hitched a ride from New
York to L.A. on the Sony jet with Dad and Kevin Costner, and a limousine drove us home to Santa Barbara. When I told Dad I didn't want
to return to Eaglebrook for eighth grade, he said, "Sorry, pal, that's
how it's going to be." I reminded him of his promise to me. He said,
"That's the way it is." I was accustomed to the strains of his marriage
to Mom; there was nothing to indicate they were any worse now, and
he didn't explain himself. He said: "I'm your father, not your friend."
My newly hormone-crazed teenage self decided that his about-face
was an unforgivable betrayal, and a turning point. From then onward,
my focus became less and less about Mom and Dad and more and
more about my friends.

That summer, I underwent a minor transformation. I was thirteen
now, a teenager. I lost my baby fat and traded in my bowl cut for a
more stylish side part. I started pushing my parents pretty hard to
give me independence. S'Estaca was a good place to spread my wings.
The families I knew there let their kids run wild, and Mom and Dad
felt some pressure to allow me similar freedom.

   I ran with a little band of fellow misfit urchins: Oro, Tom, Asher,
Aidan, and Sasha. Our parents were all hippies or artists. Dad had a
Zodiac with a 30-horsepower engine and a steering wheel connected
to the throttle, and I'd take it out every day, stopping to pick up my
friends at the beach, then heading away from shore to go wake boarding and kneeboarding. At night, while our parents partied at home,
we'd party in town until after midnight. The local police force seemed

to consist of one old guy, and you could sit at a bar in Spain at thirteen and order a Bacardi and Coke. As long as we were staying out of our parents' hair, they didn't focus too much on where we were. When I came home late, I'd try to avoid them so they couldn't smell my breath. It all seemed harmless at the time, and I have only the fondest memories of those days in Spain with my parents, but in hindsight I was clearly whetting my appetite for mood-managing chemicals, and for friends who shared that appetite.

In Deià that summer, I developed a major crush on Galen Ayers, who was worldly and multilingual and head-turningly beautiful, with blond hair and blue eyes. She was also fun and sweet and laid-back, a hippie artist in the making. Her father was Kevin Ayers, the influential British psychedelic-rock musician who'd cofounded the group Soft Machine. But she'd been raised largely by her mother and stepfather, Axel, who owned hotels in Deià. Late at night, our crew would break into one of them, the Residencia, to go skinny-dipping in the pool. Or else we'd go down to the beach at Cala Deià and swim in the ocean, which glowed magically with bioluminescent plankton.

That was also the summer when Uncle Billy died. Granny was heartbroken. I took it hard too. We were in Spain when we got the news, and I was very dramatic in my reaction, tearing off on my dirt bike to find a spot in the hills to sit and be alone. It was the first death I'd experienced, and I felt a keen sense of loss, but I was at an age when I was still learning how to grieve, and I tried to watch Dad and the other adults to see what they did. I felt particularly terrible for Granny, who I knew had just lost the love of her life.

It was also that July Fourth weekend, back in Santa Barbara, that I had sex for the first time. It was with a girl I'd been seeing named Tricia, on a damp mattress at the home of my friend Sean, who still wet his bed. I liked Tricia, and thought she was attractive, but those factors were secondary to my determination not to be a virgin anymore.

The whole thing was awkward. The time and place and activity were negotiated by our mutual friends. I didn't even take off my boxers. Afterward, I got up and said I'd be right back, then left and didn't return. I felt guilty, but not enough to do anything about it. Maybe I was afraid of the intimacy; I just knew I felt more comfortable with my friends who were waiting for me outside. The next day, Tricia had a friend call to say that she'd taken a test and was pregnant. Not realizing that such early detection was biologically impossible, I freaked out and told her to get another test. Later the same day, the friend called to say Tricia had taken another test and the result was again positive. I was hugely relieved when it turned out, not surprisingly, that she had invented the pregnancy to get back at me for taking off on her, which I deserved.

It was a season of firsts. Later that summer, a woman in her twenties named Stephanie—who would soon pull a Mrs. Robinson on me—drove me and her younger brother Leland to a keg party at Top of the World, a piece of open parkland in Montecito where kids went to drink. There was a knot of wild boys there, white gangbangers from Santa Barbara, and because I was an unfamiliar face, and probably seemed awkward, they started paying attention to me and giving me unfriendly looks. One of them walked over. With no warning, he punched me in the face. I came to on the ground, seeing lights and tracers and feeling like The Dude in *The Big Lebowski* after he gets coldcocked. It was the first time I'd ever been knocked out. The guy was already walking away. My immediate reaction wasn't fear that he was going to come back. It wasn't embarrassment that I'd just gotten clocked. It wasn't about the throbbing ache in my jaw. It was: *That's who I want to be like, that motherfucker right there.* I wanted people to see that I wasn't a pussy. I could come from a rich and famous family and be just as bad as everyone else.

I was becoming more detached. That year, a friend gave me a huge dog named Lobo, who was half timber wolf. He was gentle, and was an outside dog, but my pet ferret, Tiki, had a strong odor. One day, Lobo got into the house, smelled his opportunity, made a beeline for Tiki, and ate her. I'd had Tiki for many years, and it was a terrible, upsetting accident, but somehow her death also made sense to me. Tiki had lived a long life, and it's a dog-eat-ferret world.

When I returned to Eaglebrook for eighth grade, I had a very different experience than the previous year. I still liked sports and was on the varsity football, wrestling, and lacrosse teams. I must have had Stockholm syndrome, because I became friends with my former tormentor, Matt, who also played football and wrestled. It somehow felt like a victory to befriend him.

But I was also smoking and drinking and skateboarding and making forbidden nighttime runs off-campus, sprinting across fields and through the woods to a store where I'd buy candy and Cheez Whiz and ramen noodles, which my friends and I would make in our contraband hot pots. Eaglebrook began to feel like the sidelines to me.

Every weekend, I'd Amtrak to New York City, my new playing field, to skate and drink 40s and smoke blunts and do mushrooms with a graffiti crew I was getting to know called BHC. Its members tagged, or signed their work, as Tone and Kaz and Chast and Deter; a couple of them later became skater extras in the movie *Kids*. My tag was SAKE, as in *for God's sake;* I liked how the letters mashed together.

Drugs went hand-in-hand with the culture of skateboarding and "writing," which was the umbrella term for all the varieties of painting graffiti. We'd go to bodegas above 100th Street to buy weed, or to dealers hanging out in Sheep Meadow in Central Park, or to an old lady who ran a comic book store near Columbus Circle and sold us mushrooms.

I liked doing mushrooms and acid. I enjoyed the way they changed how things looked, with colors becoming brighter and patterns coming to life. Tripping, I could sit and stare at a wall for what seemed like hours. Every experience felt like a vision quest, where I'd make new mental connections and have psychological epiphanies. The revelations would stay with me for days, I remember, though I can't recall any specifics now.

As I got more interested in drugs, I became less interested in seeing friends from childhood. I still considered them friends, but we were into different things. They were squares, and I wasn't. My new friends and I would gather in Hell's Kitchen, where several of them lived, or skate around the Cube sculpture on Astor Place, in the East Village. I began to learn little lessons of the street. Once, I was with Tony, aka Tone, when a kid came up to us and said, "You guys write?" I assumed Tony would say yes and talk about where and what we tagged. When he didn't, I was about to start talking myself, but Tony cut me off and said: "Nah, we don't write." He knew that the kid was fishing to find out whether we'd written over something he'd written. That was how beefs started, and Tony had the survival instincts to head off that possibility.

Eaglebrook went through ninth grade, but when I returned for my third and final year there, I only lasted a month. I had a little stash spot in my letterman's jacket, an inside pocket torn at the bottom so I could reach through and move contraband around the lining. I kept a small bag of weed there, along with a couple of starter-kit pipes, bulky and ridiculous-looking contraptions pieced together from PVC tubing that gave off toxic fumes when heated. Someone must have told someone else about it, because when I was in class one day, Mr. Kilroy, my adviser and the husband of Mrs. Kilroy, our sexy medieval history teacher, searched my room and found it. I was called to the headmaster's office. Mr. Chase had the evidence sitting on his desk. The school had a zero-tolerance drug policy, and he said he was expelling me.

7

2005: Spin Out

I used to go up to Mom's house in Santa Barbara fairly regularly. I love it there. It's beautiful and peaceful and home to me. It's where I finished high school and began to find myself, and some of my oldest friends are there. It's also where I really started heading down the path to losing myself. Sometimes Mom is around, but often she isn't.

Now, with my ex Amanda living there, I no longer feel welcome, but one weekend when Erin is back east seeing family, Curtis and I drive to Santa Barbara for a visit. On Sunday, Curtis returns to L.A., and I stay. I've agreed to drive Mom's dogs to the vet's office with Amanda the next morning. That night, I stop by the house of Doyanne, one of three beautiful sisters I'm friends with, to say hello. She has sugar cubes of acid she's been saving to do with her boyfriend, but she asks if I want to do them with her.

By the time I get back to Mom's house, it's the next morning. The LSD has pretty much worn off, and the last thing I want to do is take Mom's dogs to the vet, but I said I'd go. Amanda is furious, screaming at me for being late. "What are you on, Ecstasy?" I'm not late. Really, she's just angry that I spent the whole night out. She's been calling me for hours.

It's raining. I've been up for three days straight, and Amanda's dead sober. When I go to get in Mom's Escalade, Amanda says: "Motherfucker, I'm driving, you're too fucked up to drive." Before we get onto the highway, she pulls into a Chevron on Coast Village Road to gas up.

"It's my car," I say. "You're not driving. I'm driving."

"You're too fucked up."

"I'm not fucked up. I'm driving."

I get in the driver's seat. On the 101 freeway, we're still arguing about who should drive. Amanda starts slapping me, and I lose control of the steering wheel. We spin out, do a full 360, skid onto the median, and hit a tree. Only Amanda's airbag deploys. She is shaken but unharmed. I'm not wearing a seatbelt, and my head bounces off the steering wheel.

"You can't be driving," Amanda says. "You're going to get arrested if you were driving. Switch places with me."

I remember the bags of coke and weed in my quarter pocket and begin picturing the imminent arrival of the California Highway Patrol. I jump out of the car, hop a fence, hide behind some bushes, dump the coke onto the back of my hand, and snort it all up. When I return to the car, a guy who saw the accident has pulled over and gotten out of his car, and he asks, "Are you all right?"

"Do you smoke weed?"

"Yeah."

I hand him the bag of it. He says, "You'd better sit down."

"Why, what's up?"

"Your head is wide open."

Blood is gushing from my forehead and dripping onto my white shirt and khakis. I sit down on the car's bumper and wait for an ambulance.

As soon as the CHiPs arrive, they separate me and Amanda. The officer questioning me says: "Who was driving?"

I say, "She was."

He is convinced I am lying—maybe the giveaway is the bleeding, steering wheel–shaped wound on my head—and keeps asking me the same question, despite my unchanging answer. Amanda tells the same story to the cop who's questioning her and threatening, "You're going to jail, sweetheart, I know you're lying."

The ambulance comes, and at the hospital I get a dozen stitches in my head. Then Mom shows up to get the dogs. In front of her, one of the cops tells me, "We're going to give you one last opportunity to tell the truth. If you don't, you're going to prison. Who was driving?"

I nod at Amanda again and say, "She was."

One of the CHiPs starts yelling at Mom: "Do you know your son's going to prison? We know he was driving. He's going down."

But Amanda and I tell the same story, and since she's driven the car before, the cops find one of her hairs on the driver's seat visor. Eventually, they have to let us go.

My world has shrunk to only a few equally drug-addicted friends. My other friends keep their distance, and my phone, which has always rung constantly, is mostly silent. Curtis is still paying rent, but my life has gotten too dark even for him, and he no longer sleeps at the apartment.

When Dad presses me to go to another rehab, this one in Arizona, I reluctantly agree, and Amanda says she'll take me there. She's a compulsive nurturer. She takes care of her father, who has had legal problems. She's been a mother to her younger sister. It's a seven-hour drive. Around the midway point, I make Amanda stop the car, and I get out, thinking I'll hitchhike back to L.A. But Amanda coaxes me back into the car and finally gets me to the clinic in Sedona.

The rehab does no good, because I'm not done with drugs yet, maybe because I feel there's nothing for me to go home to. I'm just returning to the same bullshit, with nothing really going on in my life, and no money in my pocket, where I'm a burden to anyone who has to look out for me. I don't believe in myself. I have no discipline. I just want to do what I know I'm best at, which is drugs.

When I return from Arizona, Mom and Dad's attitude is understandably to stand back and see what happens. And what happens is I slip right back into my habits. My relapse starts with self-pity: *No one cares about me. No one loves me.* I start getting worked up. Then it's a short step to what makes me comfortable. Even though I've started to loathe the cocaine—what it does to me, how I act on it—it has a gravitational pull I can't resist. I must have some kind of demented death wish. Every shot, I want to take myself right to the brink of overdose. If that doesn't happen, I immediately reload and do another one.

While I was in Arizona, Amanda found me an L.A. apartment on Craigslist. It's on Orange Grove Avenue, off of Sunset, conveniently around the corner from Amanda's place on Hayworth Avenue. Erin is visiting friends in Chicago, and when she comes back to L.A. I spend weeks hiding her from Amanda. Amanda hates Erin, who has replaced her in my life, and whom she unfairly faults for my worsening drug problem.

When Amanda finds out that Erin is living with me, she starts showing up all the time. I'll have people over, and Amanda will suddenly arrive and bang on the door and kick it until I let her in. Then she gets up in Erin's face and screams at her, saying the meanest things she can think of: "Loser! White trash! Trailer trash! Get the fuck out of here! Nobody likes you!" Erin sits there and takes it.

One day, Erin and I are in my bedroom, three days into a bender and double-fisting two large vodka cranberries each, when I hear Amanda yelling out front. The door is locked, and she goes around the house and starts banging on the kitchen door. It's locked too, and on a chain, but Amanda takes a rock, breaks the window, and lets herself in. I hear her throwing things in the kitchen. I quickly lock the bedroom door but Amanda breaks it down. When she comes in, I am sitting on the bed, and Erin is on the other side of me. Amanda smacks the drink out of my hand, dousing me.

"Fucking relax, Amanda!" I say.

She leaps at Erin. I jump up and get between them. Amanda is brandishing a keychain with a solid metal ball on it, a miniature morning star, and she swings it, hitting the left side of my head, just below the temple. I come to lying on the floor. I've only been down for a second or two, but Amanda, scared, has fled. I feel a throbbing ache on the side of my head, and Erin drives me to an urgent-care place on Sunset. The specialist says my jaw is broken, and I need to get to an emergency room immediately. But my jaw doesn't really hurt anymore, and I go home and shoot up instead. Later, when I run my finger along my jaw, I'll feel a noticeable space where it's supposed to connect to the cheekbone, and sometimes it will lock up on me.

Finally I say, "Erin, Amanda is a bully. You're an athlete, and you're twice her size. She's never played a sport. You could kick her ass. The next time she comes over, say, 'You know what? Let's fight.'"

That sinks in. The next time Amanda comes over, kicking the door and screaming and trying to get at Erin, I say, "Hold on, Amanda, Erin's coming out, she wants to fight you." I open the door to the bedroom, where Erin is tying up her hair. And *vroom*: Amanda takes off.

Really, it's just me and Erin now. I almost never talk to Mom or Dad. They still think I'm addicted to heroin. If they only knew how much worse liquid cocaine is. Dad has me on a tough-love allowance, and what money I get I immediately spend on drugs. There's nothing left for me to buy a new pair of shoes or go out to dinner. In a city that runs on cars, I'm carless. I walk to the few auditions I still book, sometimes traveling miles on foot, and show up to them sweating. The only offers I'm getting are for B and C movies and reality shows. I'm sitting around feeling like a schmuck, which exacerbates my cocaine use, which just makes me more disgusted with it. I am optimistic to a fault, perhaps, but sometimes I think: *Maybe this is my lot. Maybe I should just accept that shit's not going to work out for me.*

I'm brimming with resentment: toward myself, mostly. In Dad's defense, what is he supposed to do? Am I owed something? Mom and Dad have sent me to a lot of rehabs. They've helped me with money. But it's always from a distance. I'm sure from Mom's point of view, she's done her best to stand by me all these years, feeling she's received little gratitude for her efforts. I do know that when Dad came to see me in New York, for what felt like our heart-to-heart, that conversation seemed to have had a greater effect than any 30-day program they ever sent me to. It's unfortunate it ended the way it did.

But Erin is still here. She's the one person who has stood by me through everything, and my feelings for her have begun to deepen. Erin knows I can't handle being alone. If we're lying in bed together, watching a movie, and she falls asleep before I do, I wake her up so I won't feel like I'm by myself. She says I have a fear of abandonment, and she's right. As far back as I can remember, I've needed someone there with me, always, someone I really care about and who I think cares about me. Her steadfastness means a lot to me. I feel a love for her that wasn't there before. For the first time in our three years together, I think of her as my girlfriend, as family.

It's only when I'm three or four days into a bender that I'm able to start enjoying it. The edginess and paranoia of the first few days are behind me. I'm out of my mind because I've been awake for days, and there are moments when I think I'm having a good time. To anyone else, I must look like a space alien. I see the wreckage of my behavior. I know I want the coke to stop.

It's during this period that I reacquaint myself with heroin, which I haven't tried since I was sixteen. I'm supposed to go to Morocco for a DJ gig. Erin has just gotten a puppy, a hot dog named Oscar, and she brings it on the flight from LAX. We're changing planes in New York, and her sister, Paige, meets us at Kennedy Airport to get Oscar, who'll stay with her while we're out of the country. But as we're checking in for the next leg of our flight, Erin realizes that she left our passports in the dog carrier. Paige's phone is dead, and we can't reach her. We drive into Manhattan for the night and crash with Blake, a coke dealer I know, figuring we'll catch a flight out the next day.

Instead, we end up holing up at Blake's apartment for a month. Besides missing the Morocco gig, I flake on some bookings in L.A., and my manager leaves a series of increasingly exasperated voicemails for me. Blake is a dope fiend, and stingy with her heroin, but she gives me a little bump. It's so small I don't think it will have any effect, but ten minutes later I feel comfortable and slowed down and leveled out. This is what I need in my life. Maybe heroin can be my savior.

For now, though, I'm not done with cocaine hell, and back in L.A. I embrace my dangerous lifestyle, going to a tattoo parlor on Sunset called Shamrock Social Club and getting a *13*—which has replaced *7* as my lucky number—inked behind my left ear.

One day, my friend Maria says, "You need money? I know how to get some." Okay. "We should stick up a liquor store in West Hollywood." She says she's done it before. We're both high. We both need money. But I don't believe that she's going to go through with it, and I roll with her bluff.

In the car outside the store, she pulls on a ski mask and gives me one to put on. I always try to act like I know what I'm doing, that *I've got this* and I'm not freaked out. But I'm high, and I'm shaken. She's going through with it. I'm trembling with fear, afraid that a cop might walk in, or that the person we're robbing could pull a shotgun out from under the counter. I have no idea what's going to happen.

Once inside, Maria flashes a handgun and tells the cashier to give her all the money in the register, which is only a few hundred dollars. I just stand there. *Holy shit, holy shit, I can't believe this is happening.* Afterward, I feel exhilaration and an adrenaline rush, which I do like. *Holy shit, that was unbelievable.*

In L.A., I often cop drugs on the street. I'll go down to Skid Row, a place rife with drugs and addiction, find someone who looks like a drug addict, and say, "Take me to where the best shit is, and I'll break you off a piece." Around eleven one spring morning, I go to Skid Row and buy five balloons of heroin and four coke rocks. Minutes later, as I steer through the intersection of Fifth Street and Broadway, I hear a siren and see police lights in my rearview. I ignore this development and keep driving—"erratically" and "straddling two lanes," the police will later claim. Eventually, I pull over near Third and Broadway. I fail a field sobriety test, and the cops arrest me. They find a bag in the car's center console, containing 1.8 grams of heroin. They also find a folded receipt containing the crack, weighing .61 grams, and a four-inch glass pipe with burnt crack residue.

"This isn't right," I say. "Why do you arrest drug addicts?"

Erin flew to Philly this morning, so I call Amanda to bail me out.

She picks me up. I'm grateful, but then she starts in with her scolding, and at the first light I jump out of the car. She starts screaming and threatening to pull my bail, but I know she won't, and I keep walking until I get back to Skid Row. I just want to get high again.

When I go to court, I'm put on probation, lose my driver's license, and am ordered to attend substance-abuse classes once a week. I go to one, give the instructor a Sony PlayStation to sign me in for the rest, and never go back.

How far can I push myself? I want to do a stickup without Maria. I've always had a fascination with guns. I had a BB gun, growing up in Montecito, and one time when I was ten, after seeing my neighbor beating her dog, my friend and I sat in my tree house and shot out her windows, which earned me a stern talking-to from Dad. I also went hunting a couple of times, once while visiting Dad on set in South Africa, and later when we visited producer Joel Silver at his house in Yemassee, South Carolina, and shot quail and pheasants.

Maria mentioned that motels are good targets, because they have cash, and I decide I'll hit a seedy place on the eastern edge of Hollywood. My friend Coco drives me. I met her in New York and have always been impressed by her. She hustled her way through Columbia University, and we've had an off-and-on romance.

I'm using an air gun, which looks like a regular handgun but is powered by a small CO_2 cartridge and shoots tiny pellets. It's only slightly more powerful than a BB gun, so I comfort myself that what I'm doing isn't so bad. Coco waits in the car in the alley behind the motel. I go in wearing a ski mask and holding my gun and come away with a couple hundred dollars. Risk and reward are clearly out of whack: this is not going to be a sustainable way to pay my bills, and I know I'm inviting disaster. But I'm doing it less for the money than for the adrenaline, the knowledge that I'm able to do it, and the bragging rights. I like confusing people, making them puzzle over how someone who came from so much privilege can do such crazy shit. I don't tell Coco, or anyone else, that I'm using a pellet gun.

I do a third stickup, this time entirely on my own. I tell Erin I'll be right back. I put a bandanna on my face, get on my motorcycle, and gun down the hill. I am scared and excited. I pull up at a nondescript motel and go into the front office. An older white woman is at the desk. I pull out my gun. She stays quiet and backs away as I reach around and open the cash drawer. She's not in mortal danger, but she doesn't know that. There's only some change and one $20 bill, which I grab. I race home, crazy with the energy rush, proud of my balls, flushed with embarrassment at my paltry haul, and ashamed at having done something so outside of my character. Doing stickups at tiny hole-in-the-wall places, not even expecting to get much money—I never pictured myself in situations like these. But things are so bad and empty for me, my life is such a mess, and the stickups at least provide crumbs for my ego, scraps of self-worth, giving me a feeling of power: *At least I have the balls to think about this and follow through on it.* Or so I console my lost self.

One of my biggest regrets, later, will be how little time I spend with my grandparents during these years, especially Granny. I've always had such a strong relationship with her, and I'd like to think that we touch base occasionally, but it's possible that as much as a year goes by when I have no contact with her at all.

At the moment, there's even more distance between me and Mom than usual. She has a lot going on. She's entangled in her custody battle with her ex-fiancé, Zack Bacon, and is trying to keep me away from him, knowing he might use my behavior to gain leverage. We rarely speak, and Amanda has recently told me—actually said the words out loud—that I'm not welcome at my own house.

Mom is now dating Michael Klein, a rich entrepreneur who's into yoga and the Grateful Dead and lives in a 13,000-square-foot guitar-shaped house north of San Francisco. He's a nice guy, but he wears a fanny pack and Birkenstocks and has little in common with Mom. He eats only raw food. Mom's raw tastes don't go much beyond sushi and caviar.

I'm skeptical of this new relationship, but when Mom and Michael decide to get married, in Santa Barbara in December 2005, I reluctantly agree to walk her down the aisle. I'm thinking: *I'm not welcome at your house, but you want me at your wedding, because it will look better to have your son there?* Mom says she'll make it easy for me, renting a tuxedo and arranging for a car to pick me up at home in L.A.

On the day of the ceremony, Amanda keeps calling—"Jesus, Cameron, roll out of bed, get in the car!" I keep saying, "Yeah, I just need another half hour." Amanda starts calling Erin: "Put him in the fucking car!" But I don't like this guy. I don't like the idea of Mom marrying him, and I don't want to be part of their wedding. I know my skipping it will really hurt Mom's feelings, but I'm angry at her. I'm angry about her relationship with Amanda, among other things. I've told her: "If you want to know something, why not come to me and ask me? Why do you have this woman snooping around my life, giving you half-truths?" And then I have my longer-standing resentment toward Mom, warranted or not, dating back to childhood. I probably want to hurt her feelings.

I never get in the car. Mom is devastated, and embarrassed in front of all her friends. I'm her only family in the world, and I blew off her wedding. The marriage lasts less than a year.

I have my third seizure in a room at the Beverly Laurel, an out-of-the-way motel where I sometimes crash. I come to on the floor next to the mini-fridge, with Erin giving me CPR. I've pissed myself, and my teeth hurt from clenching, and our friend Jill is crying hysterically, but I'm pleased that Erin has followed my edict and not called an ambulance.

My reaction, as with my earlier seizures, is to worry that everyone around me is going to be scared and nervous and come between me and my drugs. I want to be getting high again. My insane behavior is scary to others but not to me, not until years later, when I won't be able to understand how I could ever have thought this way.

Just when it seems like my death is preordained, and that I'll be found impaled on a steering column or slumped over with a needle in my leg or sprawled on a bodega floor with a cop's bullet in my head, something unexpected happens that causes my life to swerve in a more hopeful direction.

Amanda, still thinking I'm addicted to heroin, reads an article online about ibogaine, a supposed miracle cure made from the bark of a tree that grows in Central Africa. It's a hallucinogen long used by tribes there as part of a rite of passage from boy to man, and is gnarly enough that it's an alternative to another rite, in which a boy kills a male lion and returns home with its testicles dangling from his spear point.

Ibogaine isn't officially recognized as a therapy in the U.S., so I agree to go down to Tijuana for it. It will get Amanda and Mom and Dad off my back. My family, still thinking I'm addicted to heroin, will pay for whatever they believe could be a cure. At a club in Hollywood, I run into my DJ friend Magnum, a musical hero of mine since I was young. He's in bad shape, addicted to I'm-not-sure-what and looking to get clean, and I convince him to go down to the ibogaine clinic with me.

Ibogaine has been called a miracle cure for drug addiction, which does sound appealing, but since I know that my addiction is to cocaine, I have more modest ambitions for the experiment: I'm mainly just curious about what could be a powerful hallucinogenic trip, an interesting and possibly enlightening vision quest.

The process is supposed to take seven days, and Amanda drives me down to a café in San Diego, where I meet a guy named Nathen, who shuttles me over the border to an unassuming four-bedroom house in a leafy neighborhood. Inside is the clinic called the Ibogaine Association.

I tell a guy in a white lab jacket who seems to be in charge that I have a strong tolerance, and he'd better give me a higher dose than most. I swallow three capsules, put on a pair of blackout goggles, and lie down on a bed on my back, as instructed.

I quickly become nauseous. I stumble with what feel like sea legs to the bathroom, where I vomit and pee at the same time, a strange sensation. I return to the bed until the nausea returns. I try walking to the bathroom again, but this time my legs buckle, and I crawl the rest of the way.

When I'm lying on the bed, goggled, there's no external sensory stimulation. For forty-eight hours, I go on a sort of instrumental tour of my brain. It is as if I can feel each localized chemical reaction taking place in my mind. I am also aware of the systematic loss of my vocabulary: I watch the words drain away into some dark recess of my brain. The visuals and thoughts continue, but now I have no words to attach to them. It's a confusing, helpless, desperate feeling.

At some point, I become aware of someone screaming pitifully, as if they've lost a child. I try getting out of the bed but can't summon the coordination to do it. I pull the goggles off. Colors are blazingly intense. Bright tracers rip across my field of vision. I feel awkward, like a newborn animal. The screaming hasn't stopped, and I become aware of a terrible stench. I want to get out of here immediately.

I sit up, swing my legs over the side of the bed, find my cigarettes, and stumble out to my room's balcony. It's late afternoon. The sun is grazing the rooftops of Tijuana. The respite from the stench, and some stilted small talk with another patient who's shown up while I've been on another planet, begins to sharpen my senses.

A nurse tells me that Magnum has been wailing for the better part of two days. That's my first indication of how long I've been lying down. That alone takes some minutes to digest. My ride isn't due for another four days—the ibogaine trip was the treatment, and the remaining days are just for recovery—but I don't think I can stand to be here another four hours.

The nurse asks, "How was it?" I just look at her, then begin to make my way to Magnum's room. He's surrounded by three housekeepers, one rubbing his back softly, one tending to the mess he's made, one standing there looking exhausted. They are tender and understanding.

I don't need to spend four days here recovering. I visualize my couch at home. I picture Junior curled up next to me, him sensing that I am healing and need love. I see myself reunited with Erin. They represent safety. I call Erin and somehow manage to communicate that I need her to pick me up, and I'll meet her at a McDonald's just across the border.

I go downstairs, where two of the housekeepers are watching a tele-novela. They ask if I want something to eat. In my pidgin Spanish, and over their objections, I insist that they call a taxi, or I'll walk to the border.

When the cab drops me off, I tell immigration officials something close to the truth: I am a drug addict who came to Mexico for a cure not offered in the U.S. It's a hallucinogen, and I am still tripping, and it has taken a lot just to get here, and I'm just trying to get home to my family. Though I meet all the criteria for the world's worst drug mule, I must look so pitiful that they don't even go through my backpack.

I walk through the tunnel to the U.S. side, where I find Erin, my salvation, waiting for me in the parking lot beneath the golden arches. I drown her in affection the whole ride back to L.A. For another week I see tracers and sparklers, the aftereffects of the ibogaine. Amazingly, my craving for cocaine has evaporated. I just have no interest in it anymore.

8

1993: Gooned

Mom and Dad were understandably upset about my expulsion from Eaglebrook. I pointed out that Dad smoked pot, but he said that he'd waited until he was nineteen before he tried it for the first time. He told me my brain wasn't fully formed yet, and that drugs would screw up my endorphins, which were responsible for my sense of well-being.

He and Mom announced that they were sending me on a three-week wilderness program in Idaho. I put up no resistance. I knew I'd fucked up, and anyway, it sounded like Outward Bound; I thought it might be fun.

When I got off the plane in Boise, I saw a man with a sign that said SUWS, which stood for School of Urban and Wilderness Survival. Beside him were two miserable-looking boys with carry-on bags, like me. We waited silently until a fourth boy arrived, wearing handcuffs and flanked by two big dudes. He'd been abducted—or "gooned" in SUWS lingo—while sleeping at his parents' house, and brought here against his will. *Wow, at least my parents didn't do that.* I got a momentary peek into the spectrum of parenting styles and felt a new appreciation for my own mother and father.

We rode in a van for two hours, then left the highway and turned onto a dirt road, eventually stopping at a rickety barbed-wire cattle

An early role, in Oliver,
with my friend J.D. at Eaglebrook.

fence with a gate. The rest of the group was already gathered there, in a clearing. There were a dozen of us, boys and girls, and two adult male field instructors—lean, taciturn guys who looked like they'd spent a lot of time outside.

It was October, in the Owyhee Desert in southern Idaho. We were each handed a set of clothes: green army fatigues, hiking boots, a T-shirt, a red hooded sweatshirt, and socks. Stacks of material were scattered on the grass. I was given a bundle of tarp, string, tape, four ounces of powdered milk, rice, lentils, flour to make dumplings, raisins for a treat, and a can of peaches in syrup. We had no packs, and I asked how we were supposed to carry our gear. "I'm glad you asked," a bald guide who seemed more senior said in a quiet monotone. "Watch closely, and I'll show you." He proceeded to patch together a makeshift pack out of the string, tape, and tarp.

That night, we hiked a few miles. Then the other guide, who had scraggly facial hair, announced that we were going to make camp. He said, "Tonight, I want you to take out your can of peaches. Enjoy them, because you're not going to have anything tasty like this for some time." When we'd finished, he told us that the can was going to be our cooking pot going forward. He gave us buck knives, and we each punched a couple of holes near the rim of our can, threading a wire between them to make a handle. A second, larger can would serve as our drinking cup and be filled with water each morning, which we'd have to boil the night before to make it drinkable.

I realized the next day that it was a lot of water. The guides insisted each of us finish our allotment before we could set out on the day's hike. Some kids struggled to finish it and vomited. Some kids threw fits, crying and screaming and cursing. But it was all the water we'd be drinking that day, and without it we'd risk dehydration or worse.

One morning, a chubby girl who was constantly throwing tantrums refused to drink her water. Then she threw it on the ground. The rest of us had to wait while she made a fire, boiled a new can of water, let it cool, and drank it. Some of the other kids yelled at her. The guides were patient and never got emotional.

The later we set out, the hotter it was and the later we'd reach that day's destination. Sometimes we wouldn't get going until two in the afternoon; then we'd stumble into our destination at ten that night, and finish our chores around three in the morning. We'd only get two and a half hours of sleep before we had to wake up at the crack of dawn and do it all over again. In case anyone got ideas about running, before we went to sleep the guides confiscated our boots.

On the second day, after we reached our destination, we were each instructed to find a piece of wood to start fashioning our fire-making kit. One of the guides demonstrated. He took a bent, flexible stick and tied a string to each end, making a bow. He then took a straight stick that would serve as a drill; and a flat piece of wood, with a shallow socket cut out, for a fireboard. Finally, he took his buck knife, which had a divot in the handle, and rested it on top of the drill. "That's how you get pressure when you're trying to start a fire," he said. As he sawed the bow back and forth, the drill spun rapidly in the socket, and smoke began to wisp upward. He took the drill out of the hole, revealing a tiny coal, which he tipped into a nest of fibers he'd made from dried grass and twigs. He blew on the nest, and as flames began to rise, he put it beneath a stack of kindling.

Now it was our turn to make bow drills. As I was cutting out the notch in my fireboard, I slipped and cut my finger deeply. I was bleeding a lot and could see bone. I was secretly thrilled, confident that I'd found my ticket out of this hellscape. This was an expensive program. They'd have to evacuate me to a hospital, probably by helicopter. I went over to one of our guides to present my program-ending injury.

"Go get me a twig this size," he said, indicating a three-inch length.

"What do you mean? Look at my finger. I need to go to a doctor."

"Yeah, no, it's too far."

I brought him a twig, and he put it next to my finger, made a splint, taped it up, and turned his attention elsewhere.

In that moment, I realized this wasn't going to be like Outward Bound. It was going to be like one of those programs for troubled teens that *60 Minutes* investigates after a mounting number of fatalities results in state licensing authorities revoking accreditation.

For twenty-one days we hiked in the desert, walking from dawn until dusk. Every night, we broke down our packs and set up our tarps as shelter. Every morning, before sunrise, we reassembled the packs. The nights were freezing. The days were blazing hot. The desert was barren. We wiped our asses with leaves. We were all dead tired and hungry, struggling to adjust to the minuscule amount of food. Several kids had panic attacks.

The days seemed to go on forever. Just when I wanted to do nothing more than lie down and go to sleep, we'd have to first do our chores, like going to the stream to get water and making a fire to boil it for the next morning.

The guides would do things like "tie" you, behaviorally, to someone who was struggling. I was one of the younger kids, but I adapted pretty quickly and moved to the head of the class. I took great pride in my bow and excelled at starting fires. I got tied a couple of times to the chubby tantrum-thrower. I couldn't go to sleep until she'd finished what she had to do. I could give her pointers and try to keep her motivated, but I couldn't do the work for her.

One night that first week, as we were setting up camp, another group of kids came out of the bushes without warning. They were in their third week. Every group spent its third week tracking the next group of first-weekers. A lot of first-week kids would run, a pointless exercise in a vast desert where there was nowhere to go. When they did run, third-weekers would have to go and rescue them. The third-weekers' visit to our camp was intended as inspiration: our ragtag group could one day—in a couple weeks—have our shit together like they did.

Our rations were insufficient, forcing us to eat ants, crickets, roots—anything we could get our hands on. We learned how to make traps to catch desert mice. You'd put two pieces of wood together to make a T, top it with a heavy rock, brace it with a thin tiny stick, and put a raisin on that. When a mouse went for the raisin, the stick would move or break, and the rock would slam down on dinner. Then we'd skin it, gut it, roast it, and get a couple of nibbles of meat. We were so hungry that if we caught one, we were eating it. One evening two weeks in, when we reached that day's destination, a bag of apples was waiting for us. We each got one. I ate the core and the seeds, too. Everyone did. That's how hungry we were. It's amazing how much you can enjoy an apple.

Then we did solos. Everyone was assigned his own isolated plot, far enough apart that none of us could see each other. Each plot was marked by a circle of stones with a ten-foot radius, and we had to stay in the circle for three days. The guides gave us each a pencil and notebook. I journaled. I did my mundane daily chores. I made my fires and tended them. I managed my sparse rations. I could eat as much as I wanted or as little as I wanted in a sitting, but those rations had to last the whole three days. The solo was profound, and it was trying. I'd never been alone like that, and it was hard to be with myself for so many hours, but I found to my surprise that I enjoyed the solitude. The silence was spiritual. I took pride in how well I was adapting to the challenge.

The third and final week, it was our turn to track the next group of first-weekers, spying on them through a telescope. By then, we were thin as twigs and caked with desert dirt, but there was a shared sense that in a short time we'd all matured and grown in surprisingly meaningful ways. Even the kids who'd really struggled and you didn't think were going to make it were coming along. We'd formed a fairly capable and cohesive unit. It was a real confidence builder, for all of us.

One morning, we woke up and set out hiking for the last time. We walked for hours, singing in the predawn darkness. Eventually, as we approached what the guides called "trail's end," we could see our families walking to meet us. Mom and Dad were there, and we hugged. Then, each kid demonstrated a skill learned over the past few weeks.

Some kids demonstrated how to make a mousetrap, others how to make the nest used to turn an ember into a fire. I'd decided to show how I could make a fire with my wooden bow. It was a windy morning. I worked on it, and I couldn't get it. I could tell that the guides were on the verge of saying, "It's okay, let's move on." But I wouldn't stop. I kept working on the flame, working on it, working on it, refusing to give up. Finally, it caught. I warmed the embers, built the fire. Mom and Dad were so proud. They had a look on their faces that I hadn't seen in a while: hopeful.

We went to the hotel where the families were staying, and where there was going to be a brunch buffet for all the kids and their parents. Before I jumped into the shower in my room, I paused to look in a full-length mirror in the bathroom. It was the first time I'd seen myself in three weeks. I saw a different person, lean and mean and dirty, a young warrior. I liked this version of me. It made sense. I felt like I'd gone through some real changes. I'd tested myself and come out stronger. I was fourteen.

Dad was between *Falling Down* and *Disclosure,* and Mom was gearing up for the release of a documentary about Dada artist Beatrice Wood that she had helped produce. While they tried to figure out where to send me next, they parked me in New York City at a place called Beekman, which was basically *The Breakfast Club:* The School. Beekman had a smoking garden, I got to make my own schedule, and kids sat on their desks in class or openly carried on side conversations. My friends and I arranged our classes so that we had a two-hour lunch block, when we'd go to the park, skate, and smoke weed. Afterward, I'd sit through math stoned, while Charlie, our teacher, gamely tried to impart knowledge to our classroom of ne'er-do-wells.

Beekman was on East Fiftieth Street, near to where many of my BHC tagger friends lived, and right in prime skating territory. The skyscrapers in midtown had staircases and fountains and rails and ramps; we were in a constant war with the security guards as we went for kick flips, really high ollies, trashcan ollies, 180 ollies, nollies (off the nose), tail slides, nose slides, board slides, and grinding (sliding on the trucks). My graffiti improved. I got the lettering down pretty well, and basics like throw-ups and big outlines and bubble letters, though I never mastered the more intricate, artistic piecing.

Post-Idaho, I had more confidence, and a newfound desire to test myself and see what else I was capable of. Skating, I'd grab onto moving buses and trucks and taxis, letting them pull me down the avenues. The taxi drivers were the craziest; when they'd see me in their rearview mirrors, they wouldn't stop or yell, they'd punch the gas. A few times, they accelerated so quickly that, if I'd fallen off, I could easily have died.

Tagging, I'd join the crew in seeking out the most hard-to-reach spots. We climbed scaffolding, so that when it was removed, people would wonder: *How the fuck did you get up there?* We wrote on the sides of interborough bridges, wrapping one end of an extra long belt around a railing and the other end around ourselves, and dangling off the side of the bridge to paint. I was fixated on pushing myself to see what I would do and what I could do. I wanted to go further than any of the kids I was hanging out with. I got off on the exhilaration and adrenaline and on the respect I earned through my antics. In my teenage mind, they made up for the baggage of my last name.

Meanwhile I was trying new drugs, expanding into ecstasy and cocaine, which I bought from delivery services in the city. My behavior, as far as I was concerned, was consistent with the warrior version of myself I'd glimpsed in Idaho. To me, SUWS had been about having a positive experience, not about turning myself around, so now I didn't feel like I was regressing. My life felt fun and relatively innocent. I was enjoying the freedom that I had.

It was also around this time that I started to get into DJing and electronic music, through Deter. His real name was Beau, and he was resident DJ for two Drum & Bass parties in the city: Camouflage and Koncrete Jungle. I'd carry his records to the parties, dance at them, and then go back to the tiny apartment he shared with his mom on St. Mark's Place, where he'd let me mess around on his turntables. Drum & Bass was good training. It had the fastest tempo of all the EDM genres—160 to 180 beats per minute—so once I mastered beat-matching in D&B, everything else came easily.

I liked Beekman, but I wasn't in a position to press the issue of where my parents sent me next, and when I was allowed to return to Eaglebrook for the second semester of ninth grade, I went, and I managed to stay out of trouble.

That summer, in Mallorca, I experienced my first love. I finally worked up the courage to declare my feelings for Galen, my longtime crush. It turned out she felt the same way, and we'd sit up in the pool pavilion at S'Estaca and just stare at each other, for hours. We began a relationship that would last for several years.

I found that I was getting less sensitive to Dad's anger. One night, Jay and I went barhopping in Deià and then dirt biking in the hills. We got back to the house around five in the morning, much later than I'd said we would, and we were loud coming in, waking Dad up. He called me to his room. He was naked—I guess he slept that way—and started yelling at me and getting right up in my face. Maybe he poked me in the chest to drive home a point. Soon, we were manhandling each other. Then I threw him against the wall.

I think we were both startled that it had happened. Neither of us said anything, and I walked out, but it was a turning point. Something fundamental and unspoken had shifted in the way we saw each other.

For tenth grade, Mom and Dad, whose marriage was still limping along, found a Quaker boarding school in Yardley, Pennsylvania, called the George School, an hour and a half from New York City. It wasn't as lax as Beekman, but it was more laid-back and progressive than Eaglebrook.

At George, I channeled my aggression into sports. On the lacrosse field I adapted my Youth Football technique. I wasn't the biggest guy on the team, but I had good stick skills, and I was decisively the hardest hitter. I played right midfield, which put me about twenty-five yards away from the center spot. Usually, the players facing off would be in there for a while as each tried to get the ball. I found that if I took off at a sprint, I could usually get there before one of them controlled the ball. Keeping my hands together, which made my checks legal, I'd run at top speed, sending my target and his pads exploding in all directions. Though the hits were legal, they were so savage that referees started calling penalties, citing me for unsportsmanlike conduct or unnecessary roughness. But I became known for delivering crushing blows, and it was an effective strategy. Once hit by me, a player who found himself in a face-off again would be anxious to get out of there as quickly as possible, which led to unforced errors. Pummeling people—leveling them—was what I was best at, and what I liked to do. Dad got a kick out of my ferocity on the field, and the coaches loved it. At the varsity banquet at George, the head coach, who liked to give nicknames, singled a few of us out, calling me Cam "I'll Slam You" Douglas.

I thrived at George, playing varsity football too, enjoying the company of girls, and making a couple of good friends. I also hung out with two janitors at the school who lived in Trenton and who I'd leave campus with to smoke blunts. On weekends, me and a couple of like-minded friends would take the train to New York, where I continued skating and tagging and increasingly DJing with Beau.

I don't remember the first time I did coke, but I really started ramping up my use that year at George. In New York, we'd buy coke in tinfoil bindles, and we'd bring a couple of them with us on the train back to George, finishing them by Sunday night. I had ADD, and the cocaine focused me. It was rocket fuel for the life I was living and liking. I was feeling myself. I was a decent athlete. I was popular. The coke allowed me to stay up for hours and made whatever I was doing more enjoyable. Coke also conferred social advantages. I was doing it with older kids, seniors, so it had an aura that I liked. And it provided one more avenue for my overall ambition, which was to bend rules, push boundaries, and be more extreme than other kids. That instinct was powerful in me.

Drugs and alcohol weren't yet my highest priority. That winter, tired after three years of wrestling, which was stressful and demanding, I switched to swimming for the season, thinking it would be more fun. I was still focused on sports and girls and skateboarding. Drugs, though, were the cause of my next move.

Since my expulsion from Eaglebrook, Mom and Dad had required me to submit to random urine tests. I failed one of these, and then—I don't remember this, but Dad insists it's what happened—I was either expelled from George or asked not to return after my weed stash was found in the giant katsura tree on the school's south lawn, which also serves as the school's logo. At that point, I convinced Mom and Dad that the best place for me was back in California. They were more persuadable than usual, maybe because they had a lot on their minds. Their marriage, which had been circling the drain for a while now, was about to take the final plunge.

9

1977–1995: Mom and Dad

My parents' marriage began, as it would end, at the Beverly Wilshire Hotel.

When Mom met Dad in 1977, she was a sophomore at Georgetown University's School of Foreign Service. She'd interned at the White House but had become disillusioned with her ambition to join the diplomatic corps. She was at home in rarefied circles, and was close to members of the Iranian royal Pahlavi family and U.S. congressman John Brademas. Her friend Stuart, a son of future Governor of Rhode Island Bruce Sundlun, was working for the Actors Studio's James Lipton, who was producing a State Department reception for Jimmy Carter's inauguration, and Mom went as Stuart's plus-one to the event at the Kennedy Center. She was nineteen.

Dad was thirty-two, and on top of the world. The year before, as producer of *One Flew Over the Cuckoo's Nest,* he'd won the Best Picture Oscar, then spent the next twelve months on a hedonistic round-the-world victory lap with Jack Nicholson, who'd won Best Actor as the film's lead. The inauguration was one of the final stops. Dad arrived at the Kennedy Center gala with Jack and Warren Beatty, and all three of them were enthralled with the ethereal young beauty in a white dress named Diandra de Morrell Luker. Dad, in particular, was infatuated and spent much of the evening talking with her on the lip of a fountain in the upstairs atrium.

Mom, for her part, had no idea who the dashing man with a beard and shag of hair was, and at first she thought he might be a well-known painter or writer. As the reception wound down, Mom invited Dad to go with her and Stuart to Pisces, a club in Georgetown. Dad said he'd meet them there later, but Mom said the club was private and she wasn't sure he'd be able to get in. Dad confidently assured her it wouldn't be a problem. Then he got there, and it was a problem—until eventually he got word to her inside and she came out and fetched him. He invited her to the inauguration the following day.

The next morning it was freezing, and Dad said, "Not to be too forward, but let's watch from my hotel room. We can open the window, look down Pennsylvania Avenue, and we'll have a good view." They spent the rest of the weekend together, and as soon as Dad got back to L.A., he called to invite Mom for a visit. Four weeks later, they were engaged. Pappy asked Dad if he was sure he didn't want to wait a bit. Dad said yes, he was sure about this.

They were married on March 20, 1977, eight weeks after they'd met, beside the pool in Pappy's backyard in Beverly Hills, with a small group of guests who included Jack Nicholson, Warren Beatty, Karl Malden, and Gregory Peck. The ceremony was followed by a big reception at the Beverly Wilshire Hotel. Afterward, Dad invited a few dozen people upstairs to a large Moroccan suite he'd reserved. There, Mom innocently asked a woman she was talking to why three people had just gone into the bathroom together.

Mom had an elegance that stood out in Los Angeles. She was long-waisted, with dark blond Botticelli curls, a patrician nose, and perfect posture. But Dad was chasing his dreams, Mom was a new transfer student at UCLA, and the culture of Hollywood, where she knew almost no one, was alien to her.

When she went to her first industry dinner party, she sat next to Walter Matthau's wife, Carol, who was in her fifties, wore white Kabuki makeup, and turned to Mom and said, "I understand you just got married. Can I give you some advice? If you want to be a really

Mom and Dad's wedding, at Pappy's house.

great Hollywood wife, you'll have all your teeth removed." Mom was perplexed. Dad had to explain the crude joke to her later.

On her twenty-first birthday, Dad threw a big party for Mom at the house they'd rented in Beverly Hills, and it was a disaster. Though Mom had tonsillitis, Dad didn't cancel the party, and while she lay ill in bed upstairs, he partied downstairs with Foreigner and other guests, nearly all of them his friends. Finally, at 5 a.m., Mom kicked everyone out. Afterward, she decided she didn't like show business or the people in it. This would be a problem, since that was Dad's life.

Dad soon bought a ranch-style house on Tower Grove Drive. It had a panoramic view and would later gain notoriety as the headquarters of

Heidi Fleiss's prostitution business. Mom and Dad were living there when Mom got pregnant.

Mom didn't have a lot of emotional support. Surrounded by ambitious and successful people fixated on a single industry, it was hard for her to carve out an identity of her own. Dad was immersed in producing and acting in *The China Syndrome,* and pregnant Mom, thinking maybe she could act, had a small part in the film.

I was born on December 13, 1978, at Cedars-Sinai Medical Center. I was a bald baby, and Mom and Dad called me Swifty, after the hairless superagent Swifty Lazar. Mom, as an only child who'd been raised largely by a governess and had no family nearby, was overwhelmed.

Soon after, with Mom not having warmed up to Hollywood, we moved to Santa Barbara. But Dad needed to be in L.A. for business, and he spent half of every week there. As his acting career took off, he'd be gone for months at a time. When he was home, and even when he wasn't, all of the attention was focused on him, which created tension between them. She didn't approve of his friends or their drug-fueled hedonism.

Six years into the marriage, when I was four, Fox greenlit *Romancing the Stone,* making it clear to Mom that her often-absent husband would be even scarcer in the coming years, and she asked him for a separation. They didn't say anything about it to me, and I was used to Dad's absences, so at the time I had no inkling of a formal change in their relationship, and within months they decided to give things another try and ended the separation.

What I do remember is that while Dad was shooting the movie down in Mexico, Mom, one of her artist girlfriends, me, and our dog got in a Toyota jeep with a tank of gas on its roof and headed south across the border, down through the Baja peninsula. We stopped in little towns, at one point having the engine changed out because ours wasn't compatible with the available gas, and at another point driving onto a car ferry, until we finally reached Careyes, a fishing village.

We watched tortoises being born on the beach. We saw migrating monarch butterflies. I learned to scuba dive in the hotel pool. And I remember the scorpions: As we rode horses one day, a scorpion fell out of a tree onto Mom's shoulder. Another night, there was a downpour, and scorpions swarmed through cracks in our hotel room walls, while Mom and I stood on the bed panicking over whether they were crawling up the bedposts. Some evenings, Mom would go out with friends, leaving me in the care of a Mexican babysitter who, although I was already five, pressed me to her naked breast and tried to nurse me.

Eight years into the marriage, Mom learned that Dad was having a fling with Kathleen Turner and told him she was contemplating filing for divorce. She gave him an ultimatum—we move east, or we're done—and so we packed up and relocated to New York, to the apartment on Central Park West, where we would live for the next five years.

Mom liked being able to reconnect with her East Coast friends, and found her footing when she got a job at the Met, making documentary films. "Hollywood isn't the whole world, Cameron," Mom said.

Mom and Dad, beyond just their age gap, were really very different people. Mom put a premium on beauty and refinement. Dad was pragmatic. He didn't really care what he looked like, would travel with just a carry-on, and could get away with it.

During this period in New York, Dad was laser-focused on his career—on escaping the shadow of Pappy and building his own identity. The perks of his exploding fame—reflected glory, a life of luxury, interesting opportunities—gave Mom a big life, but his success also meant that he was busier than ever, away more often, and more stressed.

The pressures of his work seemed to translate into pressure on their marriage. Even when he was physically present, he could be emotionally absent. Mom felt lonely and neglected, and she blamed the whole culture of Hollywood, with its hedonism and thirst for the adulation of strangers. She thought Dad didn't understand how difficult it was to be his wife. I think she felt that her main job, for many years, was to do damage control.

Dad, for his part, felt unappreciated and thought Mom was ungrateful. When they'd fight over his inattention, or over his drinking and drugging, he'd say: "Where do you think this all comes from?" Over time, a lot of resentment built up between them, and they lived largely separate lives.

I'd always adored Dad and put him on a pedestal, but for a while I was angry with him, seeing him as the engineer of Mom's misery. In time, I came to see that Mom's version of the story wasn't the whole story. Dad wasn't the only one with distractions. Sometimes, there'd be men at the house, and Mom's whole demeanor would change, including her accent and mannerisms. Eventually, my anger flipped toward her. And because she was the more present parent, she probably unfairly bore the brunt of my confused pain.

In early 1992, when I was thirteen and before *Basic Instinct* came out, as Mom tells the story, Dad took me to a screening. She didn't want me to go, but Dad told her he'd rather I see it with him than hear about it from kids at school. Mom says I returned home crying and made her "promise you'll never go and see that movie." She swore that she wouldn't, and to this day she says that she still hasn't seen it. I don't remember any of this happening, and Dad says, "Cam, I did *not* let you see *Basic Instinct* when you were thirteen."

The fall of 1992, after we got back from Mallorca and the Summer Olympics in Barcelona, was when Dad checked into the rehab clinic in Arizona for his supposed "sex addiction."

My general strategy was to try to tune out whatever they were going through, but I knew things weren't good between them. I was conscious of whenever something particularly bad happened, and aware of Mom's tactics, and of what she caught Dad doing, and of what she was doing. I just chose disengagement over the emotional distress I saw other kids whose parents had bad marriages go through.

Finally, in the summer of 1995, when I was sixteen, Mom hired a P.I. to tail Dad, and she later showed me telephoto surveillance shots of him at the Beverly Wilshire with another woman.

Mom had threatened divorce for years, and I think she was hoping to use the pictures as leverage to rein Dad in. In the past, her ultimatums had worked, at least for a time. Maybe because Dad felt guilty—he was the bad guy, in Mom's framing of their marital problems—he kept coming back, trying to make up for his behavior.

For a long time both of them resisted ending the marriage. Each had been traumatized by their own parents' divorces. Mom had been shipped off to boarding school, and Pappy has told a story about paying for Granny, after their divorce, to bring their sons to visit him in Paris: "One day we were walking in the Bois de Boulogne when Michael put my hand in Diana's and said, 'Now the family's together.'" They thought a divorce would harm me. But this time, when Mom finally filed for divorce, Dad, I think to her surprise, agreed. He was tired of that dance. Dad now thinks they should have divorced years earlier.

It's sad to think back on, but when they told me they were getting divorced, it didn't knock my socks off. Actually, I welcomed it. I loved them both, and wanted to be around them if they were happy, but since that was so rare, and my exposure to them was mainly when they weren't happy, none of us was happy. I wondered if it was normal that I was relieved. I'd seen divorce crush other kids.

I say all that, but when I reflect now on the direction I was going in then—a trajectory on which I was about to skip the rails altogether—I have to think that their marriage was slowly wearing away at me, and that I was sitting on a lot of unacknowledged rage. My behavior, which was about to become dramatically more aggressive and reckless, clearly had something to do with what was happening at home.

2006: More Cheeva

I bogaine, praised for helping addicts to kick heroin, is for me the thing that, by disrupting my cocaine addiction, helps me to embrace heroin. This is a good thing, at first. It's arguably irresponsible to do a PSA for such a harmful drug, but initially, for me, heroin is a godsend. It medicates my unease in a much less violently destructive way than coke did.

On the West Coast, heroin is sold as tar—soft, tacky black balls that melt in the sun. People call it *dope, brown, negra, cheeva.* Tar is less refined than the white powder sold on the East Coast, and cheaper. I don't have much disposable income at this point, and I cop on the street, a few balloons at a time. I break off a little piece of tar, put it in a spoon, draw some water up into a syringe, and squirt it onto the cheeva. The water turns a muddy color. Holding a lighter under the spoon, I heat it. The impurities cook off, leaving clear maple syrup–colored liquid and a few burnt solids. Then I take a cotton ball or the cotton from a cigarette filter and stick the needle into it, using it as a filtration system as I draw the liquid up through the cotton. I find a vein in my leg, put the needle in, pull back on the plunger—people call this "flagging"—and look for a ribbon of blood, evidence I'm in the vein. Then I press down, and lift off.

In the beginning, when I shoot up, my eyes are pinned, but the symptom soon fades, and no one can tell I'm high unless I really overdo it. Erin, who's right there with me in the transition from coke to heroin, is happy with the change. On blow, I could sometimes disappear for days. On cheeva, I'm never away from home for more than a few hours. Instead of clubbing, Erin and I spend hours at Amoeba Music, a huge independent record store on Sunset, going through racks of vinyl, and at 24-hour newsstands, where I buy muscle car magazines, science magazines, music magazines. At home, on my PlayStation, I devote whole days to *Oblivion*, a new medieval-fantasy game.

Suddenly, I can function again. I go from hiding in my closet to wanting to go out, even just to eat. Friends find me calm and sweet. I build, and rebuild, relationships. I see my family. I'm focused and go to business meetings. I stop drinking. My life feels like it's coming together.

"You're back," a friend says.

Money is still a problem. Not a problem like I can't pay my rent or buy food. But I'm supporting both Erin and Jay, who has joined us in California after his roommate in New York descended into a drug-induced paranoid psychosis, putting tape on everything he owned and hurling his laptop off the Brooklyn Bridge. To me, Jay's return now is a member of my family coming home—but it's expensive, because I'm bankrolling all of our drug habits as well. And I'm no longer earning the income I was when I was DJing. Cash is always tight.

A 9-to-5 job is out of the question. There's no way in my current state that I could get one, much less hold it down. But even if I quit drugs, I'd be unlikely to get one. The closest I've ever had to a regular job was working construction with a friend one summer and a stint in high school when I volunteered at the Motion Picture & Television Country House and Hospital, a retirement home in L.A. for show business people, a gig I really liked. For money, I've DJed and I've acted. The luxury of never having been forced to punch the clock has left me highly resistant to doing it.

Now, though, I remember an encounter in New York, right before I moved to L.A. I ran into Alex Rose, who'd been my trainer at the David Barton Gym on Astor Place when I was getting in shape for *It Runs in the Family*. He made music on the side, and we became close friends. I was vaguely aware that he also sold crystal by the ounce for Emmanuel Marais, a big dog in dealing crystal to New York's gay club scene. Emmanuel is in his mid-forties and has a heavy Parisian accent. He studied at the Sorbonne and was a food entrepreneur until he fell on hard times after 9/11. He's done well enough selling crystal that he has homes in the Catskills and on Fire Island. When I saw Alex in October, he said that if I got to know anyone out in L.A. who could get quality Tina—as crystal was called in New York—at a good price, he and Emmanuel would be interested in buying it.

Until now, I've dismissed the idea, not wanting to cross that line. I see the pellet-gun stickups I've done as just little stunts to feed my ego, not real crimes. They were the acts of a kid dying for attention, unable to get any from anyone, done to bolster his opinion of himself. Even if I'd gotten caught, I assumed I'd never get much time for the crimes of a drug addict, armed with an air gun, who netted maybe $100. Moving weight is different. I know that on the other side of this line is the potential of serious prison time.

But I'm really feeling broke. Erin and I have sometimes bought blow from my pal Gabriel, our landlord's handyman, who is five years older than me. He was born in Mexico but grew up in L.A., and he lives with his three children and his parents and brothers in a house north of the city. He and his brother, Carlos, work at a hardware store in Hollywood by day and deliver drugs at night. Gabriel is tough but has a good heart.

One day, over Erin's objections, I ask Gabriel if he can get me an ounce of good crystal. I explain why. He's interested, and I tell Emmanuel I'm going to send him an ounce, on me, so he can sample "my product." Most guys who sell drugs in quantity are older, started as street dealers, and gradually worked their way up; since I'm trying to bootstrap myself straight into a wholesaling role, I'm trying to act the part of someone for whom giving away an ounce is no big deal.

Mom and Dad after my first sentencing.

So I'm doing it. I'm crossing the line I wasn't going to cross. I consider what that means. I know this isn't going to end well. Then I bat the thought away and forget about it. But it lingers, out of mind, as a feeling of deep foreboding and persistent anxiety.

I'm still auditioning for movie parts, in a half-assed way, and the producers of a budget-slasher flick called *Shrooms* cast me in the lead role. It isn't a step forward, careerwise, but it is a step, as well as a payday I desperately need. Dad is happy that I've gotten a part; maybe he's hoping this is the start of a turnaround. For the two-month shoot in Ireland, the producers will fly me and Erin first-class. Travel poses a new problem, now that Erin and I have a twice-a-day cheeva habit.

On the date of our departure, Saint Patrick's Day, we pack needles in our checked luggage; if they're discovered, we'll say they're for fertility shots. We stuff an orange pill canister with tar, and Erin inserts it between her legs, tampon-style. She is terrified that we're going to get caught at the airport, but body X-rays haven't yet become a standard security measure, and we sail through the TSA checkpoint at LAX.

The drugs should last us two weeks, and we arrange for Jay to FedEx us periodic shipments after that. Jay will also take care of Funny, our rabbit, and ship the ounce of crystal to Alex, for Emmanuel, once Gabriel comes through with it.

The first week in Ireland, we're fine. We're out in the countryside, over the border into Northern Ireland, and I go through rehearsals and fittings. I'm playing one of a group of American college kids who go hunting for psychedelic mushrooms in the woods and are murdered, one after another, by a serial killer. When I'm not working, I retreat to our hotel room to play *Oblivion* and shoot up.

Erin and I need to replenish our supply soon, but Jay is suddenly hard to reach. I call Gabriel, who says he gave Jay the ounce of crystal to ship to Alex. I call Alex, who says he never received a package. I call my landlord, Carine, who says she hasn't seen Jay in days. Fucking Jay. He's a meth fiend, and he has clearly gone AWOL, holing up somewhere and going on a bender with my ice. He's fucked me twice over, and also left Funny to fend for himself. I ask Gabriel to send us some cheeva instead, but he gets cold feet. I plead. He still won't do it.

Erin and I are down to our emergency reserve of cottons. We moisten and mash them to squeeze out whatever trace of heroin residue remains, which yields a couple of small, weak shots.

We start to get sick. We catch a ride to Dublin, an hour-and-a-half south, and roam a neighborhood that looks promising for a street score but come up empty. We decide to go to Germany for the long weekend. We have friends there, club people who we figure can hook us up. But after flying to Düsseldorf and driving to Cologne, where our promoter friend Loki lives, we find out that our friends only have coke connections. We get sicker and sicker. Andrea, my booking agent in Germany, takes us to a soccer game, where Erin and I keep trading commiserating looks: we feel terrible, almost out-of-body. We're both at a point where we shouldn't even be seen in public.

The afternoon of our flight back to Ireland, Loki suddenly says, "You guys should get going." The clock says six, but Daylight Saving Time has just begun, and it's actually seven. Erin and I grab a taxi to the airport but miss our flight. *Fuck fuck fuck.* Erin calls the head of production for *Shrooms* to say I won't make the first day of filming. By now, we haven't shot up in four days and are having serious withdrawal symptoms. My nose is running. My eyes are running. I'm getting cold sweats. I'm shaking. Break dancing when I was a teenager, I did some damage to my tailbone, and now my lower back starts spasming. I can't get comfortable. We sleep at the airport, or try to, and I spend a lot of time in the men's room, throwing up and pissing out of my ass, sometimes simultaneously. My body is screaming for heroin.

I know I'm in deep shit with the producers. When Erin and I land back in Dublin, a driver from the production is waiting for us with a van. During the ride north to the shooting location, I lie on the floor, feet on the ceiling, muttering incomprehensibly. The driver keeps looking at Erin, wondering what's up with me. "He's just exhausted," she says. "We slept in the airport last night and didn't get any sleep." Eventually, I feel so terrible that I ask the driver if he knows of a methadone clinic on our route. He says he doesn't. I'm skeptical. Heroin is epidemic in Ireland and especially in Dublin, a major port for it.

"Hey," I say, "please don't tell the producers I asked you that."

The driver nods, noncommittal.

I'm on a roller coaster of pain. I've heard people say that withdrawal is like the flu, times one million. I'm sweating and feverishly hot, and at the same time I'm freezing. I'm convulsing uncontrollably. I feel like I'm dying. I want to crawl out of my skin.

By the time we get to the hotel, it's dark out, and Paddy, one of the producers, calls up to our room and says they want to talk to me. I'm sprawled on the bed, blackout drunk because I've been drinking to try to feel better. Erin pokes me and says I have to go downstairs.

"This is serious, Cameron."

I tell her she needs to talk to them. I can't.

Erin goes down and tells Paddy and Bob, another producer, that we have food poisoning.

"We know what's going on," Paddy says. "Cameron's a liability, and he's off the movie." They're sending us back to the U.S.

Erin will explain all this to me tomorrow. Tonight I continue to speak delusional nonsense, and I shake and writhe and flail so much that I keep hitting Erin, until she gets up and moves to the other bed.

"What the fuck, Cameron?"

It's the next morning. Dad is on the phone and livid. Someone from the production has let him know what happened.

He gives me an ultimatum: Get on the plane, come back to L.A., go straight into inpatient rehab, and send Erin back to Pennsylvania, or that's it—he's not going to give me any more help or support. It's not an unreasonable demand, and I might be ready to get clean, but I'm not willing to cut ties with Erin. She has stood by me through everything, and I feel that she deserves my loyalty.

Dad starts talking about Uncle Eric again. "You saw what his problems did to Pappy and Oma. In their eighties, they were still going to rehabs and family therapy sessions to talk about what they'd done wrong. I'm not going to let myself be drawn into this behavior anymore. It's ruining and disrupting my life. I have young children and a wife who I need to protect. They've always been supportive of you and shared their love. This isn't fair to them."

"Don't you love me anymore, Dad?"

"Of course I love you, Cameron. You're my son. But I'm not going to nurture a relationship with you, because I think you're going to die. I don't want the same life Pappy had. I don't want to be going into my seventies and eighties trying to solve your problems. I've been seeing a therapist about it."

"What?"

"I think you're going to overdose, or someone's going to kill you, or you're going to kill someone. I'm trying to prepare myself emotionally for that."

11

1995: King of the Shits

Returning to California for eleventh grade, I was ready for a change of mindset. Mom wanted me to go to Laguna Blanca, a private school in Hope Ranch, but I told Dad that I wanted to go to Carpinteria High. Most of my friends, and all the ones who were more interested in getting into trouble than in studying, including my fellow Sewer Rats Dave and Jay, went to Carpinteria High. And it was a public school. By now, being a tough guy had become a priority for me, and you couldn't be a tough guy if you went to private school. Maybe because Dad felt guilty for forcing me to go to Eaglebrook, or for his years of absence, he sided with me and overruled Mom.

I'd been brought up traveling all over the world, surrounded by extremely smart and successful and beautiful people—intellectuals, artists, leaders—in a cultured environment. I'd gone to elite private schools—Birch Wathen, Eaglebrook, George—where I'd been offered a level of education that the public schools around here didn't come close to. I had grown up in the most rarefied enclaves, in exquisitely beautiful homes. And I was aware of how fortunate I'd been to experience all of that. But I also found myself drawn to the rougher, more struggling life of the poor-to-middle class.

Carpinteria was the sheep town near Santa Barbara, rife with lower-middle-class delinquents. The high school had surfer kids. It had cowboys from ranches up in the hills. There weren't many black kids, but there was a significant Mexican gang presence. The bad kids, some of them members of the local Mexican gang called the Carpas—and not the rich preppies of Santa Barbara—were my people.

I took pride in navigating that world comfortably, in having street instincts that were authentic and allowed me to blend in. I didn't feel like I was posing or slumming. I was making a choice based on what I wanted to do, rather than following a script determined by my education and upbringing. It was a way to feel free of the weight of my last name and the expectations that came with it. At the same time, ironically, I was unwittingly practicing the family craft—acting—and doing a good job of it.

I'd been stubbornly committed to the idea of going to school with my Santa Barbara friends, and now that it was happening, just as Mom and Dad were finally pulling the trigger on a divorce, I made a conscious decision about how I wanted to be seen—as a wild, dangerous kid—and acted accordingly. My friends who'd stayed in California had avoided the softening influence of East Coast prep schools, and I was insecure about my own toughness compared with theirs. They still thought New York was crazy, the concrete jungle, and I tried to confirm that idea, carrying myself in such a way that guys in Carpinteria would look at me and respect me and want to hang out with me.

My friends came from families of average means; I was an oddball. I learned that I had to be just a little bit wilder than everyone else, a little bit meaner, to get people to go from *Oh, that Douglas kid, he's a fucking rich spoiled pussy* to *Oh, that Douglas kid, he's the real deal*. We surfed and fought and did coke. I'd played football since I was ten, and I started out the school year on the Carpinteria High team, the Warriors. But skateboarding, more conducive to partying, was becoming a much bigger part of my life, and I soon quit football so I could devote myself to my new lifestyle.

Quitting the football team was a big deal for me. I'd never quit a sport before, and I took pride in that fact, but I told myself that I was quitting now because of my parents' divorce. Maybe, in a roundabout way, I was; somehow, I felt that the divorce justified doing what I really wanted to be doing, which was running around with my friends, getting high and drinking 40s, and not spending a couple of hours after school every day at football practice. Some of my football teammates pushed back, challenging my decision, but when I hit them with the divorce, which was so public, what could they do except to express sympathy and say they understood.

I knew this was a pivotal moment. It was an outwardly insignificant shift that was committing me to a doomed path. Even then, I was conscious that things were going to be different going forward, and not necessarily for the better. I was giving up on normal life and saying: *Fuck everything.*

After I quit football, I'd still show up when everyone congregated for Friday night games, but I felt guilty being there, reminded of my choices, and I'd try to leave before the game started. I spent some of my newly free time on music. I was increasingly interested in DJing and break dancing, which I explored with a different set of friends, foremost among them Isaac, who'd grown up poor until he was eight, when he went to live with his godmother, a gay Native American woman whose tribe had money. Dad had bought me a set of turntables, and I'd make mixtapes and play parties and small raves.

Mainly, though, I was focused on being a badass. This involved sleeping with girls but not having relationships with them. If I had a girlfriend, I'd have to hang out with her. I wanted to hang out with my skateboarding friends. I loved my friends like they were my family, truly. I think I would have taken a bullet for a few of them.

Ice plants, a succulent groundcover, grew wild all over Carpinteria. As a surface, they created a low-friction cushion. We'd take the trucks and wheels off our skateboards, strap a couple of feet of inner tube under the deck, and slide down hills blanketed with the plants.

Paul, a core member of our crew, was goofy and maniacally indifferent to safety. He had a 1950s Ford pickup truck with a passenger door that didn't close, and he liked to make sharp left turns, flinging his passenger outward as the door swung open. When this happened to me, I found myself outside the car, clinging to the door, until Paul pulled me in by my belt. Another time, we were with Jay and Hans, one of our wilder, more aggressive friends, doing mushrooms at Tar Pits, a Carpinteria beach. We were under a tree, up on a tall bluff that abruptly plunged to a section of sand where there were huge boulders. Paul started bouncing around, flapping his arms as if he could fly. He walked to the edge of the cliff, stood there a second, and stepped off. He landed on the rocks and should have died, but he only broke several bones.

Recklessness was the norm in my life. It was present in the way I rode my motorcycle in Mallorca, in the way I drove a car in California, in the way I interacted with people if I went to a party where I didn't know anyone. It was just how I approached the world. The very real possibility of something going terribly wrong felt okay at the time, but maybe it's also what, together with years of drug addiction, later morphed into the intense anxiety I always felt.

I was the ringleader of our group—the maker of plans, chooser of destinations, finder of trouble—and the one most likely to keep a bender going for days on end. A lot of the time, we'd all hang out in my pool house. I had good manners and an easy rapport with adults, and my friends' parents would say things like, "Cameron's such a nice boy." Mom disapproved of my friends, and Dad called me King of the Shits, but given all that was going on with them, they were hardly present to impose structure on my life.

In that particular California environment, you gained respect by having the courage to stand your ground and fight, not run.

Until now, my fighting experience was limited to:

- some little-kid fights in football
- a couple of fights at Eaglebrook
- the time my tagger friend Tony and I got jumped by some guys, and I swung my skateboard around violently to fend them off
- wrestling, which was fighting minus punches

Dad and me.

One weekend that October, I went to Avofest, the California Avocado Festival, which shuts down Carpinteria every fall as tens of thousands of people crowd the streets, listening to music and sampling the World's Largest Vat of Guacamole.

Jay and Jesse and a girl named Kate and I were running wild, stealing beer from a grocery store, acting like we owned the place, and generally being hooligans. Having recently arrived from New York, I still had a conspicuously East Coast style, defined by polo shirts and a baseball hat worn askew. We were getting dirty looks from a bunch of Carpas. At one point, I got separated from my friends. I was looking for them on Linden Avenue, the festival's main drag, when two Carpas rolled up on me, calling me "kid" and telling me to get lost.

"You got a problem with me, motherfuckers?" I said. "All right, let's go handle it, let's do it."

I was apprehensive, and hoping my aggressive talk might scare them off, but it didn't. We headed down a side street, and I just started throwing punches at one of them. I must have surprised him, because

I quickly got the upper hand and was giving him a good ass-kicking. His friend jumped on me, and I threw him off and started beating him up, too. Then an older, larger Carpas member came out onto a porch across the street, holding a baseball bat. At that point I took off running, but I was pretty pleased with myself—this was the first time I'd beaten two guys at once—and when I found Jay and Jesse and Kate, I bragged about my performance.

Twenty minutes later, I noticed a couple of cops pointing at me from across the street. I thought maybe I was being paranoid. Five minutes after that, I was in handcuffs and being charged with disorderly conduct and public intoxication.

I was put in Juvenile Hall, which was in Goleta, for the rest of the weekend. I was anxious going in—would there be a whole other level of more intimidating tough guy here that I hadn't encountered before?—but was relieved to find myself among the same kinds of kids I was already hanging out with, and it felt like a badge of honor to cross this new threshold.

The cells in juvie had toilets in them, and I learned to hang a sheet for privacy. Juvie was also my first exposure to strict racial segregation, aimed at keeping gangs apart. The two main ones in Santa Barbara were the Eastside gang and the Westside gang, both Mexican. There was also a white Northside gang, but most of the kids in juvie were Mexican.

On Monday, I went before a juvenile-court judge and was released on probation.

I think Dad chalked up the incident to standard-issue teenage misbehavior, but I could almost hear Mom's bubble popping. I'd by now been kicked out of more than one school and become an apprentice juvenile delinquent, but until my arrest she had seemed to be in denial about what was happening. She'd introduce me to her society friends and talk about where I'd be "going to school," even as that path became increasingly unlikely. She kept asking if I wanted my childhood bedroom redecorated, but I insisted she leave the painting of a carousel on the wall and not throw out the big stuffed polar bear I kept in a corner of my room, or the gorilla who sat on my shelf wearing a three-piece suit, a cigar in his mouth. My attachment to the gorilla, at least, wasn't due to regressive fantasies about my childhood; the vest's watch pocket was where I stashed my drugs. After the arrest, Mom struggled to reconcile my imaginary future and my real present. She seemed not to fully understand the seriousness of my situation. One time, she brought thirty burgers and fries for all the kids in juvie, which was sweet but of course not allowed. I'm pretty sure the staff ate the food.

12

1995–1996: The Most Troublesome Douglas

With my Avofest victory, even the kids from Carpas started to respect me. As I grew wilder at the school we all went to, I became friends with some of them. Even at George, I'd been wearing my socks pulled up, but now I started blending more cholo elements in with my polo shirts: wifebeaters, sagging blue and brown Dickies khakis, bandannas, plaid flannel shirts, and Nike Cortezes, the official Cali gangster shoe. Cortezes were super light, and great for break dancing, and I liked the way they looked. Mom and Dad might make a comment about my clothes now and then, and if I needed to dress up for something of theirs, I would, but that was the prevalent style for kids in that place at that time.

A concrete storm trench across the street from Carpinteria High was the preferred battleground for students. It was off campus, so no teacher was going to arrive to break things up. Every day, there'd be a fight there with a crowd looking on, and I was in a few of them.

There was always some kid looking to score points off my last name, and part of what animated my fighting—what made it mean so much to me and gave me so much satisfaction—was the feeling that I needed to carry my last name in a way that was respected in that world. It was a world that no one in my family had really experienced, with the possible exception of Pappy when he was young and poor. But I parked myself in it. That was important to me. I wanted people who lived in that element to say: "Cameron Douglas is not a coward. Cameron Douglas will *go there*."

If you challenged someone to fight in the storm trench, they knew there was no getting out of it, and that there'd be an audience. I looked for any reason to demonstrate my fierceness. If someone so much as mentioned my family, or gave me a look, or did anything I could take offense to, I'd fight. Some kids would talk endless amounts of shit and then not show, knowing they'd be embarrassed. I began to see that there are people who can pull the trigger, and people who can't.

I wanted to prove that I was as tough as the tough Carpinteria kids, and that desire emboldened me. I was drinking regularly, and using coke and some crystal, which only fueled my aggression. Down in that ravine, I got my ass kicked plenty of times, but as I started fighting more often I found that, because I'd wrestled competitively for a couple of years, experience tended to give me the upper hand. A fight might start standing up, with a couple of punches, but generally it would turn into grappling on the ground, where I knew what I was doing. I realized that even getting beaten wasn't the end of the world. I became a bully of bullies, seeking them out and baiting them; if they went for it, we'd fight, and if they didn't, I'd ridicule them.

Carpinteria High had a lot of tough gangbanger kids, but I became known as the crazy white boy. If you were looking for a fight, you were going to find one. If you were coming at me with your friend, I'd be coming at you with a rock, and I was going to hit you with it, in the head. I usually had a buck knife or switchblade on me. In my car I kept a baseball bat, and also a roll of quarters. If I was getting ready to fight, I'd grip the quarters in one hand and a cigarette lighter in the other, giving my punches instant knockout power. I learned to take my shirt off before I fought, so that it couldn't be pulled over my head and used against me. An older kid taught me how to do a head butt if someone was right up in my face.

In the years since, Dad has asked me how I became a good fighter.

I've said: "I'm not a good fighter. I'm just not afraid to put my chin down and swing my fists around." And that's what I did. It turns out there are only so many people who are willing to go to that extreme. For whatever reason, I was one of them.

I was endangering myself and other people, but I didn't think I had a death wish. I was just being a wild and crazy teenager. The mood among me and my friends wasn't dark. We were having fun, and what we found most fun was doing things that made us feel more alive, more sure of ourselves, more full of ourselves—testing ourselves and pushing boundaries.

Jesse and I knew a kid named Griffin at Santa Barbara High whose dad had a big weed stash, and we went to his house to take it. We weren't friends, but I'd been there before, and I knew where Griffin's room was. We scaled the second-floor balcony and found the sliding door to the room open, then made our way to his dad's bedroom closet, where we found a good half-pound of weed in a basket. Before leaving, we went downstairs and grabbed a couple of beers from the fridge.

Griffin was part of a white gang that called itself the Militia. Soon after our break-in, we heard that his crew was having a keg party, and Jay and Jesse and Sean and I went, and Griffin came up to me and said, "I know you fuckin' robbed my house." I wasn't sure how he knew, and we were surrounded by his gang, but I said, "If I thought that you robbed my house, and I was standing right in front of you, I'd be down your throat so fast you wouldn't know what happened. So what are you doing flapping your jaws? If you think I did something, let's do something about it. Otherwise, you're a fucking bitch." I was taking a chance, but I also had a reputation that preceded me for being volatile and aggressive. Griffin started mincing words, and I started pushing him. I said, "You say that one more time, I'm going to fucking blast you just for saying it." He walked away. My friends and I waited just long enough so it wouldn't seem like we were fleeing, and then we left. As soon as we got in the car, everyone looked at me and said: "Dude, are you out of your fucking mind?"

"Did it fucking work?" I said. "Right. So shut the fuck up."

Fortunately, I never hurt anyone too badly. Sometimes when I came out on top, the other kid would turn around and want to be my best friend; and sometimes when I lost, I'd find myself drawn to developing a friendship with the other kid. Scrapping became a social tool for me, the way I established myself in peer groups.

At home, too, I was rewarded for my toughness. If Dad had a friend over, he'd say, smiling, "Hey, Cam, tell that story about that fight you got into the other day."

I was a chronic truant. I knew where the best parties were, and most weekends I'd lead a caravan of half a dozen cars down to L.A. to a rave; so many of our friends wanted to go with us that one night a kid named Kevin rode the whole way in the trunk of Jesse's Mustang, which hadn't had its shocks replaced in a long time. On Halloween, I was the kid in a hoodie with a bandanna over my face so you could only see my eyes, reenacting the vandalism scene in *Stand by Me* as we drove down a street and I leaned out the window with a baseball bat, taking out one mailbox after another. When I added a few stints

Knucklehead me with Mom.

in juvie to the mix, the kids I was hanging out with looked at me in a respectful new light.

That fall, I had my first experience with heroin. It held a certain allure for me. It was another line to cross, one more step away from people's expectations of me, so I was curious to try it. My friend Jaime was in Carpas, and his uncle, who was also in the gang, shot me up. I was afraid of the needle but eager for the experience, and I was pleased that these two gangbangers deemed me worthy of inclusion.

I wasn't prepared for how physical heroin would be. I felt it saturate my body, and I threw up, but then I felt warm all over, and relaxed and happy and content. Wow. *Wow.* The feeling carried over to how I associated with people: I was more at ease talking to them and being around them. I wasn't worried about getting addicted; at that time, heroin didn't really suit me. It's a private, antisocial drug, and I wanted to be out and about—snowboarding, having adventures—not staying home and nodding out. Cocaine was the drug for that—until it wasn't.

The terms of my probation included a curfew and random drug testing, and I continued to rack up violations, spending increasing amounts of time in Juvenile Hall, with the stays lengthening from a weekend to a week to a month. My general strategy, going into new situations like juvie, was to try to avoid people finding out who I was. Douglas was a common enough last name, and I usually had about two weeks before everyone figured out my background, which gave me enough time to get established, make connections, and have people form opinions of me that didn't have to do with my family.

In juvie, everything was geared toward rehabilitation. A nice man named Peter Claydon came to visit me once a week. He was slight and soft-spoken, with a big head of curly hair and a British accent. He was a psychologist who specialized in troubled youth, and he was always taking notes. He was very interested in my anger. "Are you sure you're not angry? It's okay to be angry." I didn't feel like I was angry. I'm sure, in retrospect, that I must have been, and was stuffing my feelings and numbing them with drugs and alcohol, but at the time I felt like I was living exactly the way I wanted to. And I felt that in a place like juvie, dutifully answering a therapist's questions was just part of the package. Really talking out your problems was what friends were for.

There was a swimming pool at Juvenile Hall, and on Sundays the staff would take a group of us there and hold competitions for candy and snacks from the commissary cart. I was a fast swimmer and could hold my breath a long time, and I won many of the competitions. I started getting pulled out to play volleyball with the staff, who called me the Great White Hope.

The din of juvie reminded me of a dog pound: animals lined up in cages flanking a center path, quiet until a handler came in, at which point they'd go bananas, barking, jumping up, desperate for food and attention. In juvie, if someone came in, everyone started screaming and yelling. When Dad came and visited me, he said, "You know why it's so noisy in here? 'Cause they can't read."

Ironically, it was during the intermittent periods of quiet in juvie that I discovered a love of books, reading Wilbur Smith's historical novels, Louis L'Amour's cowboys-and-Indians novels, Stephen King's *The Green Mile,* everything by Tolkien, and nonfiction books about history. Books made me feel less alone. Each one was a spaceship or time machine that took me out of my current situation to a different place or period, or a powerful lens that brought the present into focus by shining a light on the past.

On home supervision, I had an electronic ankle-bracelet monitor. The probation office installed a receiver in my house, connected to our phone line. If I went beyond a 100-foot radius when I was supposed to be at home, the receiver would alert the probation office.

During these periods of relative freedom, I had to attend a group called Klein Bottle, on Milpas Street. The counselor was a recovering addict named Dave Vartabedian, a California-ized Armenian with dark hair and a mustache who'd spent seven years in state prison and now worked with at-risk youth. When my driver's license was suspended, he'd pick me up from school, making sure I went straight home. I looked up to him. But when he showed us pictures from prison, I thought: *Seven years in prison . . . What the fuck?* I couldn't imagine what that was like, how someone survived it, how anyone could fuck up so badly that they ended up with a sentence like that.

In November, Dad went to South Africa to shoot *The Ghost and the Darkness* with Val Kilmer, about the Man-Eating Lions of Tsavo. Over Christmas break, Mom and I flew to visit him on location. While Dad worked, Mom and I took a lot of pictures with local tribespeople. It was our last time together as a family. As far as I was concerned, the divorce was long overdue.

When Dad was back in Santa Barbara, his oversight of me was light and sporadic. In an effort to maintain his relationship with me, he had rented a place in Montecito not far from our house on Hot Springs Road, and the probation office installed a second ankle-monitor receiver connected to a phone line there. I stayed with him when he was in town, and it sometimes felt like we were two bachelors palling around. When I missed curfews set by Dad, usually because I'd been out making mischief with friends, I found that an excuse which worked on him more often than not was saying that I'd been with a girl.

I'd always been afraid of his anger, but during that period when the divorce was happening, I think he just didn't have the energy to be my disciplinarian. He probably felt some guilt. We didn't spend much time together, and maybe he wanted what time we did spend together to be harmonious. We were both trying to avoid confrontation. I never lost respect for him, but I was willful. I don't know that his discipline would have had any effect.

When he wasn't present to check my behavior, Mom lost any control over me. When she spoke to me in Spanish around my friends—she hoped I would become bilingual—I'd redden and answer in English. At the time, for me and my friends, nothing was more important than being who you were and standing firm on what you believed. I was full of shit, of course. Motivated by my need to belong among my friends, I wasn't standing firm on what I believed. I was being someone I wasn't.

One night, the Santa Anas were blowing, making their ethereal gusting sound, and I was drinking beers with Jay and Isaac down at the pool house. This was nothing new, but for some reason Mom lost it. She called probation, and a home supervision officer came to the house. He asked her if this wasn't something she and I could work out between us, because the penalty for violating my probation, at this point, would be harsh and complicated. But she insisted he take me back to juvie. She was my legal guardian, and he had to defer to her request. I was taken back into custody.

A few days later, I was brought to the courthouse, shackled to a line of other juvenile defendants. When my name was called, I shuffled into the courtroom. I knew Mom was in the room, and I suspected she felt guilty. No doubt she was expecting me to be released back home that day. But when it was my turn to face the judge, he said that Mom clearly couldn't handle me, so the state was going to take that responsibility out of her hands. He was making me a ward of California.

When he said that, I glanced back at Mom, the architect of this disastrous development. She looked stunned, and I could see panic building in her eyes. I glared at her: *I hope you're happy now.* I felt bitterly, self-defeatingly joyful: she had gotten what she deserved. It hadn't yet sunk in that I was the one who'd have to carry this weight. When the guards re-cuffed us and led us outside to the bus that would take us away, I stared straight ahead, not looking at Mom, who years later wouldn't remember this day at all.

13

1996: The Juvie Archipelago

After I was made a ward of California, I was sent to a short-term group home, a rehab in Oxnard. From there I moved on to drug rehab at Hazelden, in Minnesota. I had no interest in getting sober, and I didn't see the benefit in talking to a shrink. In one of the group meetings I had to attend, we were given an exercise: *Draw a picture of where you might be if you continue heading in your current direction.* I drew a prison wall with a prison tower. I didn't really think that was a possible outcome, but I thought drawing it made me look tough and would show the lightweights around me that I was the genuine article.

I was supposed to go home after thirty days, but then the administrators told me they were going to move me into their extended program, which had no fixed duration. I didn't like the sound of that. I called a taxi and told it to wait a block away, then I ran across a field to meet it. I called Emmy, a friend from the George School, to ask her to buy me a bus ticket. I don't remember how the situation was resolved, but according to Hazelden's records, I left "at the request of the staff." Dad says I had violated Hazelden's zero-tolerance substance policy.

Next, I was sent to a group home in a poor section of St. Paul. Sherburne House received kids from different states' juvenile systems.

During the day, we'd be bussed to a nearby school, and once a week we were driven fifteen minutes away for an AA meeting. Soon after I arrived, I received a fax from Dad, who was on vacation with his friend Jean "Johnny" Pigozzi, an automotive heir and playboy and a very sharp guy:

> *Dear Cameron, I've been thinking about you a lot. I'm sending this fax to you by satellite on Johnny's boat. I don't understand how these things work—but we're a hundred miles from the nearest road, off the coast of Baja in Mexico! It's been very quiet for the four days I've been here; getting a lot of rest, snorkeling for sea urchins, reading a good book, and a couple of scripts.*

Dad was often doing that, telling me about the latest amazing, far-off place he found himself. I tried to think positively about it. It made me happy to think that someone I loved was enjoying himself. I also wondered whether he was hoping to motivate me by showing me what I was missing.

> *I'll be back tomorrow night and will call you. I hope things have calmed down for you Cameron—that you're able to let go of some of the anger. You have a lot of family and friends who really care about you—and it is going to get better! I pray for you every night—and can't wait to see you real soon! Love, Dad*

Everyone was always telling me that I was angry. I felt offended by the idea. Having other people telling me what I was feeling: *that* made me angry. *Why the fuck does everyone insist that I'm angry?*

One day, bored during an AA meeting, I wandered out back. The woman who lived above the meeting room was just returning to her apartment, and we talked a bit. Liz was eighteen and had a hustler vibe. We made a plan to meet again when I returned the following week. This time she invited me up to her apartment, and we had sex. I started taking an hour out of each AA meeting to go upstairs and hang out with her. By now, I'd stopped taking sex for granted. A relationship might last only a few days, but for me it was always romantic.

It was as important to me as the sex, if not more, that there be an emotional connection.

By Sherburne House criteria, I was doing well—participating, going along with the curriculum, and, as far as they knew, staying out of trouble. But I'd noticed that a couple of boys, including my friend Victor, a wild, good-looking, wealthy kid from New York City, had been there for as long as two years, which seemed forever to my seventeen-year-old self. I had no intention of staying there anywhere close to that long. I went to the head counselor, Neil, and asked how soon I could leave if I kept doing everything right and didn't get into any trouble. He was noncommittal: "We'll just have to see how you progress."

That was the thing with the juvenile system and its focus on rehabilitation. It depended on involuntary, open-ended, *Cuckoo's Nest*–style commitments to institutions that had full discretion over how long they kept you. Their funding was based on how many kids were there, and the facilities were often run by adults with their own psychological issues.

"Two months? Four months?"

"I can't tell you that."

"What, six months?"

"I don't know, I don't have an answer for you."

Fuck that, I wasn't going to be there for years. I started bucking, hopping the fence and running to a little liquor store down the street, where I'd grab 40s for me and Victor and another friend of ours.

I eventually told Liz that I was thinking about running away, and she said I could stay with her while I figured out my plans. A few weeks later, in the middle of the night, I climbed out of the second-floor bathroom window at Sherburne House, dropped to the ground, and was on my way. It took me an hour to jog-walk across town, and when I got to Liz's place, just before dawn, I rang the buzzer. No one answered. I kept ringing. Still no answer.

It was the middle of the summer, and I waited there all day. Eventually, a kid who rode past on a BMX said I could take refuge on his screened-in porch nearby. It had a couch I could sleep on. The next day I was back at Liz's door, buzzing and waiting.

Finally, she showed up. I was so relieved. When I popped out of the shadows, wide-eyed, I think I scared the shit out of her. A guy was with her, and she told him she'd see him later. I went upstairs with her, sprawled on her couch, and cracked a cold beer. At that moment, I felt safe and content, and I spent the night. But the next day, when Liz took me to lunch, she was distant, and I started feeling paranoid.

That evening, at her apartment, she got a phone call. A few moments later she said she had to go downstairs, and she'd be right back. She left the door to the apartment open. My spider sense tingled. Then I heard a police radio. I grabbed my jacket, darted out the door, and ran down the hall, away from the staircase. Around a corner, there was a door slightly ajar. I slipped through it into a room where a fat man on a couch looked up in surprise. I put a finger to my lips. "Don't worry," I said quietly, "I'll be out of here in a moment." He didn't look like he was buying it. I could hear the police down the hall, confused that I wasn't in Liz's apartment.

I made for an open window, climbed down a fire escape, and sprinted back to the BMX boy's porch. All I had with me was my address book, in my jacket; the boy and his obese mother let me use their phone. First I got in touch with Chuck, a kid who I'd met at Hazelden and was now living in a halfway house in St. Paul, and he came and picked me up and gave me a ride to the bus station. Then I called Mary, my friend Jesse's mother, back in Santa Barbara. She bought me a one-way Greyhound ticket to New York City. Soon I was on a bus heading east.

When the bus made stops, I was careful not to get off, but in Cleveland I decided to stretch my legs. I was standing on the sidewalk, shaking out my cramps and talking to a girl from the bus, when a police detective approached me and started asking questions. I told him I was with my older sister, and we were on our way to New York. He looked at the girl standing next to me and got a blank stare that didn't give him confidence in my story. He told me to get into the back of his cruiser while he investigated further.

I returned to California in handcuffs. As I strode through LAX, flanked by police detectives, I enjoyed imagining the scenarios people in the airport had to be conjuring about who I was and what was happening. I rode in the back of a police car from LAX to Santa Barbara Juvenile Hall. The window in back was rolled down a few inches, and I held my cuffed hands outside the car so that people could see them—maybe in a bid for sympathy, or in the vain hope that someone would rescue me.

At that point, I was designated to spend four months at Los Prietos, a boys' work camp that was part of the Santa Barbara juvenile system. It was tough there. My head was already shaved, but everyone else got sheared when we arrived. We slept in barracks-style housing, and the program was like boot camp. Los Prietos stood on seventeen acres in the Los Padres National Forest, and we spent most of each day clearing trails and removing dry underbrush that might fuel wildfires. We had to do calisthenics every morning. There was a pool, and we'd box underwater, to dampen the force of our punches. Then it was off to bed, to start all over again in the morning.

Mom and Dad and Pappy and Jojo and Granny all wrote me letters during this period, but the ones that really stuck with me were from Granny, who was unfailingly supportive, encouraging, inspiring, and filled with wisdom.

Boys' camp felt like pre-prison. In juvie, there'd been some pretty innocent kids. But here, there were boys on their way to more serious incarceration. There were also a lot of knuckleheads, kids who couldn't or wouldn't follow the rules and viewed this as a notch in their belt. I was one of those knuckleheads.

My various internments weren't respites from my fighting lifestyle but opportunities to practice it. The kids called juvie "gladiator school." We were all pretty proud to be there, and we all had troubled father-son relationships. Each of us was seeking an identity, looking to test ourselves, and fighting was the best way we knew how to do it.

Entering the system, I hadn't been afraid to fight, but my experiences there made me much more comfortable with combat, and even with getting beaten up, because for me fighting was less about victory than about balls. I had many opportunities to sharpen my skills. I got into fights at Juvenile Hall, at Los Prietos, and at Sherburne House, where my nickname was Bear, because of how rough and physical I was.

It was in these outposts of the juvenile justice system that I fully internalized an essential truth of hand-to-hand fighting: Sometimes the stronger kid prevails, but usually it's the *fiercer* kid—the one who's there to win—who comes out on top. That seemed to come naturally to me. I started to grasp the importance of shock-and-awe in fights. I'd skip the whole pushing-and-posturing thing. I wanted to move first and get the first blow in, especially with someone I thought could hurt me.

After a few more months back in Juvenile Hall, I was released to Mom's house, but I still had to show up for school every day at La Posada, a trailer behind Juvenile Hall, where the principal doubled as my probation officer.

I'd taken a sick satisfaction when I was made a ward of the state, right in front of Mom. I had tried to tell her that reporting my home-

On a boat with my friend Jay, whose face has been obscured to protect his identity, and Jann Wenner.

probation violation would have serious consequences. A *home super-vision officer* had tried to tell her. But she lived in a world of her own at times, and we'd both suffered the consequences. Now our relationship was less mother-son than *I am the man of the house, in her house.* I loved her, but sometimes I didn't want to be bothered with her.

During this period, Mom had an ever-shifting cast of houseguests and hangers-on. One of the best of Mom's inner circle was Suzan Pelfrey, her on-call shaman, who lived up in Ojai and whose guidance Mom sought on decisions big and small. Then there was Ann, a plump, long-haired, beatifically smiling yoga teacher who was a lovely, grounding presence in the house and who also had a stash of psychedelic mushroom powder. My old friend Isaac and I would go into her room in the main house at 2 a.m. and wake her with a short break dancing routine, then cajole her into giving us some of the magic dust.

After Ann left, a smooth and handsome didgeridoo player named Patrick moved into her room. He'd come down to the pool house when my friends and I were hanging out there, and at first I liked him, but then his sponging became excessive. He convinced Mom to bankroll a didgeridoo album. Eventually, Jay got into a fistfight with him, and he moved out.

Finally, Mom became involved with a man I did like. Todd Raines was a property manager in Santa Barbara who lived in a beautiful house he'd built himself. He was a genuinely good guy, a hard worker who'd made his own success and had some tough breaks. His wife had died, and he was raising their kids by himself. He was a good father, and he loved Mom and was loyal to her. He always treated me like a friend, and he and I hung out a lot together. He and Mom would date for several years and eventually become engaged.

My sojourn as a ward of the state had not reformed me. When I was seventeen, over Halloween weekend, Dad took me and Jay to Las Vegas. We checked into a suite at the MGM Grand, and then Dad headed off to the blackjack tables. As he left, he said, "Just promise me one thing: no fighting."

"Of course. Yeah. Sure. Absolutely. No problem."

Jay and I ate some mushrooms, then headed to the new Scream Park, which had just opened on the lot next to the hotel. Ahead of us, in the line for bumper cars, was a group of teenage tag-bangers, Southern California quasi-gangsters/quasi-graffiti-artists, with a couple of girls. When the gate opened and the scramble for cars began, one of the tag-bangers and I were stragglers, and soon it was just the two of us, with only one car left. I shoved him out of the way and got into the car. The bar clicked shut, locking me in. Then he slapped me, which was much more disrespectful than if he'd hit me, and got in the passenger side of one of his friends' cars.

When the announcer said, "Everyone go in the same direction," I spun my car around and floored it, heading against the flow of traffic and straight at the kid who'd slapped me. I sideswiped him as we yelled at each other. When the ride stopped, I leaped out of my car and ran over to him. A bunch of other people got between us, and one said, "What are you doing? There are police everywhere here." This snapped me back to reality, and we went our separate ways. For the next hour, I was enraged. I couldn't stop thinking about how the kid had slapped me.

An hour and a half later, Jay and I were in a zigzag line for the Haunted House when I heard, "Hey bitch, fuck you." It was the group from the bumper cars. I jumped out of line and said, "You know what? Let's go," and we all headed to the parking lot. On the way, I said to the girls in their group, "Listen, as soon as I'm done beating your friend up, we have a nice villa with a Jacuzzi." The girls giggled. The guy was fuming.

The moment we reached the parking lot, we started fighting. I got him down on the ground and held him there with one arm, punching him with the other. People were telling me to stop, and pulling on my shirt, and one of the girls was kicking me, but I was fully in the grip of the mushrooms by this point and in such a fury that I just kept hitting this kid.

Suddenly, I felt a sharp pain in my left arm. I jumped up and turned around. A kid was standing close to me, holding a knife. He'd been aiming for my liver and hit bone instead. Blood was pouring from my elbow. The other guys picked up rocks and started throwing them at me. Jay had taken off, and now I was getting hit in the head with stones. The guys ran at me, jumped on me. I fell to my hands and knees, and they were on my back, punching and kicking me. I broke away and managed to outrun them, but I was leaking blood from my arm and from my eye, where I'd caught a solid punch.

Back in the hotel room, I got ice, yelled at Jay for ditching me, and braced for Dad's reaction. When he came in, he said, "Oh hey, boys . . . Man, I had a good night. I did pretty good at the tables." Then he saw me, and my shiner, and the big knots on my face.

"What the fuck?! The one fucking thing I asked you not to do!"

He called for the hotel doctor to come up, and the guy gave me some stitches in the elbow. When I went back to school, one of my eyes was still completely red.

Dad was angry about that one for a while, and I think seeing the damage to my body scared him. It was one thing for him to hear about my brawls and imagine them in the abstract, but another to see the ugly outcome up close.

I still had a strict curfew, but it was overseen by home supervision officers I knew from juvie, who were fond of me and lenient about enforcing it. I was smoking pot and snorting crystal and its dirtier cousin, crank. I was playing a game of chicken with myself that I was determined not to lose. I was crashing high school and college parties late into the night, but somehow I also kept making it to school in the trailer at La Posada the next day.

Every morning, on the bulletin board, there'd be a list of names of people who had to give urine by the end of the day. If your name was on it, you couldn't use the bathroom until you'd provided a sample. It was stressful, but I passed every time. With only three weeks left at La Posada, I'd almost made it. Then my supervision level would be almost back to normal, and I'd at last be able to return to Carpinteria High.

14

2006: Oblivion

In Dublin, Erin and I have the whole day to kill until our flight back to the States, and to ease the pain we order two double vodkas each, charged to the production. Room service brings the four drinks, we chug them, and we order again. The sickness is getting worse. I'm puking all over the floor, rushing to the bathroom with bouts of diarrhea, babbling. Now I'm plastered, too.

The flight is another eleven hours of misery. Erin asks a cabin attendant if she has Advil. "We have food poisoning," Erin adds. The woman scrunches her face in sympathy and keeps serving us booze.

This whole time, I'm torn about Dad's ultimatum to kiss Erin goodbye and keep a relationship with him, or stay with her and go my own way. I can't believe I blew the acting job. I chew over what Dad said. He's always been kind of distant—and in fairness, I've given him plenty of reasons not to trust me—but the whole conversation is difficult to swallow on multiple levels. Comparing me to Uncle Eric, yet again, is sobering. And now he's giving up on me? There's part of me, I think, that has given up on myself. I know I've blown so many opportunities. I'm not living the life I feel I was meant to or that the people who love me want me to; and I'm not having the kind of relationship with my family that I'd like.

But I also have a lot of resentment toward Dad. I'm only skimming by financially, but he continues to restrict my access to some money Pappy put in trust for me. I understand his reasons. And in fact he has helped us get a better apartment to move into when we return from Ireland. But it all feels infantilizing. And now he's cutting me off. In my anger, I find resolve: Time to get serious about making money and taking care of myself and my family of friends.

Right now, to me, "getting serious" doesn't mean abandoning the path I'm on. It means committing more fully to it. In these early days of my new addiction, I see heroin as the missing piece of the puzzle. What happened in Ireland wasn't a sign that I should quit using; it was a sign that I should stop trying to live a normal life. Withdrawal from heroin may be terrible, but the heroin itself is making me feel *more* competent, more able to take care of the things that I need to take care of. I'd felt utterly lost on cocaine. Compared to that, heroin is a safety blanket, and right now I'm focused on the moment when we land. Gabriel is supposed to pick us up at the airport. "He better have cheeva with him," I say to Erin.

"Cameron, you're five days into detoxing, why start using again?"

It's true. We're through the worst of the withdrawal. After another two or three days, we'll probably be in the clear. But physical discomfort wins the moment. "Fuck it," I say.

Erin and I emerge from the terminal like walking dead, pale and sweaty and rank, shrinking in the morning light. Gabriel is at the curb, standing next to his Jetta, and helps us with our bags.

"You got cheeva?" I ask.

"Nah, bro." He shrugs.

I'm furious. I tell him to drop us off and go get some. At least we have our new apartment. Erin calls the new landlord to say we're back early, and to ask if we can move in now. But the landlord says Dad called and broke the lease, and we no longer have the place.

Motherfucker. This is real. He knows I have no money and nowhere to go, and he is cutting me off. How can he do this?

I have Gabriel drop us at the Rodeway Inn, a cheap hotel on Beverly Boulevard. Erin calls her mom, who lets us use her credit card to pay for a night there. Then I call my friend Adam in New York and he wires me $2,000, which will cover a room for a month.

It takes Gabriel a long, painful hour to bring us the dope. Finally he arrives, I shoot up, and the world feels tolerable again.

I need money fast, and I still owe Emmanuel the ounce of crystal that Jay was supposed to send to him. Gabriel fronts me a replacement ounce, then Emmanuel gives me the green light and sends me money for another pound. The shipment brings me, the middleman, $10,000 in profit, which I split fifty-fifty with Gabriel. Within a couple of days, Erin and I have $15,000 to live on. After months of scraping by, we're suddenly flush.

In the first weeks after I return from Ireland, Dad and I don't speak. Then, as a conciliatory gesture to him, I agree to meet again with Candy Finnigan, the interventionist.

When we meet in West Hollywood, I look at her and say, "You know, Candy, this isn't going to end well." I have a sense of foreboding about my life, and about my relationship with my family.

"You're not a psychic," she says. "You don't know how things are going to end."

Candy exudes a sincere desire to help me, and she sends me to a doctor for a Suboxone prescription. I get the prescription, but I don't fill it.

I know Dad is trying to help me, but if help means not using drugs anymore, then I'll pass. Drugs are still the one consistent, dependable thing in my life, and cheeva is all the medicine I need. And now I have income. Emmanuel's orders become regular, and my crystal operation quickly expands. Within a month, I'm shipping him three to four pounds a week. Dad and I meet for dinner a couple of times. I tell him I'm taking the Suboxone, and he can see that I'm doing well and look healthy. Appeased by my meeting with Candy and apparent

With Dad, Dylan, Catherine, and Carys.

sobriety, he invites Erin and me to move out of the Rodeway and in with him in his rental.

My feeling is: If it seems to everyone else that I'm doing great, and I feel like I'm doing great, then what does it matter whether it's Suboxone or heroin? If I'm doing well, I'm doing well. I'm under the misimpression that there's nothing a doctor can prescribe me that will affect me in the way that I need to be affected. Many years later, I'll learn I was wrong. I'll wish I had taken the Suboxone, once I know what it does. But right now I have zero trust when it comes to authority figures. My knee-jerk reaction to people who are supposedly trying to put me on the right path is: *I don't believe them. They're all full of shit.* I'm also afraid of the withdrawal.

At Dad's rental, Erin and I have our own little wing, and Dad gives me one of his cars, a big, older, gunmetal-gray BMW with a V12 engine. Dad works days, but we spend many afternoons and evenings together. He's inclusive, insisting we join him for dinner. A couple of weeks later, Catherine, my stepmother, and their kids, Dylan and

Carys, arrive, and it feels like we're a little family. Sometimes Erin and I babysit my half-siblings. Though there's unspoken strain among us all, Dad and Catherine are both making an effort.

This is actually some of the best time I've spent with Dad that I can remember. I'm present and available. I'm not going out every night, or sleeping all day. I run errands during the daytime but have no urge to be out and about after dark. Every day, when Dad comes home from work, I'm there, we sit down, and we hang out. It's a nice time, and I'm really happy. As Dad's work in L.A. ends, and he and Catherine and the kids get ready to return to Bermuda, Erin and I find our own place in Laurel Canyon. I leave a card for Dad that says *"Muchas Gracias"* and has a picture of a Chihuahua in a sombrero.

Dad,

I just wanted to let you know how much it has meant to me for you to open up your house to me and in doing so opening the doors to a fresh, new loving and strong bond that I have been missing so much. This was a very special time for me and fills my heart with a feeling that I have been missing for a long time. I love you Dad. Have a kick ass day. Sincerely your son,

Cameron

15

2006: Logistics

My new place, on Cole Crest Drive, is a classic Hills house on stilts, with floor-to-ceiling windows and sliding glass doors, a pool and wraparound deck, and an exhilarating view of the city below. Best of all, from my wary new perspective, the house is invisible from the street. There's no parking spot, just a gate, and then a long, narrow staircase, built into the side of a slope, that leads down to the house. On the day we move in, I have to call the Realtor, because I can't even find it.

As I'm building my business, I take a lot of precautions. Erin and I wear gloves and wipe down outgoing packages with disinfectant to avoid leaving fingerprints. We buy a vacuum sealer to shrink-wrap our drug shipments, thinking that will keep police dogs from detecting them. I minimize the time I'm in possession of crystal, shipping it as soon as I receive it. Nothing on the packages can be traced to me, and I keep a buffer between me and the transactions. To receive cash, I have P.O. boxes under different names and in several locations around L.A. I keep most of the money in those boxes, staggering my bank deposits to stay below the $10,000 single-deposit threshold that triggers a bank's reporting requirements. I pay for shipments using an MTV corporate FedEx account number I have from a friend, and I address the packages to a P.O. box in New York that Emmanuel has under a false name. I use an anonymous e-mail service that has its servers offshore. To communicate with Gabriel and Emmanuel, I cycle through burner phones and devise codes for surreptitiously communicating each new phone number to them.

Anytime I get new crystal, I test it before shipping. I tweak and play *Oblivion* for twelve, sixteen hours straight. Sometimes I play a noble hero, other times a mercenary thief.

I'm low-tech in my packaging. I put two, three pounds of meth in a Ziploc bag, inside a box, inside another box, confident that this will defeat the X-ray machines at FedEx, and the shipments keep going through without a hitch.

For a while, everything goes smoothly. Having started doing this out of desperation, I continue to do it for the income and the lifestyle. My attitude is Fuck It. I've given up on any semblance of a normal life, and this new one seems to be working.

I think of myself as being more in drug logistics than drug sales. I never cut drugs up or sell them to users, though I've been known to slice open a key and throw it on the table for guests. I get drugs from point A to point B. I know some people here and some people there, and by putting them together I'm able to support myself and my friends and our drug habits, plus some toys and trips.

Do I have a knack for logistics that I could apply to a more law-abiding pursuit? Nothing else would bring me the kind of money I'm making now. And I don't want to be in the professional logistics business. I don't want a 9-to-5, or to be a private investigator. I want to be an artist, or I want to be a drug dealer. And being an artist isn't accessible to me. If you want to make art and have a sustained career and be good at it, you can't be a drug addict. DJing and acting aren't viable options either. Heroin muffles passion. Anything that inspired me before, now takes a back seat to my job of getting and staying high. Heroin is a ball and chain, not conducive to the sustained focus and presence of acting, or to traveling from place to place as a DJ, as I've confirmed with my performance in Ireland. Drug dealing, on the other hand, lets me keep getting high, stay where I am, focus on making as much money as I can, and push forward in building my business.

———

I'm becoming more aggressive, more demanding of respect. A girl I know in Hollywood, who used to be in a novelty pop group, now has a busy trade in meth, coke, heroin, and 8-balls, and she and some of the girls who deliver for her have been getting robbed. I offer my protection, for a fee. Gabriel contracts with some buddies to go and scare the last person who robbed her and to ride with her drivers on their riskier deliveries. Our longer-term plan is to take over her territory. As I embrace my new career, I find myself wondering: *How is it that I'm not in prison? If I'm not, who is? What did they do, and what do they look like? Am I like them? Do I just not know it yet?*

One weekend, Erin and I are up in Carpinteria, and I run into a friend from high school, a white kid who was associated with the Carpas gang. Kevin and his wife and kids are staying at the same motel as us. He's clearly struggling, and he says he can get me a pound of crystal for $11,000. Compared with the usual $12,500 I pay, it's a great price, and because I've known him for so long, I break one of my cardinal rules and front him the cash. For insurance, he points to his family. They're in the room next door to us, and he's not about to take off without them.

As the afternoon turns to evening, Erin and I periodically check to make sure the family is still there. I'm starting to get a little suspicious, because Kevin isn't picking up the phone when I call, or else he picks up and gives me some kind of runaround. When I have to leave to do an errand, I tell Erin to keep an eye on his family.

When I come back to the room, Erin is passed out and the family has left. I start calling Kevin, and when I get him on the line he invokes the standard drug-dealer sob story, claiming to have been robbed. He's down in Oxnard, and I somehow convince him to meet with me to talk.

As Erin and I get near to the bar where we're going to pick him up, I tell her to move into the back seat. When Kevin gets in, I'll lock the doors and Erin will hold a gun on him, and we'll take him to see

Gabriel, who'll have ideas on how to handle this. Kevin is standing with a couple of Mexican gangbangers when we arrive, and he gets into the car. I start to pull away.

"What's up?" he says.

"Dude, I'm going to tell you right now: Erin's behind you, she's holding a pistol on you, we're going to take a little ride and figure this out."

I start picking up speed. I've locked the doors, not realizing that any door can still be opened from the inside. He simply opens his door, jumps out at more than twenty miles per hour, gets to his feet, and takes off running.

I go looking for him but don't find him, and never get my money back.

In November, I invest in a nightclub, Stereo, which a friend is opening in Chelsea in Manhattan. I put in $150,000 and Gabriel puts in $50,000, and we fly into New York for opening night. I'm moving three to five pounds of crystal a week. I make $10,000 profit from each pound, meaning a net weekly profit of $30,000 to $50,000. As a cash business, the nightclub will be good for laundering our profits.

But even though I'm done using coke, I become increasingly aware during this trip east that it isn't done with me. It has taken a lingering toll that is only now revealing itself. Visiting New York, I run into people I've spent years with who greet me as a close friend, and who I can't quite place. I cross paths with women and know that we have years of history but not what that history is. *Did we have sex? Did we work together? Are we friends?* This happens a lot and creates awkward interactions. It feels as if an alien entity hijacked my body and lived my life for me, while I slept. It's sobering to think I was so out of my mind, and how narrowly I escaped permanent injury or worse.

If I'm seeing Pappy and Granny during this period, it's very rarely. A couple of times, I go with Dad to see Pappy on his birthday. None of them knows I'm using heroin. My dad thinks I'm taking Suboxone and everything is under control. To explain my newfound prosperity, I tell Dad that I'm organizing parties, which is plausible given my DJ history. He seems to buy it. He sees that I'm living in a nice place, and have some nice toys, but he doesn't know the kind of money I'm making, or the extent to which I'm taking care of other people. He invites me and Erin to join him and his family over the Christmas holidays, first in Bermuda, then on a charter cruise around the Bahamas. Just before leaving L.A., Erin and I send a pound of crystal to Emmanuel. During our layover in New York, I receive an e-mail from him: "Please call me ASAP, still no package / your east coast friend." Erin checks FedEx tracking and sees that the package has been delivered to an address in L.A. When she Googles the location, we're in for a shock: our crystal is sitting in a branch of the Los Angeles Police Department.

16

1996: Booty Juice

On a rainy day in late October, when Dad was busy shooting *The Game,* and I was three weeks out from completing the La Posada program, I went to my friend Isaac's house for our friend Arianne's birthday party. I was still wearing an ankle monitor and was allowed to drive only between home, school, and AA meetings, so our friend Sean, whose soggy mattress I'd lost my virginity on, drove me and my new Doberman puppy, Sultan, to the party in Mom's car, a GMC Jimmy.

At Isaac's house we drank 40s and snorted crank, and by the time Sean and I left several hours later, we were both pretty faded. He was driving us down State Street, the main drag in Santa Barbara, when he rear-ended a stopped car at a red light. Our car's back window was open, and Sultan bolted. Sean jumped out of the car too, and fled the scene. I would have joined them, but the car was registered in Mom's name, so running away wasn't an option.

It was a minor fender bender. I was still on home supervision, and I thought I could keep this from becoming something bigger. I slid behind the wheel, intending to pull alongside the driver of the other car and talk before police arrived. Suddenly, a man in a suit with an earpiece lunged through my window and tried to grab the keys out of the ignition. I panicked, unsure whether he was a good Samaritan or a lunatic, and punched the gas.

I flew down State Street, blowing red lights, thinking I'd made a clean escape. Four blocks away, as I screeched left onto Cabrillo Boulevard, I clipped a taxi. I lost control of the car and spun through the intersection, crashing into the Dolphin Fountain, a local landmark featuring a trio of breaching dolphins.

I must have been out for a while, because when I regained consciousness my face was mashed into the pavement and a cop's knee was on the back of my neck. Complicating matters, it turned out that the man who'd lunged through my car window was a U.S. Secret Service agent in the advance detail of President Clinton, who'd be stumping at a local campaign rally a few days later. And after I'd floored the gas, the agent had held on to the car, and I'd dragged him until I crashed. Miraculously, neither of us sustained serious injuries. But I knew I was in deep shit. Dad drove up from L.A. late that night.

I was furious with Sean for ditching me. He had his license, and was allowed to drive, and at worst would have gotten a misdemeanor DUI charge. The stakes were much higher for me. But Sean ducked my lawyers' calls, and I was sentenced to four years and change in the California Youth Authority. CYA was where the kids Los Prietos couldn't reform got sent: kids who did drive-bys and stabbed people and committed sex crimes. Repeat offenders. CYA could hold you until you were twenty-five, and it was famously vicious. People got killed in CYA. Prison gangs started there.

While I waited to be designated to a CYA facility, I was back in juvie, in Goleta. San Marcos, a high school, was next door, and I was brought there in shackles to take my GED exam. At night I'd lie in my rack, listening to the San Marcos Royals football games—*"First down . . . Diego Viera makes the tackle"*—which somehow drove home how badly I'd fucked up, and how much I was missing out on. It was a nice time of year, and I was stuck in this tiny cell, and I felt something rare for me—regret. I was scared about what lay ahead. But Dad had assembled a high-powered team of lawyers to represent me, and thankfully they were able to convince the judge to send me to an educational lockdown facility instead of CYA. I turned eighteen right before I was sent off to Utah, wearing handcuffs.

Me and Dad, 1996.

The writer Sean Wilsey, in his memoir *Oh the Glory of It All*, describes the "therapeutic boarding school" he attended in California—the Cascade School—as a cult-like, militaristic penal colony for alienated teenagers. But when the teachers at Cascade wanted to really scare the kids, Wilsey writes, they'd threaten them with a more extreme alternative called Provo Canyon School. "'If you don't make it here, then you're going to Provo,'" a teacher named Neil liked to say. "'And at Provo they'll bend you over a bunk bed and shove a dick up your ass.'"

I was going to Provo. It had separate boys' and girls' campuses and a five-level system. Everyone started out at Level 0 and was released at Level 4. How long you stayed there depended on how fast you could work your way up the levels.

Level 0 was Orientation. They shaved our heads, replaced our street clothes with gray sweat suits, left us in a room watching *The Price Is Right* for hours, made us walk everywhere in a single-file line, and wouldn't let us call our parents. The idea was that you'd earn small rewards for each new level you attained.

The staff were mostly Mormon, and many of the orderlies were hulking South Pacific Islanders. In Orientation we met the department heads, and each of us was assigned a counselor who'd oversee our particular case. A staffer named Cynthia was especially friendly toward me. She was in her thirties, blond, Mormon, and kind of hot. On a cross-country ski outing soon after my arrival, I thought she was acting flirtatiously.

By this time, I felt like I connected well with girls and women. I preferred their company to boys' and men's, and sometimes felt that I brought out a mothering instinct. They saw potential, and at the same time they thought I was lost or crazy, and they wanted to be the one to change me. They felt that I needed them. I probably did.

That night, I asked a kid who'd been at Provo for a while if this was typical behavior for Cynthia, because if it wasn't, I thought she might be into me. "Don't get too excited," he said. She had a husband and kids, and "that's what she's like with everyone." I set aside my daydreams of erotic private lessons, reviving them only for jerk-off sessions.

If you failed to comply with any of Provo Canyon's many rules, you'd be told to "take a chair," which meant sitting in a chair facing the wall until a teacher deemed you sufficiently chastened. You also might be put "on investment," which meant getting sent to the Investment Unit, either "short-term" or "long-term." Investment was a big locked room where all the kids who'd been sent there had to sit on a bench, staring at a wall. Short-term meant you had to do this for hours. Long-term meant you had to do this for days or weeks. You were forbidden to make eye contact with one another, and a guy sitting at a desk up front monitored you the whole time.

I got sent only to short-term a couple of times, once for getting into a fight on the basketball court. But it was pretty fucked up. If you spoke while you were on investment, the monitor would reset the clock and you'd have to start over from the beginning. If you acted out or were disruptive, a staffer would "dial 9," calling in reinforcements who'd stab you in the ass with a syringe full of "booty juice" (the antipsychotic drug Haldol) and put you "on observation." That meant isolating you in the Solitary Room in back, which was a concrete cell with a drain in the floor that was your only option if you needed to relieve yourself.

Unlike all the other places I'd been, which focused on reforming budding criminals or rehabilitating drug abusers, Provo also had students with serious emotional problems, and the tough-love approach didn't seem to help them. Once, when I was on short-term investment, a kid named Roman, who seemed not to be all there, wouldn't stop asking questions, and stood up. The monitor told him to sit down, and when Roman refused, orderlies literally dragged him to the Solitary Room, where he screamed bloody murder. It sounded like they were beating the shit out of him.

I had it easier than other kids. At eighteen, I was older than most of them and had my GED, so while they were at the Learning Center taking high school classes, I had my own schedule. I could bounce around and audit courses as I wished, which usually meant English or art, which was taught by a woman who played Enya CDs relentlessly. I also took some home-study courses from Brigham Young University, and I spent a fair amount of time doing odd jobs for staff, which put me in their good graces. I wasn't doing any drugs for the first time in a while, and I started a regular meeting for students, focused on substance abuse. I was a role model, someone the staff turned to for help handling other kids.

One day, Cynthia asked if I'd like to play chess sometime. My fantasies instantly revved up again: *She wants me.* But a couple of weeks passed with no follow-up, and I began to think my imagination was overactive. Then, as I was going into the chow hall one day, she saw me and challenged me to a game right then. *It's on.* We headed toward the staircase to her office . . . and passed it. Damn. *It's not on.* We were going to play in the Learning Center. She found a vacant classroom, where she pulled two desks together and began setting up the board.

The door to the room had a huge window that large guards—paid to patrol the corridor to make sure teachers were okay—could walk past and look through at will. This wasn't fertile *Penthouse* Forum territory.

We were still developing our pawns when I felt something brush my leg. Was Cynthia playing footsie with me? No. It was my hormones again. I really needed to stop thinking that there was—

Holy shit! Her legs had clamped around one of my legs. Staring at me, she said, "Cameron, you have really cool eyes." I leaned in for a kiss. She leaned in and kissed me back. *Holy shit! And phew! And holy shit!* After a few seconds of this, we broke off the kiss and, with the door's large window in mind, began packing up the chessboard. She asked if I wanted to finish our chess game at a later date. *Yes!*

I didn't see her for a few days. Then, when I did, she was aloof. Another two weeks passed, and I began to question whether our kiss had even happened. One day, when I was in line in the chow hall, I felt a tap on my shoulder and it was Cynthia, who asked if I'd like to finish our chess game. I followed her out of the room. This time, we took a right toward the staircase that led to her department's offices. Instead of her office, though, she took me to my counselor Stephen's office. He was gone for a week at a convention. There was a couch in there, and we fucked on it.

Cynthia and I started having hardcore, uninhibited sex every day. At first, it seemed like a dream come true. Cynthia would appear in the dorm, in the chow hall, at the basketball court, and call me out. We had sex all over the compound: in her office, in an auditorium bathroom, in a recreation shed where all the balls were kept. Once, I convinced her to have a three-way with me and my friend Danny, a charismatic, athletic kid from Orange County, in the activities shed.

Though Cynthia had a family, and was in a position of authority, she was clearly developing strong feelings for me. I started to dread her impromptu requests that I stop whatever I was doing and come with her. It felt like I was her indentured servant, if not her sex slave. She made a poor effort to conceal what was going on, as if she couldn't help herself. She'd come to my unit at night to fetch me, and the unit cop would wink at me and say, "Cameron, time to get back to work again, buddy."

Eleven months after I got to Provo, I had worked my way up to Level 3 but was mysteriously unable to progress to Level 4. Staff who were in positions of authority had to unanimously agree to advance a student to Level 4, and a staffer I was friendly with told me that Cynthia kept blocking my advancement. She wouldn't sign a release form. I explained to Cynthia that in order for there to be anything between us, she needed to let me go. She relented, and not long afterward Dad flew to pick me up in a small charter plane that took us from Provo to Santa Barbara. On the flight, I told Dad about my exploits. "Sounds risky," he said, "but I can't be mad at you." I basked in his pride. We were both optimistic about my future.

The graduate.

17

1997: Hands Over Your Head

B ack in California, I still had a few months of probation left. One of my first priorities was dealing with Sean, who'd ditched me on the day I dragged the Secret Service agent four blocks. I heard he was living at his father's house off of Sandyland Road, in Carpinteria. He was a big, tough, athletic guy, and I went there planning to stab him, but when I arrived he took off running.

Then I moved to L.A. and got a small apartment on the Westside with my friend Josh, a graffiti artist I'd met at Provo, and Jamie, a skate buddy from Carpinteria. I started to focus on music again, skated a lot, took some courses at Santa Monica College, and partied every night.

Early one morning, when half a dozen friends were passed out in our living room, there was a knock at the door. I knew it was Cynthia, from Utah. She'd been in town for six days and I'd been ducking her; and a few minutes earlier, she'd called from a pay phone on the corner. I'd told her I didn't think it was a good idea for us to see each other, and she hung up, pissed.

I wasn't sure how she'd found my apartment, which looked like all the others in our huge apartment complex, but the knocking continued. I lay in bed, wishing her not to be there, hoping she'd go away. She knocked more aggressively, pounding now. *Boom boom boom.* I got up and tiptoed to the door and looked through the peephole. My friends were looking at me in drowsy confusion. I shushed them. I still thought maybe she'd go away, but then she started kicking the door.

After one kick, I opened the door and let her in. As she stood there in jeans, a flannel shirt, and hiking boots, looking like an Outward Bound guide, Josh said, "Holy shit, Ms. S., fancy meeting you here!" She suddenly looked vulnerable. I could see the realization hitting her: *What the fuck am I doing here?* I thought she might have a breakdown. Then she said, "Does anyone want to order a pizza?" To save her from her own painful awkwardness, I whisked her into my bedroom and had a talk with her. I told her she was embarrassing herself. I reminded her that I was eighteen, and that she had a husband and children back in Utah. I told her to go home, and she did.

Though I was partying a lot, I was more focused than I'd ever been. DJs were starting to make big money. I'd been DJing for years, and I thought that was what I wanted to do with my life. When I joined my friends Jay and Paul to go snowboarding in Big Bear, I discovered they'd gotten deeply into prescription drugs. Paul had robbed a series of pharmacies at knifepoint, and had stockpiled a lot of pills, and in Big Bear he and Jay spent all their time in the house, out of their minds. I wasn't into zoning out and playing video games all day—I wanted to get things accomplished—and I left them there and hitch-hiked back to L.A.

One of my roommates had a little gun that we kept under the couch for protection. We had a house rule: the gun was never to leave the premises. But one evening, after drinking two 40s with our neighbor Ron, a big dude who also skated and had just come home from prison, I decided for some reason that I'd wear the gun in the waistband of my pants when we went out. Ron and I skated and drank our way down Sunset Boulevard to West Hollywood, planning to make a little video. We went into Mel's Drive-In, got some food to go, and left without paying. There was a commotion as the owner saw us leaving and tried to block us, but as soon as he spotted the pistol at my waist, he stopped pursuing us. At that point I had a moment of clarity and decided to empty the gun's chamber and clip, leaving the bullets on the ground.

Twenty minutes later, Ron and I were a few blocks away, drunkenly eating our food at a picnic table and listening to the Beastie Boys on a boom box. My back was to the street. Suddenly, I heard a rustling in the bushes behind me and voices yelling. I turned around and saw four LAPD cars at the curb and a couple of cops on their knees pointing shotguns at us. The diner's owner must have called 911. A spotlight blinked on, and an amplified voice said: *"Slowly stand up, and put your hands over your head."*

I was trying to figure out what to do with the gun in my waistband, and even though the cops were yelling that I needed to have my hands over my head, I kept reaching down toward the gun. I wanted to throw it. The cops started screaming: "Keep your fucking hands away!" Finally I put my hand into my waistband and tossed the gun up the hill, and started walking backward with my hands in the air. This was the era of the trigger-happy LAPD, and it's a miracle they didn't shoot me. I was probably saved by my skin color and the neigh-

Up to no good on the Lower East Side.

borhood we were in. In the car to the precinct, a cop told me I'd come very close to being shot.

Ron was out on parole, and his mother wrote me a letter saying the police were trying to pin the gun charge on him, which would mean he'd go back to prison for a long time. She asked if I would please testify that the gun was mine, and I did, writing out an affidavit.

I got lucky. Emptying the gun's chamber and clip had been a smart move, because a loaded firearm would bring much more severe charges than an unloaded one. Since I was still serving out my juvenile probation, the new charge was treated as a violation of that, rather than as a new adult crime. So although I was sentenced to four to six months behind bars, and I'd serve the time in the Santa Barbara County Jail, once I was released I'd be off probation, my case closed.

Mom and Dad were predictably disappointed. They'd allowed themselves to hope that, post-Provo, I would put away childish things and be a productive citizen of the world. But I was caught up in my lifestyle, forming tight bonds with a like-minded group of friends, and didn't give a fuck. And now I was eighteen; Mom and Dad weren't legally responsible for me, and I wasn't legally accountable to them.

County jail, on a hill overlooking the 101 freeway, was my first taste of the adult penal system. I was a boy among men, many of them on their way to or from prison. Here, I could see the color lines drawn even more starkly than in juvie. The Mexicans and blacks couldn't stand each other, and Mexicans and whites sometimes formed alliances. Generally, you'd eat with "your own kind."

I was in gen pop, which sucked because it meant that other than during the limited hours when I was allowed to go out to the yard, I was indoors all the time. I took part in the jail's drug rehab program, mainly because I liked the guy who ran it, Dave Vartabedian, who I knew from juvie days, and because my participation would reduce my sentence. I got a job in the kitchen, waking at 4 a.m. to stand on the dishwashing line and work the sprayer until 11 a.m. After breakfast, we'd set up an assembly line in the chow hall to make sandwiches for Juvenile Hall, the same one I'd spent so much time in, which was across the road from the county jail. One guy laid down a slice of bread, another a slice of cheese, another a gob of mayonnaise, and another the bologna or turkey or mystery meat of the day. The boxes the meat came in were stamped FOR INSTITUTIONAL USE ONLY.

My first few weeks in County, I was able to keep my identity under wraps. The jail had registered me under my middle name, thinking that my last name might put me in danger. But when guards addressed me, I was sometimes slow to react. They'd be doing roll call, and I'd be dead-tired from getting up for the 4:30 a.m. kitchen detail. Someone would elbow me, and I'd snap to. "Morrell! Morrell! Are you fucking ignoring me?" the sheriff would say. "No, no!" I'd say. "Here! Here!"

Then, through Dave's intervention, I got moved to the Honor Farm, the cushier section of the complex. The Honor Farm had vending machines. I could move around freely and go outside when I wanted. The yard was wide open, with a volleyball court and a small weight pit, and oversight was so lax that it felt almost like the movie *Stir Crazy*. Guys on kitchen duty walked to the fence near the loading dock to see their mothers and girlfriends, who'd hand them packages, often containing drugs and other contraband, which the guys would bring back to the unit.

My lawyer visited and said the police were targeting me for a series of pharmacy robberies in the area. Several witnesses had picked me out in multiple pictures. I said, "Listen, I know who did them, and it wasn't me." I figured my face looked familiar to the witnesses not because they'd ever seen me, much less seen me robbing pharmacies, but because of my resemblance to Dad and Pappy. "It's not looking good for you," my lawyer said. I couldn't believe it; I was going to get charged with robberies I had nothing to do with.

When Jay and Paul visited me, Paul was so fucked up on pills that the supervising officer said, "Either your friend has to pull it together, or he has to go." I told Paul about my lawyer's visit, and how witnesses thought I'd done the pharmacy robberies. Paul had brought a little supply of pills to pass to me, but once the guards started watching him closely, he was able only to drop a couple of Xanax pills in my soda. My short career as a pharmacy-robbery suspect came to an end when, while I was still in jail, Paul decided to rob one of the pharmacies again. This time, Marcus Allen, the former Raiders running back and Heisman Trophy winner who lived in Montecito, happened to be in the pharmacy and chased Paul down and tackled him, holding him until police arrived.

In the Honor Farm we wore blue jeans, a blue collared shirt, and workboots. We slept in barracks-style housing in a room with maybe twenty bunkbeds and forty people. The bathroom had no stalls or even dividers, just a line of showerheads with four nozzles each and a row of toilets without partitions. I learned how to shit prison-style: underwear hiked to upper thighs to mask my groin, and pants up around the knees.

Keeping my underwear and pants high was partly for privacy and partly so that I could stand up fast if I needed to. In front of the toilets was a row of sinks. If you were on the toilet and caught a guy at a sink looking at you in the mirror, it was a red flag. The number one rule in prison is to mind your own business. You notice everything, but the other person shouldn't know you notice. You don't want to get caught looking at someone unless you're prepared to rape them or beat them up.

In the absence of partitions or any other accommodation for human shame, not to mention odor control, prison custom was to keep your arm behind you and flush, repeatedly, as you voided your bowels. If someone was lax about flushing while shitting, there'd be a loud chorus of "Water down! Water's free! Flush the toilet!"

The Honor Farm was a whole compound, separated from the main prison by a huge wall; a tunnel connected the two units. One day, standing in line to exchange my linens and get a fresh set of clothes at the jail laundry, I was talking to the person ahead of me when I saw a guy drop from a tree that grew on our side of the wall but whose branches loomed out over the other side. Then another one did the same, and another, and another. On the Honor Farm side, we were all cheering, "Yeah, go! Go! Go! Go!" The men took off running and stole a car outside the probation office. Police caught two of the guys immediately. They caught a third guy a few days later. A week after that, in L.A., they captured the fourth and final man at large. He was at his girlfriend's house, the most obvious possible place.

Even the Honor Farm felt serious. One time, Sammy, an older Mexican gangster, and another Mexican gangbanger went into a closet to fight. They really went at it. Sammy was bigger, and I feared for the smaller guy's health. But he was tough as shit, and he made it through without being seriously hurt. It reinforced my belief that while size mattered, fierceness of character was a significant factor in a fight's outcome. Fights were different here than in juvie, more savage. People would bite ears and gouge eyes. Essentially, anything went, because you were fighting for your life.

I got along with most people. As one of the younger inmates, I felt almost like a mascot. But maybe because of my youth, a bigger, older surfer dude with a shaved head, who seemed pissed off at life, kept giving me a hard time. He probably thought I'd be scared and take whatever he dished out. You could still smoke in jails then, and one day a few of us were out on the yard talking when this asshole, out of nowhere, put his cigarette out on my arm.

I didn't pull my arm away. I waited until he was done. Then I went to town on him, punching him in the face. He went down, and I got a few more punches in before other guys broke it up. I hadn't been acting like a tough guy in jail, but I'd gotten into decent shape working out in the weight pit, and I felt pretty good about the beatdown I delivered. I felt bionic, unable to be defeated in any way. Afterward, Sammy named me El Tigre, and all the Mexicans started calling me that.

Dad visited once while I was in county jail. We met in a private room, but he'd arrived in a chauffeured town car. Afterward, another inmate pulled me aside and said something about it. "So what?" I said. From then on, my identity was known, which inevitably prompted fights.

Mom had flown to India right before I went to jail, for what was supposed to be a quick trip. Three months later she was still there, and I received a visit from Todd Raines, her fiancé, and his kids. Todd and Mom had just moved into a grand, newly built house together. The house was probably a stretch for Todd financially, but Mom had insisted, and he loved her.

Now he'd come to tell me that he'd run out of patience. As Mom kept extending her stay in India, a rumor was circulating that she was spending a lot of time with a young maharaja, and Todd believed it. It wasn't the first time something like this had happened, and Todd was weary of feeling like second fiddle. He was crushed, which broke my heart. I'd come to genuinely love him, and his kids as well. I was sad for Mom, too. Without knowing the nuances of their relationship, I didn't think she'd ever find a man more suited to her standards, and I believed she'd come to regret losing Todd.

Mom got back from India just in time for my release from county jail. At 3 a.m., I walked with my little bag of personal property through a tunnel and out into a parking lot with huge lights. Mom was waiting in her Range Rover, and she brought me back to the house. My probation was over. For the first time in four years, I was not under a court's supervision.

Soon after that, Mom hosted a long-planned housewarming, an opulent soiree for all of her and Todd's friends, a Who's Who of Santa Barbara. I was surprised to see Todd, but he hadn't yet dropped the hammer on her. I also didn't realize just how deeply stung he felt.

I left the party when it was still going strong, to meet up with friends. When I came home later that night, I found Mom crying hysterically. She said that Todd and another woman had been on the dance floor, getting hot and heavy, and she'd gone over and demanded that he stop and come with her to talk elsewhere. He'd refused, then shared a deep, passionate kiss with the woman. Mom, mortified, had fled, weeping. Now she tried to get me worked up, decrying Todd's malevolence and expounding on her own victimhood. I sensed that she was hoping I would rise to defend her honor. But I loved Todd, and was offended by her behavior, and this time I felt indifferent to her predicament.

18

2007: Inspector Gadget

The cruise with Dad, island to island, is beautiful. I shoot up in my upper thighs, where the track marks won't be visible under my shorts. My addiction is growing, but I can still pass as sober, and we all get along. One night during dinner, Neil Young's "Old Man" is playing, and Erin mentions that I listen to the song all the time. Dad starts tearing up. Then he comes around the table and gives me a kiss.

The crystal intercepted by the LAPD doesn't get tracked back to me and Erin, but clearly we need to be more disciplined and creative. When we return home, we put more effort into our packaging. We mix the meth in with innocuous products like jars of scented bath salts, and we experiment with other ways to conceal it—in a bag of candy, in a gumball machine, in a VCR. We do some Googling and learn that carbon paper helps thwart X-ray machines, so we wrap the drugs in that and have Emmanuel use it to wrap the money he's sending as well. I add a few extra ounces of crystal to each new shipment to Emmanuel, to make up for the intercepted pound he already paid for.

In the spring, Alex introduces me to a guy in New York named Trevor Mitchell, who wants to buy pound quantities of crystal. He's very smart and well educated, and he, like Emmanuel, wholesales to the gay club scene. I meet him at his apartment in Chelsea, and he gives me $72,000 in cash, telling me to hold on to it: He'll let me know when he's ready to start receiving shipments. Returning to L.A., I smuggle the money in a cereal box.

A few months later, Erin and I return home to a message on our answering machine from Alex. It's cryptic. He says he has been arrested by the DEA and sent to rehab, and that I should watch my back.

Alex has called a few times in the preceding months, seemingly to talk business, and now I wonder whether he has been working for the DEA. I replay the conversations in my mind. I'm always careful about what I say on the phone—anyone listening in would hear vague references to "seeing my friend" and "sending gifts" and "picking up paperwork"—and I feel confident that even if those calls were being recorded, I didn't say anything incriminating. But after Alex's warning, I decide to put a hold on my meth distribution business.

While I figure out how to proceed, I make some cash robbing a couple of drug dealers. These new robberies are another line crossed. I'm in a different frame of mind now. My pellet-gun stickups were the desperate acts of a lost, lonely, cocaine-crazed maniac grasping for some tenuous sense of power, a feeling that I still had some balls and wasn't a total failure. But they were gateway robberies, getting me past a threshold of timidity.

Now I'm fully committed to my criminal lifestyle. I carry a real gun. I have a purpose and a plan and a willingness, probably, to fire the gun. I need money, but I'm also pragmatic. I don't try to go after Pablo Escobar. I go after people who have something I can use, but who I think will put up minimal resistance, like a guy I know named Karl. A friend and I drive to his house in Hollywood, do a bump of crystal in the car, put on ski masks, and come in the door brandishing guns. I feel kind of shitty doing this to Karl, who's a peaceful guy, but that's what makes him an easy target, and if you're in the drug game, these are the things that come with it. It's as simple as that. Drug deal-ers can't call the cops on you. That's why that world is so violent. You're on your own, and you take care of yourself. If you present yourself as a target, you're going to get targeted, eventually. Where you're weak, that's where you're exposed. And there are plenty of drug dealers out there making a lot of money who don't take very many precautions. That emboldens me. We tie Karl up and take all his shit, which is a relatively modest haul: two ounces of crystal, half an ounce of heroin, and $2,000 in cash.

Next, a buddy and I hit a dealer who lives in an apartment building in Hollywood, and who stiffed me on an ounce of heroin. My friend Lisa texts me that she's partying with him, and she leaves the garage door open for us. We come up through the elevator and walk into the apartment. Half a dozen people are sitting around a coffee table getting high. We tell them to lie down on the floor, then I go into the bedroom, where Lisa has told me the guy keeps his drugs and money. The haul is about twice the cash of our last hit, and includes an unreg-istered Glock 27. Money isn't my only motivation: I also just want to see if I can pull these things off.

With our meth network blown, the pal and I decide to start ship-ping coke instead. It will be to an entirely different set of customers, through an old Dominican friend of mine in New York. This business takes off fast, too. We're soon shipping two, then four, then six to eight kilos a week. We make $7,000 in profit per kilo. But my coke custom-ers are harder to deal with than my meth customers. The crystal guys were club users grateful for the vastly superior, cheaper crystal I was sending them and happy to front the money. My coke customers are street-savvy, expect me to front the product, and are less forgiving of logistical snafus and delays. They're also more demanding about the quality of the product.

I figure that if the DEA has me in its sights, they'll lose interest now that I'm done selling meth and their leads have gone quiet, but I become more careful. I pay a guy at the airport to load the coke right onto the plane for me. And I hire Leo, an old friend of Dad's in Santa Barbara, to help me improve on my shipping methods. Leo is a Vietnam vet who wears graduated-lens sunglasses morning, noon, and night. He's an amazing machinist, a garage tinkerer and beach guy who's made the legal portion of his living inventing and fabricating things like ride plates for Jet Skis. I drive up to meet with him and give him $10,000 to see what he can come up with. Soon, Leo is modifying stereo equipment to contain hidden compartments and experimenting with different X-ray-proof linings. He makes me a stamp with a double-diamond insignia, which I plan to use to brand the keys I'm selling.

I also get serious about countersurveillance. Having spent years associating with drug dealers, I have some familiarity with the cat-and-mouse measures they take to keep from getting caught, but I now spend hours browsing websites that sell espionage and counterespionage equipment. I mount cameras outside the house on Cole Crest. I buy a bug detector and white-noise makers, which generate a cone of silence with a five-foot radius. I get a malware program that lets me text someone, and when they open the text I instantly have full access to their phone. I come close to buying a paramotor: a propeller-powered paraglider that fits in a suitcase, and that I could wear on my back if I ever need to escape quickly from the Cole Crest house. I spend hours at the Hollywood Spy Shop on Sunset Boulevard. Erin takes to calling me Inspector Gadget.

I now have her hire people who don't know me to do pickups and drop-offs at the P.O. boxes, and I monitor the couriers by hiding tiny digital trackers in both drug shipments and stacks of money, which transmit their speed, altitude, and location. I have half a dozen pre-paid Virgin phones, each dedicated to a single supplier or customer and coded with a different-colored star sticker: gold for Emmanuel, green for Gabriel. I insist that anyone I do business with do the same, communicating on phones they use only with me. All of this—the evolution in my approach, my tactics, my technology—is really just an effort to make me feel like I'm going to be okay, when I know, deep down, that I'm not going to be okay.

I'm now making more money than I need. I set some of it aside but spend most of it, living extravagantly and buying a Ducati motorcycle and a 1962 Chevy Nova, which I spend tens of thousands of dollars to soup up. Displays of material wealth are a tightrope, since Dad knows I don't have regular work. I don't want to come off as too flashy, which would spark his suspicions, but I want to show that I can survive and even thrive. Erin and I still have his BMW, but during his trips out west from New York, I make a point of displaying the Ducati and the muscle car and the glass-walled luxury rental perched in the Holly-wood Hills. He has no idea they're the spoils of drug money.

My anxiety about a possible federal investigation intensifies. One day, I'm circling the BMW with my bug detector, and it lights up like a Christmas tree. In the wheel well, I find a GPS locator. I get an adren-aline rush from the spy-versus-spy, but my paranoia is constant and mounting. Erin starts to worry about my mental health. She catches me standing on the roof of the house wearing tighty-whities, holding a handgun, and doing bug sweeps.

I'm being watched. I'm being followed. One afternoon, I leave a newsstand I frequent on a corner near Fairfax and Beverly, and to avoid traffic I turn into a parallel alley that goes toward Laurel Can-yon. A car is parked at the alley's entrance, in view of the newsstand, and as I roll slowly past it, threading the narrow alley, I see two big guys with cop mustaches in the front seat. They look furtive. We make eye contact, and there's a moment of mutual understanding: they're here to watch me, and I know it.

Soon after, I'm on my way to a club with Jay, and we pull into a gas station; Jay waits in the car while I go to buy water, passing a home-less guy who asks me for money. Inside, I stop to browse the magazine rack. Through the window, I can see Jay and the car, still at the pump.

Suddenly, the homeless guy is standing next to me.

"Nice wheels," he says.

I ignore him.

"Hey can you help me out? I'm trying to find a place to stay. I'm waiting for my friend."

Crickets from me.

"Yeah, because I'm waiting for him to take me to the meth house."
I look at him. "What?"

"Yeah, the meth house, where they make it."

I give him a closer look. His eyes have the aviators' tan line shared by every cop in California, from wearing sunglasses all day.

I say, "Dude, I don't know what you're talking about or why you're talking to me."

"I can get good prices."

"Get the fuck away from me."

I decide that we should have better guns for protection. Erin and Gabriel and I go to a shop in Burbank, off Ventura Boulevard, and I buy a Glock 17, a Special Forces–style Desert Eagle handgun, and a Mossberg shotgun with a pistol grip. My criminal record could pose a problem, so I have Erin put two of them in her name and Gabriel put the third one in his name.

I keep the Mossberg, loaded with six 12-gauge shells, under my bed, within easy reach if I'm ever attacked while sleeping. I have a battle plan. If someone comes for me, I'll get behind the bed and start firing.

Soon after buying the guns, Erin and I go to get the one Gabriel's holding, and he says he sold it for cash. It emerges that he has secretly been harboring a grudge toward me. A few months earlier, the guy who'd gotten us involved in the Stereo nightclub deal in New York fell out with his partners; since Gabriel and I never had paperwork documenting our investment, we've stopped receiving dividend checks and no longer get our calls returned by the partners. Gabriel claims I assured him he'd make his money back from the nightclub. He borrowed the money he invested, he says, and now he's getting heat from his lenders.

I'm already concerned about Gabriel's increasing flakiness. He has always impressed me by saving money, but his lifestyle has begun to change. He has become friends with a party kid, going out to nightclubs and doing Ecstasy and GHB, a drug that comes in clear plastic water bottles. You pour out a cap and drink it. If you don't do too much, you feel great, but drink one cap too many and you're pissing in your pants and passing out. At three-thirty one morning, Gabriel is arrested at Avalon, a club at Hollywood and Vine, with dealer-level quantities of crystal, coke, pot, and Ecstasy; a pipe; and $2,130 in cash. He's slipping as a business partner, too. He's not coming through reliably with coke, and my East Coast customers make it clear to me that this could become a problem. I tell Gabriel he's putting me in a bad position, and that I'm going to find a new supplier. I start buying directly from Gabriel's source, a slight, older Mexican guy I know as Nero.

A month later, I'm still unsure about Nero, whose product can be uneven, and one evening I meet with two Mexican guys at the Cole Crest house as potential alternative suppliers. I made the mistake of mentioning the meeting to Gabriel, and I'm in the middle of it when he shows up drunk. "What the fuck are they doing here?" he says, staggering toward me.

"Take it easy, Gabriel."

"Where's my fucking money?" He's slurring. *Wherzhmyfuckinmoney?* He's standing right in front of me now.

My backpack is next to me, and he knows that's where I keep my cash. He reaches into it and pulls out $30,000. "I'm going to take this," he says, and turns away. I reach into the backpack, pull out my Glock, and point it at him. He embarrassed me. He chumped me. I want to shoot him. But he's my friend and I love him, even now.

"This one time, Gabriel, I'm going to let you get away with this. I could shoot you dead right here, and you'd be a lowlife who came into my place drunk and tried to take my money. I think I'd be okay." If this is what it takes for me to be done with him, then so be it. I'll write it off as a loss.

The two Mexican guys don't seem equipped to meet the demand of my customers. I stick with Nero as my supplier.

Two days later, Erin goes to one of the P.O. boxes where I keep cash and finds it empty. I had a little more than $150,000 in it, and it's gone. It wasn't all my money. Most of it was cash from my New York customers for kilos of blow.

Gabriel. In the past, I've sent him to pick up money from the box, and he's the only person with access to it besides me and Erin. My customers in New York are serious people, and when I tell them what happened, they want to go to Gabriel's house and deal with him directly.

"You can't do that," I say. "He's there with his children and brothers and mother and father. I'll go talk to him."

I drive to the Garcias' house.

"Dude, that's not all my money, you can't take that. You know how this shit works. These people are really upset about this. They want to come here and get the money and deal with you. You've got to give that money back."

"Fuck you," Gabriel says, "and fuck them."

I end up covering the loss myself, which really puts me in the hole.

During this period, when I'm comfortably in my heroin addiction, and my business is keeping me busy, my relationships with family and old friends are distant but stable. Even Amanda has pulled back. She's got a new boyfriend, and she and I are now able to have a friendly relationship without all the drama. She'll come over to Cole Crest and we'll sit down and talk, while Erin stays in another room.

Periodically, the Douglases get together for a family portrait, and in the fall the extended clan gathers for one in Montecito, at the beautiful home of my uncle Peter, Pappy's first son with Oma. Peter's whole family is here. Pappy and Oma are here. Dad is here with Catherine and their kids, Dylan and Carys, who are seven and four. Jojo comes with his girlfriend, Jo Ann. I come with Erin.

It's been a real production getting everyone here, and there's a makeup artist.

With Dad on Lake Shasta.

Carys gives me a big hug. "Hi, princess," I say.

Peter is always on the cutting edge of technology, and he has a new marijuana vaporizer, the first one Dad and I have ever seen. It's a big, cone-shaped, tabletop thing called the Volcano. It fills a balloon with smoke, which you then inhale. Dad and I take a couple of good rips, then kick back, taking in the scene and laughing.

I love getting together with my family, and though I haven't been seeing Dad often, it feels great to be hanging out with him and getting along.

I'm shipping four to six kilos of cocaine a week now, and in general Nero doesn't want to screw me, since I'm a source of regular business. But at least once, my New York customers have sent coke back to me, leaving me sitting with trash, and Nero was difficult about reimbursing me. So I become more demanding, getting to know coke like some people know wine. I gauge quality by look, taste, touch, and sometimes chemical reaction, dropping a piece into a cup of bleach and watching for the telltale tracer as it spins to the bottom, which indicates purity. There are a lot of ways to disguise poor coke quality, and a key might have been "re-rocked"—reconstituted into a brick after being cut with other chemicals—twice but still look shiny and fluffy. A high-quality surface layer might conceal a shitty core. My tried-and-true method for detecting manipulation is to slit open a kilo, dig into the middle of it, put a small piece on my tongue and hold it to the roof of my mouth. The more smoothly it dissolves, the better. Buttery is good, grainy bad. Since getting into kilos, the best coke I've seen is super oily and creamy. I call it the Cheese, because if you took a slicer to it you'd peel off something that looks like a shaving of Parmesan. Someone could fake that consistency, but the chemicals used to do it would have a giveaway sweetness.

Nero doesn't always get his coke from the same source, and anytime he brings me product with a stamp I haven't seen before, I'll test it myself by injecting it. Sometimes I'll mix it with heroin for a speedball. I'm not worried about relapsing, because my coke addiction shook me up to such a degree that it really doesn't appeal to me anymore. But my heroin addiction is up to around a gram and a half a day, which should last an average person three to five days.

I'm starting to have visions of kingpin grandeur. Maybe this is what I'm meant to do, and if so, taking it to the next level will probably mean moving out of the country, possibly to Europe. Drug enforcement is laxer there, and it's easier to run an illegal narcotics business. The officials you need to corrupt to carry on as a drug trafficker seem more corruptible there than in the U.S.

In July 2007, as my coke business is ramping up, Erin and Jay and I drive to Carpinteria with the dogs to try to open up a new distribution channel, which will involve shipping kilos to Europe in scuba tanks custom-fabricated by Leo. I like coming up here to see old friends. Jay and I are at the Palms Bar late one night, and we decide to go back to the place where we're staying with Erin, the Sandyland Reef Inn, to do a shot. By the time we've both found veins and shot up, it's after 2 a.m., but our plan is to return to the Palms. As soon as we come out of our room, a police car comes into the parking lot. I say to Jay, "Just keep walking." The moment we get in the Beemer, the cruiser pulls up behind us, blocking us in.

One of the cops says we're parked illegally. He shines his flashlight into our car. He sees blood on my hand and arm. I say it's from playing with my dog. I say that my girlfriend is staying at the motel. The cops notice a syringe on the back-seat floor. I say I'm a Type A diabetic. They arrest me (a rude way for me to find out there's no such thing as Type A diabetes), and Jay and drive us away as Erin watches from the balcony of our room. We're booked at the Santa Barbara County Jail, where I spent four months when I was nineteen. The cops test the syringe and find that it contains 0.25 milliliters of liquid cocaine. I'm charged with possession.

I'm freaked out mainly because I'm going to have to go through heroin withdrawal. After forty-eight hours in jail, I can feel the symptoms coming on, and I know it's just going to keep getting worse. Finally, my friend Jesse's mom, Mary, cosigns a bail bond for me, putting up her house as collateral. Mary has always been there for me. She bought me the bus ticket when I was in Minnesota. She loves me. I think she has sympathy for me because of my unusual childhood, and she doesn't blame me for my choices. She wants to help, to be there for me if she can, and I'm grateful. I don't subscribe to the tough-love philosophy. It didn't end well for Uncle Eric, and it hasn't worked too well for me either. It's not to say I don't believe in structure and discipline, but if you love someone, you're there for them. That's how I see it. But I guess it's a hard line to walk.

As soon as I get into the Beemer with Erin, I say, "I hope you have cheeva for me." I do a shot before we're out of the parking lot.

I ultimately plead to a lesser charge of disorderly conduct.

Erin tells me that TMZ has posted my mug shot side-by-side with a headshot of Rachel Maddow under a headline wondering whether she is "Michael Douglas' Son?"

Dad calls to say that he's heard I'm being investigated by the DEA.

"Get out of your house immediately, they're coming for you."

He's in town and staying at the Beverly Hills Hotel. When I get there, I see that he's with a man I don't recognize. Mom is here too. Uh-oh. This is their second double-team in two years.

Dad sighs.

"Jesus, Cameron, you're dealing now? This needs to stop. What's going on?"

"What's going on is that you guys cut me off, and before that you gave me just enough money to barely get by, and this is what's allowed me to come back in the last few years."

How about getting a real job? I didn't graduate from high school. I could pump gas, but I guess my ego's too big for that. Maybe I think I'm better than that.

The guy Dad is with extends a hand. "Earl Hightower," he says. He explains that he's a drug interventionist, but he's here because he's heard that the feds are watching me.

Dad pleads with me to get out of the country.

"This is a federal case, Dad. If they want to get me, they'll get me anywhere. But the investigation is about crystal meth, and I'm not selling it."

I'm not. I'm selling coke. But the jig's up with Dad. Clearly he now knows that I'm not making a living organizing events, and I doubt he still thinks I'm taking Suboxone.

19

1998–2004: False Spring

There was a moment, after my juvenile legal troubles ended, when the future didn't look so bad. Galen and I had been in love since I was fifteen, staying in touch by letter and phone call and seeing each other during the summers. After I got out of county jail, I moved to London with her and Jay but had trouble finding DJ work. Then I had a health scare—a painful lump on one of my balls—and flew to New York to deal with it. It turned out to be benign, an overlooked war wound from a brawl with some bouncers at a nightclub in Palma, but then I just stayed in New York, because things started going well for me.

In November 1998, Limelight, the Chelsea nightclub housed in a former Episcopal church, reopened two years after being closed by police following a grisly murder of one Club Kid by another. Amanda was in charge of booking acts, and on the strength of a Drum & Bass mixtape I gave to one of her promoters, she hired me to play in the club's H. R. Giger Room, a VIP lounge on the third floor decorated with the Swiss artist's phantasmagoric sculpture and furniture. D&B was huge in the U.K. but hadn't blown up in New York yet.

At the time, I had spiked, bleached-blond, Eminem-like hair and wore saggy Tommy Hilfiger jeans and a gold chain, and Amanda didn't seem to take me seriously when we first met. I was acting goofy, break dancing, showing off, and I went over and said: "Do you want some yayo?" Yayo was coke.

"What?"

"Do you want some yay?"

"I'm sorry, I can't hear you."

Clearly, she didn't party.

"I said, do you want some champagne?"

I'd learn that despite having grown up around clubs, Amanda had never done any drugs. She was only four years older than me, but she was an adult, and a responsible citizen. Maybe that's what drew me to her. I wanted this DJ thing really bad, and I made the young, selfish move of just ignoring the relationship I was supposedly still in with Galen in London, where I'd left all my clothes as well as my best friend.

When Dad filmed *Wonder Boys* in Pittsburgh in 1999, he got me and my old friend John jobs as production assistants on the three-month shoot. Limelight was willing to pay my airfare to return to New York every weekend to spin at the club, which gave me a rare feeling of being valued for my talent, and fueled my sense that I was carving out a path of my own. Then Limelight hired me to play a second night and started flying me back and forth twice a week. Then I added a third night, playing house music at a Sunday gay party in the Chapel, Limelight's second-biggest room. For John, who'd go on to become a successful film producer, the *Wonder Boys* gig was a step toward his dream. But my heart was in DJing. I left the production before it had wrapped, and through Amanda I picked up Saturday night at another club, the Tunnel.

Once I was back in New York full-time, living in Dad's apartment on Central Park West, my old home, my DJ career really took off. I was playing at all the big clubs then—Tunnel, Limelight, Centro-Fly, Halo. I played 2 a.m. to closing at Spa, which made stickers with my name on them. When Galen visited from London, we saw each other, and the feelings were still there between us, but I was too attached to my professional aspirations, and by then in an unhappy relationship with Amanda that I was afraid to end. Eventually Galen got tired of waiting for me and returned to the U.K. For the first time in my life, it seemed like people were paying attention to me for something other than who my father was.

I was doing coke pretty much daily. It was inextricable from the club/ DJ lifestyle that had me staying up all night and sleeping all day. Amanda and I moved in together, into her friend's sublet in an apartment building on lower Fifth Avenue, but it took her a while to realize I was using. I was hiding it, and at first she attributed my all-nighters to my having a lot of energy. But as she realized what was going on, we started fighting about it.

"Don't knock what you haven't tried."

"Well, only losers do drugs."

"Really? What's going on in your life that's so great?"

Soon she was doing coke with me. She took to it, and would go on multiday benders. Our relationship was stagnant, and the coke made Amanda more sexual. But the whole thing felt awkward, something she was doing in order to connect with me but which wasn't true to who she was. And I was being manipulative: her doing coke made it okay for me to keep doing coke.

I still felt in control, despite the occasional hiccup. In October 1999, I lent my car to a coke-dealer friend who was under police surveillance. When he returned the car to me, outside of the Fifth Avenue building, I was arrested in the lobby and charged with possession. It was the first time I'd been arrested in New York City and led to my first experience with the *New York Post*: "Michael Douglas' Son in Coke Arrest."

Amanda called the lawyer Ben Brafman, whom she knew, to represent me, and he said: "Boy, did you luck out." The *Post* could be unpredictable in its cover choices, but the Yankees had won the World Series the night before, so my bust ended up buried inside the paper. It was embarrassing, and Amanda was horrified, and Mom and Dad were worried, but Amanda and I placated them.

My relationship with Dad was filled with unspoken tensions. Pappy had created a trust for each of his grandchildren, and on my twenty-first birthday I was supposed to come into mine. But Dad would use my arrest, two months before I'd gain access to the money, to convince me to sign over control of it to him. Dad was such a monumental figure to me that he held major sway over my life. At the same time, I chafed at his hypocrisies. One day, when he was researching his part in *Traffic*, in which he'd play a judge whose daughter was an addict, he asked me: "So, what's it like?"

Amanda and I moved to an apartment in a loft building on West Thirty-Seventh Street called the Glass Farmhouse. Every now and then, something would happen to remind me of the hazards of the path I was on. One night in 2000, I got a call from the sister of my old friend Paul from Santa Barbara. There was panic in her voice.

"It's Paul," she said. "I don't know what to do. His lips are turning blue!"

Why is she calling me first? "Call a fucking ambulance!"

She hung up and called back a few minutes later.

"The ambulance is on its way, but he's not waking up."

The next day, another friend of ours called to say that Paul had died. I knew I should be sad and upset, and I acted as if I was, and on some level I must have been, but I didn't really feel anything. I wondered why that was. It worried me. But that was what having a drug addiction did for me, taking the bite out of everything else by substituting its own rote mood patterns for the vagaries of authentic emotion. It might be ugly, but it was predictable. That was its allure.

When Dad married Catherine in November 2000, he asked me to be his best man. It made me so happy. The whole thing was planned with the precision of a film production. At the post-ceremony dinner, I would be third in line to give a toast. I intended to write something the night before, but then I stayed out partying and never got around to it. All right. I'd speak from the heart and trust that I'd land on my feet. But a couple of hours before the wedding, I started getting nervous. I was in my room at the Plaza, and the only paper I could find was a receipt roll. I started writing out a toast, which grew longer and longer. I planned to unscroll the paper as I read it.

Then, at the dinner, the two people who gave toasts before me spoke off the cuff. Both were practiced public speakers, including Catherine's maid of honor, Anna Walker, a British television personality. I suddenly realized that I couldn't follow them by reading my chicken scratch off a receipt roll. Instead, I got up and just spoke from the heart. It was a clutch moment, addressing a crowd of three hundred people who included some of the biggest personalities out there—Sean Connery, Jack Nicholson, Sharon Stone, Steven Spielberg—all quietly waiting to hear what I had to say. I felt pretty loose, and it went really well. I got some laughs. I made Dad proud.

If I'd been inclined to acknowledge it, there was no shortage of evidence that coke was taking a toll on my life. I played a private party at MAGIC, the clothing trade show in Las Vegas. The next night, I was supposed to play at Avalon, a club in Boston, but I didn't want to interrupt my partying, so I sent my friend Serebe to handle the technical DJing, and Jay to pretend he was me. Then I took my $8,000 payment from the MAGIC gig and played blackjack at a casino; up $16,000, I bet the whole $24,000 on a single hand, which I lost. The episode ended with Curtis and me doing mushrooms, flying back to L.A., and emptying the pool at the downtown Standard of other guests when we jumped in naked.

Then my friend Isaac, who was getting married to Carmina, a girl I'd gone to high school with, asked me to be his best man. I was honored. The wedding was in Santa Barbara, and I flew out from New York with Abby, a sweetheart who joined me at the last minute. I went to the rehearsal. But on the wedding day, I was on a coke bender and too paranoid to leave Mom's house and go to the ceremony. Instead,

I sat in my room all afternoon, my head in my hands, looking at my watch in turmoil, hating myself, struggling to grasp my inaction as the phone kept ringing, and I kept not answering it.

Eventually, when it was too late, I called and apologized profusely. Isaac wasn't mean about it, but I knew Carmina was really upset. I was eaten up about my failure to show. I was so ashamed. This was the first time I thought that maybe I did have a drug problem.

I was already realizing that I didn't want to be with Amanda long-term. I depended on her in a number of ways. I was afraid that without her, my career would fall apart; she was my executive function, guiding me in every decision, making sure I was booking jobs and following through. She was my emotional anchor, too.

At the same time, I was miserable, resenting her and cheating on her. This yielded predictable results. When I'd stay out all night and get home late the next morning, having ignored repeated calls to my cell from Amanda, she'd hit me and slap me and scratch me. Sometimes she did it in public. I didn't know how to handle her violence other than to grab her and hold her until she stopped.

Occasionally, I'd work up the nerve to break up with her, only to become unmoored when she was gone and beg her to come back. Once, to convince her of my sincerity, I put out a cigarette on my chest, over my heart.

Four years into the relationship, I hated her, mainly because I also loved her and hated myself—for lacking the courage to break up with her and for constantly lying to her and for unfairly letting her keep believing we were going to be together forever. I was so afraid to break up with her that over the next year I kept psyching myself up to say something. Every time I hugged her, I told myself, "I can't stand this woman, I can't be with her."

My fights with Amanda had gotten so bad that after I came home at seven one morning, and we had another screaming confrontation, she convinced Mom and Dad, and even me, that I'd reached some kind of bottom and needed to go to rehab.

Dad also made rehab a condition of my being considered for a role in a film he was going to do with Pappy. For years, they'd talked about making a movie together, and one was finally coming together. *A Few Good Years* was a comedic drama that echoed some of Dad's personal history, focusing on a middle-aged son struggling to escape the shadow of his successful but neglectful father. Dad, trying to steer me away from the club scene, mentioned that there might be a part in it for me.

I spent a month at Crossroads, the drug treatment center started by Eric Clapton on Antigua. It would have been a great place to get sober long-term, had I wanted to get sober long-term. Instead, I played a lot of beach volleyball, had a fling with a starlet who was also in rehab, and let my nose take a break from drugs, knowing I'd soon go back to my normal routine.

When I came back from Crossroads, I auditioned for the role in *A Few Good Years*. Other actors, including Casey Affleck, read for the part, but it was obviously mine to lose, given that this was a Douglas family affair. Granny, with whom Pappy was still very friendly, was cast as his wife in the movie too.

Then I went to Japan to tour as a DJ, and at a club gig in Osaka I ended up smoking crystal and eating mushrooms. I was over there when I got a call to let me know I had the part. I was thrilled, but I can't say that I fully appreciated my position of privilege. Instead of simply being grateful and humbled by my great luck, I saw any acting opportunities that came my way through the narrow prism of my family. Pappy had done a lot for Dad. I felt that I was entitled to as much, if not more. Dad *owed* me.

Having had thirty days of clarity during my rehab, and with a surge of confidence from being cast in *A Few Good Years,* when I got back to New York I found the courage to finally end things with Amanda. We'd been together for nearly five years. She deserved to move on with her life. I deserved not to feel like a piece of shit. She moved out of our apartment on Thirty-Seventh Street.

I vowed never to put myself in that position again. I would never have a girlfriend. Even as I was making this vow, the post-breakup dysfunction with Amanda, which would go on for years, was already beginning.

Making the movie, which was eventually released as *It Runs in the Family*, was an amazing experience. During the two-month shoot in New York in the spring of 2002, I learned so much watching Dad and Pappy work—about acting, of course, but also how to carry yourself and interact with coworkers and treat people. In one scene, the three of us were jammed together fishing from a little boat in the middle of a lake. It felt so good to be their colleague, and to feel their pride, and to spend so much time together.

Doing well on the movie was a priority, but there was a day when I hadn't slept and had to do a scene in which my character was late to pick up his grandmother from her dialysis at the hospital and felt guilty. It was a demanding scene, calling for a wide range of emotions. I was nervous that this would be the moment when I was revealed as a fraud who couldn't perform and was wasting everyone's time. Instead I sailed through, and for the first time in my life I began to think of acting as a real option for me.

In the years since I'd left California, when I was eighteen, my relationship with Mom had been off-and-on. She was still cultivating drama with men. On Mallorca, once a year, we threw a full-moon party at S'Estaca and attended a second one at Son Marroig, another mansion that had belonged to a Habsburg. One year, when Mom was dating Sacha Newley, the son of Joan Collins, Sacha came over to me, upset because Mom seemed to be ignoring him while flirting with another guy by the fire. I went over and told the guy, "This is my mother; she's spoken for," and then said to Mom, nodding toward Sacha, "C'mon, you've got this guy over here, who you brought to Spain."

I don't recall Mom's response on that occasion, but I think she always appreciated that I was protective of her and willing to set clear boundaries with grown men. I think it made her feel loved and cared for.

Another time at S'Estaca, Mom and I got into an argument in front of one of her gentlemen friends, who stepped in and said I needed to not speak to her that way. We were standing on a pier.

"Go fuck yourself," I said.

"It's okay," Mom told him, trying to lower the temperature. She knew which way this was headed.

The guy edged forward on the pier until he was in my face, and I threw him into the water. I said, "Don't ever get between me and my mother again." By the time I was making *It Runs in the Family,* Mom was consumed by her relationship with Zack Bacon.

Soon after shooting wrapped on the movie, I went to Brazil to DJ a wedding and play a few clubs and parties, and I ended up having one of the most amazing travel experiences of my life. For a month, I was largely incommunicado. Mom and Dad had no idea where I'd gone, and when I got home, they were relieved.

Mom had never liked drugs, had had a lot of conflict with Dad about them, and saw me repeating his ways. Dad, on the other hand, seemed to have settled into a view of my drug problem as being a manageable if unfortunate undercurrent of my life. I was booking lucrative corporate DJ gigs. I'd exceeded expectations in making the movie. Yeah, I could be wild, but I was keeping my priorities in order.

Right before the release of *It Runs in the Family,* Dad invited me to take a bunch of friends to Wildcat, his ranch in Aspen, without him. This meant a lot to me. We all did mushrooms and snowboarded and played on Dad's virtual-reality golf system, hitting balls against a screen on the wall onto which you could project any course in the world. In pictures I have from the trip, my friend Curtis is wearing heart-shaped sunglasses and I'm driving a car shirtless, with a bright boa wrapped around my neck. Dad's caretaker Mike, who spoke with a cowboy drawl, was there. When I talked to Dad, he just said, "I asked Mike how things were going, and he said, 'Those boys are havin' a pretty good time up there.'"

It Runs in the Family wasn't a good movie, but I got favorable reviews—"a splashy acting debut" (*New York Times*), "the film's big emotional moment is handed to him, and he comes through beautifully" (*Los Angeles Times*), "Cameron Douglas's unforced portrayal . . . feels like the channeling of his own genuine, though flawed, humanity" (*Washington Post*). A movie career seemed right there waiting for me.

In the week leading up to the premiere, I received several invitations to try out for compelling new projects. Acting had felt comfortable to me, and I'd taken to it, but the job had come so easily that I undervalued it, let the attention go to my head, and made little effort to take advantage of the opportunities that followed.

After a three-day coke bender at the Winter Music Conference in Miami, I was due in Chicago to appear on *Oprah* with Dad and Pappy. I missed my flight out of Miami and had to catch another one the next morning. The strawberries in Oprah's greenroom were the biggest I'd ever seen, like little crab apples. Oprah herself, when she came in, made a comment about them, saying that when she saw the strawberries she knew someone important had to be coming in. By this point in the promotion of the movie, I was comfortable doing press, but it was still impressive to be there, knowing Oprah's influence and vast audience.

I was burning bridges in my DJ work, backing out of already promoted gigs at the eleventh hour. With doors now opening for me in the acting realm, I freaked out. I was feeling the weight of the moment: I was the next generation of a storied acting family, and everyone around me expected me to take my place in the dynasty. At the same time, I was very concerned that the responsibility of a career might get in the way of feeding my addiction. Ambition and a serious coke habit couldn't coexist, and the coke was my priority.

I was also naive. Because I was receiving accolades after expending only modest effort, my head got big, and I thought I was more special than I was. I failed to understand that the industry has no time for that, because there's always someone else there to take your place. For a week, I stayed at the Mondrian hotel in L.A. I didn't have a car, and my friend John came down from Santa Barbara to drive me to auditions. Agents were courting me, and I chose a two-woman team at William Morris. But after I got food poisoning and broke out in hives in the taxi to meet them, I called to cancel the meeting, not a great first impression. Then I got close to being cast in a Spike Lee network pilot, but I partied late the night before the final audition and choked.

Having been poised to move up in the movie business, I would take many steps down, appearing in a straight-to-video National Lampoon–branded comedy called *Adam & Eve*, directed by Jeff Kanew, a friend of Pappy's.

As I retreated further into my growing coke addiction, I developed acute paranoia, which was compounded by two very real threats. I

Shooting Adam & Eve *with Emmanuelle Chriqui.*

was still living on Thirty-Seventh Street, where I had a whole turn-table setup, and because I often stayed up DJing through the night there, I antagonized fellow tenants, including a local newscaster who started agitating for building management to evict me. There was also Amanda. When I'd finally summoned the courage to end our relationship for good, she'd assumed that, as in the past, I wouldn't be able to stick to it. When I did stick to it, she went crazy. She started staking me out, waiting outside the building and berating mutual friends she saw entering.

I turned back to booking DJ gigs, met Erin, and she and I moved into the apartment near Washington Square Park, along with Jay, my DJ friend Eyal, and his girlfriend, Adi. It had a pressed tin ceiling with skylights cut out. The decor was a hodgepodge: besides the large, hand-carved opium bed from Bali, which Mom had originally imported for a furniture store she owned, there were Christmas lights, a Jim Brown blaxploitation poster, a painting of a wave, a poster that said SEXY, conga drums, and a huge African tribal mask. There were skateboard decks all over the place, and in back Eyal and I set up a music studio, with turntables and foam soundproofing. In my bedroom, I hung a photo of Dad smoking on a couch at S'Estaca and a picture of a chameleon, because my friends sometimes called me "Cameleon" in honor of my ability to adapt to any milieu, whether a White House reception or a correctional facility.

I still had trouble being by myself. It wasn't solitude that was the problem. If I were dropped on a desert island, I'd be okay. It was more an inability to tolerate the idea of people not wanting to be with me. If there were people around who *could* be with me, and they weren't, that made me intensely anxious, and sad, and filled with a feeling of loneliness. When I was alone, I felt like I had somewhere to go, something to figure out. So I always had a little group around me. Women I slept with accepted my post-Amanda terms of engagement, or disengagement. Dad viewed my roommates as freeloaders—the new Shits. As far as I was concerned, we were a family.

———

My coke use took a turn. I'd been disenchanted the few times I'd tried crack. It always ended with people bickering over who'd get the last hit and desperately searching the couch and carpet for crumbs, and it produced a hangover three times as awful as powder cocaine. But then Jay stole Adi's fertility needles and introduced me to shooting coke.

Cocaine, when injected, feels like an entirely different drug. Your blood brings it up into your tongue, and you can taste it. It's a surge of feeling. You hear sounds that aren't there, like train whistles. Once I'd shot coke, any other way of doing it felt like a waste.

At first, I thought the needle was romantic. I'd hide my behavior, going into the walk-in closet, which had a chair and table and built-in shelves, to shoot up. But I also sort of wanted people to know what I was doing. The needle and what went along with it—the pain, the blood—had an aura, evoked a struggling, misunderstood artist. It set me apart from normal people who do drugs from time to time. It was exciting and new and dangerous. And it laid down a marker: if what I was doing was going to be an issue for you, then I didn't want you around me. Partly I was weeding out people who might judge me, and partly I was testing the loyalty and love of my friends.

Then I became a slave to the needle and was incapable of hiding it. I'd go into the closet for hours, scrawling gibberish in notebooks and eventually emerging in some crazy costume—ski goggles, tighty-whities, dress shoes. I'd think I was being hilarious. Everyone else was just scared of me and for me.

My paranoia got worse. Because the first couple days of a bender were the most intense, I had to be up on coke for at least three days before I started having a good time and not giving a fuck. The first twenty-four hours, I'd be a mess, always worried someone had called the police. I'd end up staying awake for days, then crashing for eighteen hours, then doing it all over again. Getting high became much more important to me than a career.

———

Eddie, my manager in L.A., came to New York the night before a gig he'd booked for me and said he wanted to come over to see me. I was days into a bender and geeking out in the closet when he arrived. I told Erin to greet him and tell him I'd been abalone diving and ruptured my eardrums, so I couldn't hang out for long. When I emerged into the living room, I had Q-tips sticking out of my ears, and I started bullshitting about having seen a great white shark but forgetting to equalize and busting my eardrums. I was still going to make the party the next night, I promised, but I couldn't talk now. It was a ridiculous story, and Eddie stared at me evenly, not saying anything. After he left, Erin said, "Cameron, what the fuck are you doing? Couldn't you at least have waited until Eddie left?" Soon Eddie stopped sending me jobs.

Then I was approached by a major booking agent who had a formula for how she represented people, starting with having professional photos taken. With her, too, I flaked on a significant booking, though I don't recall the specifics, and after that she, too, dropped me. I can only imagine all the promoters around the world who hate me because they spent money on plane tickets and developed events around me, and then I let them down.

I slowly lost my friends. They didn't want to be around me anymore. Even Jay, who I still considered my best friend and brother, would do something passive-aggressive every now and then, seeming to betray a resentment of me as his benefactor. I'd gone on a safari with Mom and Zack Bacon and his daughter, Isabel, a few years earlier and come back with a cherished video of me wakeboarding on the Okavango Delta in Botswana. Just days after I showed it to Jay, he recorded over it. It felt like only Erin was truly loyal to me, and I prized that. It was me and Erin against the world.

Everybody has their own threshold with cocaine, the dose beyond which you'll seizure. I crossed mine near the end of my time on University Place. It was the middle of the night. Erin shot me up in the closet and walked away toward our bed. She'd later tell me it sounded like I was laughing. Then I fell to the ground. She rushed over. I was rigid and convulsing. Erin ran across the apartment to Eyal's room and woke him up. He stayed with me while she called 911. The paramedics arrived, but by then I was coming out of it. The EMTs said they needed to bring me to the hospital, and Erin rode with me in the ambulance. As soon as we got back to the apartment, I shot up again.

It wasn't long afterward that Uncle Eric's housekeeper found him in his one-bedroom apartment on Twenty-Ninth Street, on the floor, apparently having fallen off his sofa. Police called his death at forty-six an accidental overdose.

20

2008: A Cascade of Unfortunate Events

Even as my coke operation has grown, my heroin addiction is getting dark. At first, it was a potent medication, with few side effects. Now it's a ball and chain that weighs 1.5 grams a day. I can't go more than a few hours without shooting up, and even that seemingly simple procedure has become a high-pressure drama.

When I started shooting coke, I had no idea what I was doing and wrought havoc on my body, blowing out the veins in my arms. A silver lining is that this has forced me to range far and wide in search of fresh veins, so I've been spared the abscesses and scarring and infections of addicts who fixate on one spot. But it now can take me literally hours, and many tries, to find a vein. It's a game of hide-and-seek. I'll see a vein, and just as the needle touches my skin it vanishes. Sometimes the veins simply collapse. I resort to going into tiny capillaries. When I miss a vein, it burns painfully. Some of the brown is low quality and stings like battery acid.

Friends come to the house to pick me up to go out, and I'll be in the bathroom still trying to get a shot in. Sometimes I make a friend wait forty-five minutes while I'm just searching for a vein. The longer it takes, the more anxious I become, which only makes it harder to find a vein. When I emerge, finally, I'm angry and sweating and frustrated and embarrassed, and getting sick because I've gone too long between shots. A couple of times, my friend Adam gets fed up and takes off while I'm still in the bathroom. If I'm shooting up with Erin, I always insist she shoot me up first, and when it takes too long I yell at her, as she sweats and shakes and tries to spot a surface vein anywhere. It's gotten to the point where I have vein envy. I appraise everyone's arms, and if they have fat, bulging veins, I'm jealous. Jay has beautiful veins. He always finds one right away, and never misses.

Finally, I have a stroke of inspiration: I find a doctor in the Valley who a friend has mentioned seems crooked, and I make an appointment. I tell him I want to inject vitamin B12 for working out and wonder if he can implant an IV port. The kind of port that old people who can't find their veins have surgically installed to take their meds. The doctor cocks an eyebrow. He clearly doesn't believe me. He just looks at me evenly and says, "Sorry, I can't help you there."

A friend convinces me to meet with a tweaker named Luke, who deals to a lot of meth addicts in L.A. He has always seemed thirsty to meet me, and I'm suspicious of him, but my friend convinces me he's good money, and we meet in a restaurant on Hollywood Boulevard. It's late in the afternoon, and Luke is talking about wanting coke. He's essentially a street dealer, and it doesn't really make sense that he'd want to do business with me, since I deal in weight. "Why would you want to do that?" I ask, and he doesn't have a good answer. He also proposes deals that make no sense, like asking me to sell him half a key for half the price of a key (usually, there's a markup for a smaller quantity), which will keep me from making any profit.

I want to see if he's wearing a wire, so I suggest we pay our bill and continue the conversation in his car, where I'll be able to use my bug detector less conspicuously than in a restaurant. When we reach his car I say, "Luke, please forgive me, but before we do anything, I'm going to do this."

I hold up my bug detector, a pocket-sized black plastic device with a silver antenna that lights up and sounds an alarm in the presence of a listening device. Luke's eyes get big.

"Is that okay?"

"Of course."

I turn on the detector and it lights up. I look at Luke. He looks at me. I get out of the car and walk away. I don't hear from Luke again.

Every time Erin and I ship drugs now, we fret over whether we've hidden them well enough. We worry that they will be intercepted. Things get so tight with agents following me, finally, that we send a last shipment of two keys, and then I stop distributing coke. I'd feel some relief, except for a cascade of unfortunate events.

Soon after we moved to Cole Crest, we took Dylan and Carys to Universal Studios for the day. When we picked up the kids at Dad's, we left nine-month-old Oscar, Erin's dachshund, there to play with his dogs. We were at Universal when Dad called.

"Does Oscar have tags? He isn't in the yard."

We rushed back.

Dad said, "You should have told me to keep an eye on him."

Erin was distraught. We searched the neighborhood on foot and by car. We drove to pounds. We posted flyers. We never found him. I bought Erin another dog, Scooby, who we keep calling Oscar or Oscy, but since then Erin has become prone to seeing anything bad that happens as part of a cosmic jinx.

Shortly before I stop shipping cocaine, Erin and I return to Cole Crest after two days in Santa Barbara, where we've been making weekly trips to pick up the machined drug-shipping devices. Erin is several yards ahead of me, and has disappeared down the steps next to the house, when I hear a scream. Despite my other security precautions, or maybe because of them, I never lock the doors to the house when I'm away. If someone wanted to get in, they could, but so far they haven't.

When I hear Erin's yelp, I race down the steps and around the corner. Erin is standing, frozen, staring at the living room's glass walls.

They are fogged over on the inside, but I can see through the glass well enough to have a view of the four inches of mud covering the entire floor. The carpets are buried. The couches are ruined. Two huge flat-screen TVs, which are only a couple of inches off the floor, are partly submerged, as is all of our furniture. We tie plastic bags around our feet and trudge through the house, seeing if there's anything we can salvage.

Our landlord says a water main up the hill burst, unleashing thousands of gallons of water. We don't have renter's insurance, and she won't do anything to help us. That night, we sleep at the Beverly Laurel. The next day, we return to do a more thorough damage assessment. I spend hours looking for a lockbox I'd hidden behind the house, containing $60,000 in cash. It's been swept away by the mudslide, and I never find it. It may still be buried on that hillside.

We hire a company to come in and clean up, staying at the Beverly Laurel while they do it, but when our lease expires a couple of months later, we move.

Even before the mudslide, I'd wanted to get away from the Cole Crest house, certain that it was the focus of a federal investigation. Our new place is on Walnut Drive, lower in the Hills, and it's a downgrade. This house isn't on stilts and doesn't have a pool. I have some cash banked, but with no new income, I need to conserve money.

With my Scarface ambitions thwarted, at least for now, I have little to fill my days, and I sit around the house in my mellow heroin haze, playing hours of *Oblivion* through a TV system that projects the game onto the wall.

I often see and hear young kids playing on the deck of the house just above ours on the hill. One day, I realize I haven't seen them in weeks.

"Erin, have you seen that family in a while?"

She shrugs. "I guess not."

"I swear to God, I saw a camera lens in the window just now, pointing this way."

"You sound like you're back on coke."

Even with the more modest house, and a lower monthly rent, the money goes fast. I'm offered a small part in a B movie called *Loaded,* playing a California drug dealer (big stretch), which brings in less than $10,000. By the end of the year, we can barely pay our rent.

To stretch our remaining cash as far as possible, we stop paying our cell phone bills, and Erin's mom mails her a TracFone just so she can check in and make sure Erin is okay. We live above a canyon, and we coast to the bottom in neutral to save money on gas. We scrounge for change in the couch cushions. At Whole Foods, we clean out the free-sample stations. Nero takes pity on us and comps us heroin.

My relationships with Mom and Dad have recently consisted of alternating closeness and estrangement, punctuated by invitations to one-off events: a premiere, a party, a vacation. Mom calls at least once a week and leaves voicemails. Every three months, maybe, I return the call. My dynamic with Dad is seething frustration on his part and wounded sensitivity on mine.

Many months after I began my research into breeds to mate with Junior, I found a dog called a Boerboel. In aesthetics and demeanor, it seemed like the perfect complement to Junior. I started out looking for an all-black Boerboel but settled on a brindled one I named Eve, since she will be the mother of a new kind of dog. She's still too young to breed, but when she's ready, I'll mate her with Junior to create the world's first Boerbador.

Dad invites me to a dinner party in Malibu at his old agent Ron Meyer's house, where there are a bunch of celebrities, and says, "Oh, Cameron, why don't you tell them about how you're going to make a new breed of dog."

I'm feeling like a failure, and anything coming out of Dad's mouth sounds contrived to needle me and treat me like a child. Probably he just thinks it's a good story, but I burn with self-consciousness.

During a storm one night, after Erin and Jay and I have moved to the house on Walnut, a eucalyptus tree falls on the roof. It doesn't cause too much damage, but coming only a few months after the mudslide at the Cole Crest house, Erin believes we're cursed. She thinks it can't be a coincidence that so many bad things have happened to one set of people, and she feels that more bad things are coming. When I shrug it off, she says I'm in denial. I have to admit that it's a pretty bad run of wet luck, especially considering that California is in the middle of a historic drought. I wonder if my years of being out of alignment with who I am and what I'm supposed to be doing are finally bubbling up and causing this turmoil. When our landlord Winn, a male model turned house flipper, comes by a few days later, he yells at us for not letting him know about the tree immediately.

I frequently experience night sweats, which I chalk up to my body purging itself of toxins. Before I go to sleep, I kneel at the foot of my bed and pray. I visualize what I want. I focus my energy on desirable abstractions like inner peace and prosperity and a sense of purpose. I'm not religious, exactly, but I figure that praying can't hurt. I'd hate to find out, too late, that it's important, and that I've neglected it my whole life. Praying is the only thing I'm disciplined about. I'm like the guy whose whole life is fucked but who religiously buys a lottery ticket every day. I'm multiplying my chances of success, covering my bases, giving this one thing my best shot. I'm sure not giving my best shot on so many other levels.

I grew up thinking that crying isn't a manly thing to do, but I do cry sometimes. Usually it's not in response to something sad or difficult but something redemptive and inspiring. I'll see a seventy-year-old homeless guy on the same corner every day, putting his best foot forward, and being friendly, and that's the thing that will bring me to tears. Maybe it's because I empathize with his struggle in a weird way, and admire the dignity with which he carries his burden.

Dad has invited me to spend Thanksgiving with his family in New York. I always rush out the door at the last minute when I have a flight to catch, and now, as I leave to go to the airport, I grab a backpack recently borrowed by my friend Patrick, who dates a former Pussycat Doll, to use as a carry-on bag. When I go through the TSA line at Bob Hope Airport, in Burbank, I'm pulled aside. A supervisor riffles through the backpack, and in the outside pocket he finds several knives, including a switchblade, apparently left there by Patrick. "You know it's illegal to bring these on a plane, right?"

I protest that the knives aren't mine, and I'm charged with disturbing the peace. Later, Patrick will write a letter assuming blame for the knives and testifying to my good character, and the charge will be dismissed. I'm released after a couple of hours, and Erin and I catch the next flight out.

When our plane lands at Newark Airport, we're five hours past our last shot, and we beeline to a restaurant that has silverware, sit down and order a Coke, then take turns in the bathroom using a spoon to liquefy tar and injecting it.

Erin and I check into the Rivington, on the Lower East Side, where a manager I'm friends with gives me a good rate. We hang out in our room, shooting cheeva. Erin is going up to Connecticut to her sister's house for dinner. Dad and I have agreed that I'll come to the apartment on Central Park West at 4 p.m. As the hour approaches, Erin keeps telling me to get moving, I'll be late. But I'm having trouble finding a vein, and I tell her to leave without me. She heads off to Grand Central to catch her train. I finally get the needle into a vein and push the plunger, then lean back on the sofa and zone out for a while before leaving.

By the time I reach the Kenilworth, my old home, it's 7:30 p.m. The doorman buzzes up and speaks to someone. "Yes, sir," the doorman says, hanging up the phone, then turns to me and says, almost apologetically, that Dad has left for his place in the country. I'm crushed. I call Erin, who's still at Grand Central. "You sound so sad," she says. She tells me she'll wait for me at the station; I can have Thanksgiving with her family in Greenwich. Erin's parents, who I'm sure suspect

With Dad, Catherine, and Steven Soderbergh
on the set of Traffic.

that we're addicts, believe Erin when she tells them she's happy, and have told me that I can call them Mom and Dad.

I feel hurt, and angry, and wronged—*Dad didn't even call to ask where I was, or give me a heads-up that he was leaving*—and we don't talk for a while. I'm incapable of absorbing his point of view, of understanding how Dylan and Carys were waiting for me by the elevator, excited for my arrival, at four o'clock, or how it broke Dad's heart to see them disappointed, or how in fact he did try calling me "ten times," in his words. He's not ready to tell me that he was upstairs when I arrived, and hadn't left for the country; he was just so pissed at me by then that he couldn't bear to see me.

A few months later, on Erin's birthday, a couple of L.A. Sheriff's cars pull up outside the house on Walnut. Erin answers the door, and Jay and I, in the back, can hear the cops asking about us and starting to move through the house. Thinking they're here because they have outstanding warrants against us, we run out the back door and take off up the hill, not stopping until we reach our old place on Cole Crest. The owner is there, who we got along well with, and we're sweating, and we try to play it off like we just happened to be in the neighborhood and stopped by to say hello and take a dip in the pool.

In our rush out of the house on Walnut, we forgot to grab our cell phones. As we'll soon learn, the sheriff was delivering an eviction notice, and Erin had to be escorted from the premises. Then she had to repeat the humiliation after the cops called Dad's business manager, Angela, and said they needed Erin to return to the house to get our guns out. As neighbors gawked, she retrieved the guns and put them in the trunk of the Beemer. Then our landlord, Winn, invited a TV crew from *Inside Edition* into the house, which he had apparently staged to look like a trashed drug den. Winn was interviewed and pointed to something that was definitely not crack, saying that it was crack.

Erin comes to pick me and Jay up. The three of us look like the Beverly Hillbillies, in a car overstuffed with our dogs, guns, hastily packed suitcases, and loose possessions. Jay goes to stay with our old landlord Carine, who he's sleeping with, and Erin and I move into the Beverly Laurel.

We live at the motel for three months. Heroin has obliterated everything else in my life by this point. I owe Nero thousands of dollars. One day, he says he can't give us any more cheeva. Erin hands him her watch, a Movado with diamonds that she was given before I knew her, and says he can hold it as collateral. I give him my Ducati, and I pawn my turntables and boxes of records that took me years to amass. Afterward, I cry.

I put everything else in storage. Mom and Dad have both relocated to New York—Mom from Santa Barbara, Dad from Bermuda—and I've decided to move back there too, which makes them happy. I'm thinking I'll go back into DJing to make some income, and possibly get back into acting, too. A production company out of England has offered me a role in a sci-fi movie.

PART TWO

Just a Dash of Good

For this trill is the only music
My soul has to dance . . .
And
My soul must dance
For my soul must Live
This
Permits my essence to breathe
Without that breath
That most beautiful part of my
    design
Will wilt and die
And
Surely with this foundation gone
What remains of God's creation
Will soon follow

So I listen
With great intent
For THE music

Where and when there is none to
    be heard
I turn within
To find my heart beating a rhythm
For my soul to dance

Flawless is God's ambition

In New York before my arrest.

21

2009: Yes It's Really Me

In New York we get a tenth-floor room at the Gansevoort Hotel, in the Meatpacking District, with a decent view looking north toward Chelsea. But even with the discount from a manager I know, it's costing $475 a night, and we're down to our last few thousand dollars. I'm already embarrassed that I've had to ask Dad to put the hotel on his credit card. I tell him I'm looking for my own place, and I'll pay him back. And the cost of our heroin habits has shot up. On the West Coast, $500 would buy us two weeks' worth of tar. Here, for powder, we're easily spending $500 a day.

I want to rent an apartment in Brooklyn, but I have no credit other than a $500-limit Visa card. My only option is to pay a year's rent up front. I could ask Dad for the money, and maybe he'd give it to me, but in my mind asking him for more help is the one route not open to me. I don't look great, and Dad knows why, but I let myself believe that by acting like I'm okay, I'm selling that I'm okay.

Despite the money pressure, though, I feel relief. I've been out of the drug business for more than a year, and now that I've moved to New York, away from the West Coast DEA, I've dodged trouble by the hair of my chinny-chin-chin. Today, I've scheduled a routine checkup for Junior, Eve, and Scooby. Erin and I take better care of them than of ourselves. At this point, four and a half years into my heroin addiction, I'm shooting up five or six times a day. I'm pale and soft, but at least diligent about varying injection sites, favoring obscure places like my ribcage, upper butt, and armpit. Erin is careless. She's out of shape and sweats all the time, and her legs are swollen and bruised in a cheetah pattern because she always injects in the same small area of her thighs.

Before we leave the room, I shoot up. I'm not expecting to be at the vet that long, but I'd rather not take any chances.

We leash the dogs and head toward the elevator.

"Oh hello, my West Coast friend."

I hear him before I see him. Erin and I are just coming out of the West Village Veterinary Hospital when that familiar thick French accent reaches me. Emmanuel. It's been a few years since I last did business with him, but even as he crosses Eighth Avenue toward us, walking his own small dog, I'm thinking, *Maybe this guy is going to somehow provide money for me.*

"This is Diva," he says, nodding at his Italian greyhound. Diva and Eve and Junior and Scooby are now sniffing each other and having a dog convention, and Erin, who's holding our dogs' leashes, stands off to the side while Emmanuel and I catch up. He suggests we have dinner later.

When Emmanuel calls at six, he proposes a Japanese restaurant, Ono. Ono is *in* the Gansevoort. What are the chances? I never mentioned where I was staying. "Great," I say.

"Look how perfectly everything's lining up, Erin," I say after hanging up.

"I don't know, Cameron." She's shaking her head. "This doesn't smell right."

Three years of surveillance by the DEA has made me habitually cautious, and I briefly consider texting Emmanuel the spyware that would give me access to his phone.

"Put it on his phone," Erin says.

I say I don't think that's necessary. "Maybe this is God's way of letting me get back on my feet."

"Don't talk to him about drugs," Erin says.

———

Over a two-hour sushi dinner, Emmanuel asks if I'm still active in the business, and I say I'm not. Then he starts talking about a deal he's involved in that isn't working out but—"Maybe is better we continue this conversation in my room?" His room? He's staying right here, at the Gansevoort.

"No way, me too."

We get in the elevator and I ask what floor he's on.

"Ten."

"No way, me too." *This is meant to be.*

I say I have to stop by my room for a few minutes, and it turns out he's in the room *next door*. What are the chances? Back in my room, I shoot up. I tell Erin how fortunate we are; all these coincidences are lining up so well. I wonder aloud if I should take my bug detector to Emmanuel's room.

"One hundred percent," Erin says.

But in my mind, I'm done with all that. And I've just done a shot, and I'm high. I say, "Nah, it's good, I've got a good feeling about this."

In Emmanuel's room, he tells me how he made this huge investment, and this guy was driving back from California with the stuff and didn't show up when he was supposed to, and Emmanuel's in really bad shape, and he has people waiting for him, and blah blah blah. Can I help him out?

Quintessential drug-dealer sob story.

I throw a price at him, $30,000 for a pound, which is high enough (normally he'd pay $24,000) that he almost certainly won't go for it. But he does. He must be desperate. This is clearly meant to be.

We talk logistics: I'll get two burner phones for us to use; I'll switch phones every two weeks; I'll text him the new phone number, flipping the sequence of digits as a simple cloaking device.

The next day, Emmanuel comes to my room with the money. He says he was only able to get $15,000, so I say I'll only be able to get him a half pound of crystal.

"Please count it," he says, pushing the cash toward me.

"No, that's fine, I trust you."

"No no no, let's count it."

"It's fine, I trust you."

He won't let it go. He takes the money and starts counting it out loud himself. Kind of weird, but my profit on this and a few more projected deals with him will be enough to get me an apartment. Everything is falling into place as I'd hoped. I hand him his burner and say he'll have the crystal in a week to ten days.

Erin and I head to California, leaving the dogs in their $475-a-night luxury hotel room, where our friend Patrick will stay with them. In L.A., we hole up at the Beverly Laurel. Erin sits by the pool while I meet with Nero in the room. A few days later, I send Erin out to Bath & Body Works, while Nero returns with a mini-duffel and pulls out a Tupperware container full of what look like shards of clear glass. I pay him $7,000 for the half pound of crystal, and he leaves. When Erin gets back, she's carrying a white gift basket: it holds a package labeled TROPICAL BREEZE, which contains body gels, lotions, a loofah, and soap; a Zen Pack with rocks, bath tea, washcloths, a candle, and shea butter; and three tin canisters of bath salts. We wear latex gloves as we empty the canisters, stuff them with Ziplocs full of the crystal, rewrap the basket with cellophane, tie it with a bow, and scrub everything down with Lysol disinfectant wipes.

Erin and I cab to a UPS store on Sunset, at the base of Laurel Canyon, and pay cash to send the basket to New York, addressed, as Emmanuel requested, to a Paul Smith at a P.O. box on Third Avenue in the Thirties.

"The bath salts are fabulous!" Emmanuel says when he calls the next afternoon.

"Yeah, I thought you would like them, my friend. I thought you would like them . . . I was so excited for you to take a bath and see for yourself."

Emmanuel and I are already talking about our next deal, referring in our communications to money as "paperwork" and crystal as "pastry." Over the next three days, as I try to set it up, I speak on the phone with Nero more than a dozen times.

—

A week later, I'm back in New York and there's a message from the Gansevoort's head of security, saying there have been noise complaints about my room and to call him. This is strange. Erin and I and the dogs are very quiet. In the afternoon, I call the guy back and he doesn't pick up, but I say I'm in the room. A few minutes later, there's a knock at the door. I'm in the bathroom and I tell Erin to answer it and say I'm not here. She opens the door, I hear someone say they want to talk to me, she says I'm out, and they leave. I come out of the bathroom. "Who was that?"

"The security guy and a couple of other guys."

"Did they look like agents?"

"No, absolutely not. Young kids. I think he was training them."

"You're sure, Erin?"

"One hundred percent."

I call the guy back and say I'm in the room again, and a few minutes later there's another knock. As soon as I open the door, I see a guy in a polo shirt and a New York Yankees hat who could not look more exactly like the central casting version of a federal agent.

Three of them, they all look like ex-lacrosse players, grab me by my shirt—I'm wearing an Urban Outfitters T-shirt that reads YES IT'S REALLY ME—and pull me through the doorway. A cop at the end of the hall has his gun drawn. They handcuff me and take me into another room and sit me down. Yankees Hat says, "Cameron"—he pulls out his badge—"I'm not with the LAPD or the NYPD. I'm a Special Agent with the DEA, and you're jammed up right now. We can do this two ways. You can make a scene, we can throw you in handcuffs, take you out the front door kicking and screaming. Or, for your family's sake, we can take you out the back way, put you in a car."

For my family's sake. Pappy and Dad enjoy media attention when it suits them, but not the sort my arrest would bring. I say to Yankees Hat, let's leave the quiet way, and they take me down the back stairwell.

In their small, unmarked sedan, Yankees Hat, whose name is Justin Meadows, tells me he never thought I'd go for their sting. After nearly three years, this was their Hail Mary. They'd tracked me using my cell phone. At the DEA's Manhattan field office, five blocks from the Gansevoort, I take off my shirt so they can photograph my torso, and I get a "whoa" or two, as they see the track-mark scarring around my ribcage and armpit.

I'm left alone in a holding cell with a bench, and every couple of hours Justin or his partner, Susan, comes back, looks at me through the bars, and asks if I want to talk.

"You probably won't get a life sentence, but I think you're looking at fifteen years."

"Every minute you sit there and think about what to do, the window gets smaller and smaller for us to give you a deal."

"If you give us a statement right now, we're going to let you go home, and we're going to make sure this never gets out."

"Think about your father, your family, your grandfather . . . How old is he?"

"Ninety-five percent of the people we arrest cooperate."

"This is a one-time-only offer."

I don't say anything. I'm processing what's happening. I'd been out of the business for two years, and they got me by creating a scenario I wasn't looking for. How did this happen? Clearly, Emmanuel fucked me. Beyond that, I don't know what they know. I'm trying to come up with a plan of action.

Each time they ask if I want to talk, I say no, and they leave, but after several hours of this I'm starting to get really dope-sick. I keep telling them I'm ill and need medicine.

"Give us a statement, and we can help you out with that."

The tone is: *We're on the same team. You fucked yourself, and we want to help you un-fuck yourself.*

My nose is running, my eyes are watering, I'm getting cold sweats, and the diarrhea is beginning. I ask an agent to bring me toilet paper. I know this is about to get a lot worse. An urge begins to rise in me to do just about anything to get out of here. I ask if I can call my father.

Justin unlocks my cell door and brings me to a room filled with desks and other agents. He hands me his cell phone and I call Dad, who's on vacation at his place in Mont-Tremblant, in Quebec.

"Cameron!" It's been a while since we talked.

"Hey, Dad, I'm in a bad situation. I need to know what you think I should do." I'm just starting to explain when Justin grabs the phone from me and says, "Mr. Douglas, this is Agent Meadows," and walks away from me, still talking. When he returns, he hands the phone back to me. Dad tells me to do whatever they ask.

I'm sick and scared, and Dad always knows how to handle tough situations. And so, with Justin and Susan watching, I waive my Miranda rights and write out a statement. I'm thinking this will get me out from under the long sentence looming over my head, but the statement is the confession of an addled mind—a soup of truths, half truths, and fictions.

They ask who my suppliers were. Gabriel fucked me, so I give them his name and Carlos's. But I don't think the DEA can do anything with this. I haven't done business with the Garcias in years, so there's no way the DEA will be able to connect them to this latest deal with Emmanuel. Maybe they'll get a little heat, but that's it.

Justin asks who *their* supplier is, and I make up a name.

"I know him as Maestro."

"Where does he live?"

"I have no idea."

I'm being so vague, and making so much up, that I'm sure the DEA won't be able to arrest anyone.

The DEA is hitting me with the pitch they hit everyone with to wear down any determination not to cooperate: *Someone wore a wire on you. Why should they go free, while you go to prison?* So why don't I just name names and enthusiastically cooperate? 1) There's a code among criminals, and I believe in it: this is a situation I got myself into, understanding the risks, and I don't think it's fair to drag other people into it; 2) I don't want to give information about some people I genuinely care about, or to live with the weight of knowing I did that to them; 3) If I cooperate with the government, I'll forfeit a lot of rights, including the right to appeal; 4) I know that the stigma of cooperating will make for a much more difficult prison experience.

Then Agent Meadows shows me a picture of Maestro, who is actually Nero. "Is this Maestro?" How do they even know about him? Is this a trick? I leap into the void.

"Nah, that's not him, I've never seen the guy."

Agent Meadows takes the picture off the table.

It's after midnight when they take me out to a car, handcuffed, for the ride to the Downtown Hospital for medical clearance. Along the way, they make good on their promise to help me with my sickness, stopping by the Gansevoort. They've called Erin, and she's waiting outside when we pull up. She hands them the bottle with my Suboxone prescription, but they don't give it to me yet.

At the hospital, I'm dry-heaving and have serious diarrhea, and

MCC.

a doctor who diagnoses me with opioid dependence gives me some shots to ease my withdrawal symptoms. He tells the DEA agents that I should continue to take the Suboxone I've already been prescribed, and says I should see a doctor in the next two days.

We drive on to the Metropolitan Correctional Center, beside the federal courthouse at Foley Square, where the car comes to a stop. The agents have left the bottle of Suboxone on the center console, within easy reach, and one of them says, "Do what you need to do, but do it quickly." Then they step out of the car for a minute to arrange my intake. I've never taken Suboxone before and have no sense of its potency. I swallow a handful of the pills.

Within minutes, I'm delirious. Inside MCC, I still have some tablets in my pocket, but when I reach for them a guard says, "Take your hand out of your fucking pocket." I hold up two fists, like I'm displaying my biceps, and he says, "Open your fucking hands." He takes the tablets from me and orders me to undress. As I pull off my clothes, I stumble into a wall. Once I'm completely naked, he has me open my hands again, squat and cough, lift my nut sack, turn my ears out, and run my hands through my hair. Then I'm allowed to put my street clothes back on.

The on-call psychologist observes me to be "visibly high," and for tonight, as a precaution, I'm put on suicide watch in a cell with a glass wall. I lie on a mat in a dreamy stupor, and watch shifts of inmates sitting outside the cell, observing me and writing in a notebook.

The next day, before I'm arraigned, I meet briefly with my lawyer, Nick De Feis, referred to Dad by a friend. Nick, who's in his late forties, is skinny, short, and balding, with the assured demeanor and careful speech of an ex-prosecutor, and mainly defends corporate clients and white-collar criminals. "Here's what's going to happen," Nick says. "Your charges carry a mandatory minimum sentence of ten years. The only way we're going to get a downward departure from that is if you help them with their case." This sounds kind of sketchy to me, but I defer to Nick.

My bail hearing will be closed. Mom is in Spain with her younger kids. She and Dad have signed my $5 million bond, so I can get house arrest, and Dad has arranged to pay for the private security guards required by the court to guard me around the clock. When I go before a magistrate, I'm shivering and can barely stand up. I'm released to home detention and driven by the DEA agents to a townhouse Mom is renting on East Seventy-First. The guards will sleep in a room opposite the bedroom I'm in.

I'm grateful to be out, but in time I'll realize the deal was a mistake. The conditions of my house arrest require me to help the government in exactly the way I don't want to. If I'd just stayed at MCC, I would have made regular bail in a matter of two or three days, and in the meantime I'd have been given methadone instead of tearing my hair out from heroin withdrawal.

Nick comes to the house. I've emerged from my haze and have more clarity, and I say, "Listen, that statement I gave the DEA has to be worthless. I was fucked up on heroin and then going through withdrawal. I want that thrown out and to start from square one."

"That's not going to wash," Nick says. "You already agreed to this deal, and they have you dead to rights." The prosecutors are claiming they have evidence that I sold over 100 kilos of drugs. Nick explains the drug conspiracy laws, which maybe I should have boned up on earlier, considering that they were the ones I was breaking. I'm shocked to learn that testimony alone, from witnesses looking to save their own skin, can mean the difference between conviction and acquittal. The sentencing guidelines call for 120 months to life behind bars. If I plead guilty and give the prosecutors "substantial assistance," I'll give up my right to an appeal, but Nick can make a strong case for less time in prison.

I'm coasting along on the decisions of others. All I can think about is alleviating the all-encompassing pain of my dope sickness.

The DEA has warned Erin that she can't tell anyone, including her family, what has happened. She's alone at the Gansevoort, and the agents ask her if she wants to see me. They pick her up at the hotel and drive her over. She's bawling when she enters. We hug, and I ask her what's wrong, but she won't say. She just keeps bawling as we hang out with the agents near us, and then I whisper, "Did you bring negra?"

She says, "Didn't they give you your Suboxone?"

She had told them, the night of my arrest, that I needed it, but other than the handful of pills before my intake at MCC, they never gave it to me. At this point, I'm extremely sick. Erin's still crying when she leaves, and as soon as she gets back to the Gansevoort, we talk on Skype. She tells me that the agents had told her, on the drive to see me, that they think her being in the city is a distraction for me. We talk about going to City Hall and getting married so she'll have the right to see me.

At Mom's, as I'm foraging for a match to light a cigarette, I luck out and discover a couple of roaches in a matchbox, left behind by house-guests. I take them into the bathroom and smoke them next to an open window, trying to let as little smoke into the house as possible.

Mom is still in Spain, and Dad is in Canada. Even if they were here, they couldn't do anything to help me address my biggest problem, which is trying to end the suffering of withdrawal from my five-year-old heroin habit. The only person I want to talk to on the phone is Erin, because she's the one person who might be able to help alleviate the pain.

Erin and I leave the Skype window open, so there's a two-way video feed between us at all times. We watch TV together. I watch the dogs running around the hotel room, and they hear my voice when I say, "I'm right here." Sometimes, during the night, I'll wake up and say, "Erin?" and if she doesn't answer, I say it more insistently and wake her up, and when she says, "Cameron," I can fall back asleep. It's hard knowing she has everything I want: freedom, privacy, drugs.

A psychiatrist named Robert Millman visits me at the house and writes me a new prescription for Suboxone, but the DEA still doesn't fill it. Erin calls Dr. Millman, and Nick, and the DEA, telling them I need my Suboxone. The agents tell her they think I'm more clear-headed without it.

By now, I've seen that friends are permitted to bring me clothes, and a couple of days later Erin comes to the house and leaves a bag of miscellaneous items for me—toiletries, snacks, clothing—with the security guard. She's put some bindles of heroin in a hidden pocket near the crotch of a pair of my pants, and sewn it shut, but as soon as she drops the bag off, the guards take the pants to the laundry room. I go in there to try to retrieve them, and a guard says, "What are you doing?" I say I'm on my way to the kitchen, and I'm just getting a pair of pants. "Nah," he says. "They all need to be washed first." When the pants are delivered to me later, the glassines are all empty. On Skype, I tell Erin what happened.

She tries again. This time, she puts the cheeva in an electric tooth-brush and drops it off when I'm at a court hearing. When I get back to the house, I know what I'm looking for. In the battery compartment, I find ten envelopes of heroin. It's not enough to get me high, but at least it keeps the sickness at bay.

A few days later, on Skype, I tell Erin, "I need you to bring me another toothbrush." She goes to Duane Reade, buys another Sonicare, opens the battery compartment, and stuffs in as many glassines as will fit: nineteen. Then she reseals the toothbrush's clamshell packaging so it looks unopened, and drops off the toothbrush at Mom's house in a black bag. When I come back from another court hearing, a female guard says to me, "Your girlfriend seems pretty worried about your oral hygiene. She brought you a second toothbrush." It's the same guard who received the first one.

I shrug and say, "Yeah, the other one broke."

"We're going to take a look at it," she says.

A few minutes later she returns. "We found something that looks like heroin in it. We let the cops know."

Fuck.

Agent Meadows arrives and field-tests it. Seven grams of heroin. "I had no idea that was there," I say. "My friend Patrick gave Erin that bag to bring over. He must have put it in there."

"We're taking you in," Justin says.

I say I just need to change out of my court clothes. I tell Erin on Skype to tell the DEA that she was just dropping off a bag that Patrick gave her. "I've got to go," I say.

22

2009: Crazy Legs

At MCC, I'm given an orange jumpsuit to put on. Twelve brutalist stories of hulking brown ugliness, MCC holds nearly eight hundred inmates, all waiting to be tried or sentenced or to testify in other people's cases. Since it's a place for pretrial detention, it's a maximum-security facility, with some of the most depraved and violent prisoners from the most dangerous penitentiaries housed alongside people like me. Or like Erin, who a few hours after I was brought back here is arrested, sweating and shaking, at the Gansevoort. In the hotel room, the DEA found empty glassines and glassines containing small amounts of heroin, marijuana, and crystal meth. I feel terrible for Erin, and I'm also scared: I know the prosecutors are going to try to pull every piece of information they can out of her, which is going to jeopardize my strategy of feeding vague, incomplete, and false information to them.

Everyone starts out at MCC in the Special Housing Unit on 9S—ninth floor, south wing—known colloquially as the SHU, or solitary. Except that solitary confinement is no longer solitary, in many cases. As a result of prison overcrowding, the practice of double-celling, or confining two inmates in one cell, has become rampant. My cell is a tiny cement box with a bunk bed, a metal toilet connected to a small sink, a steel door, and a narrow opaque window near the ceiling that reveals only whether it's light or dark outside. My cell-mate, Juan, is a friendly guy from the Bronx who's in for some drug-related crime or other.

Going from the comforts of Mom's house to the privations of this cell is a shock. Guards pass our meals to us through a slot, and the food tends to be just a colder, more congealed version of the slop non-SHU prisoners receive. We get no recreation time outside the cell. We're locked in twenty-four hours a day, seven days a week. The unit is surprisingly loud, as prisoners communicate by yelling from one cell to another, and some inmates scream just because they're angry or out of their minds, a feeling I'll come to fully understand. I can't have visitors, and I'll be allowed only a single fifteen-minute phone call in my three weeks here.

"Is this even legal?" I ask Juan.

"Right? And we got it good compared to the guys up there," Juan says, nodding in the direction of the staircase that rises from the unit's corridor to two sets of metal doors: behind them, there's an even more restricted unit, a wing of six cells known as 10S, or 9½, where the highest-risk prisoners are held in true isolation. That's where Joaquín Guzmán Loera, the stumpy, escape-prone Sinaloa Cartel boss better known as El Chapo, will be held a few years from now. The fluorescent lights are kept on twenty-four hours a day, and guards monitor the prisoners through two cameras in each cell. Another resident, a terrorism suspect previously held at Guantanamo Bay, will later describe Gitmo as more pleasant.

Without heroin, I'm crawling out of my skin. The MCC doctor puts me on a seven-day course of tapering, twice-daily doses of methadone, which offer some relief, but after all these years of not missing a day of injecting heroin, I'm in bad shape, with torrential diarrhea. Juan is understanding. As I learned to do in county jail, I hang up a sheet when using the toilet, holding one arm behind me and pushing the flush button over and over, while I do my business, to minimize the odor.

On the top bunk, I stare at the ceiling. It's cement in a honeycomb pattern. Hot water pipes, painted glossy red, run across it. I close my eyes and allow myself a sliver of fantasy, imagining that when I open them the honeycomb is gone, I'm back in my own bed at the Gansevoort, and I can say, "I was only dreaming, thank God." I'm praying this is simply the most realistic nightmare I've ever had. But when I open my eyes, I'm staring at the concrete honeycomb and the red pipes, and the weight descends again on my chest. I'm really here. This is happening.

Hey Pop . . .

I'm sorry about all of this, I really am . . .

I really was shooting for bigger and better. Also please apologize to Pappy, Granny, and the rest of the family for all this, I feel really ashamed for being the source of any embarrassment and/or shame . . .

Thank you for your support and standing behind me on this one. It means the world to me.

Your son,

Cameron

DJing in Hamburg.

My meetings with Nick in the attorney consultation rooms are the only times I get out of my cell. It's humbling and scary to see how muscular the other prisoners are. I'm in the worst shape of my life, bloated and with no muscle tone. In this environment, where you're either prey or predator, that's dangerous. You want a potential predator to worry that you might not simply roll over for him, so he'd be better off pursuing a softer target. I'm still going through withdrawal, but I start working out with Juan, who does a typical prison routine: 500 to 1,000 push-ups in a two-hour session, in sets of 30. My first set, I make it to 15. The second set, I get to 10. The next one, I can do only 7. I go until around 100, when I can't do another push-up. I'm surprised and concerned by how weak I am.

At my first proffer meeting with prosecutors, they put my initial confession in front of me. I'm not too worried. Gabriel and Carlos, the only real people I named, have gone AWOL, and the prosecutors assume they've fled to Mexico. Maestro is an invented name.

The prosecutors remind me that if I go to trial, I could face a sentence of up to life in prison. Because of the intercepted toothbrush, they've already added a charge of heroin possession to my indictment. Now they want details about exactly what I did and how I did it. Dates and places. Weights and dollar amounts. Methods of packaging and shipment. They need to know exactly what I'll testify to at any trial of my suppliers.

I'm dragging my feet and not being forthright. Little of what I tell them is entirely true, and they catch me in blatant lies. I refer to Trevor Mitchell—who gave me $72,000, and who I never sent crystal to—as someone I know only as the Professor. My reticence is misplaced: I'll later learn that he's CW-2, one of the cooperating witnesses who helped the DEA build a case against me.

I'm going along with what Dad and Mom and Nick are telling me is the smart course of action, but afterward I tell Nick I'm uncomfortable with how things are progressing. He stresses that it's extremely unlikely Gabriel and Carlos will be found. Even if they are, they'll almost certainly cooperate, so the case won't go to trial. I can't comprehend how they could even be indicted, based on my drug-addled, half-fictional confession, and I'm momentarily pacified.

At least I'm not an informant. An informant is out on the street, backstabbing people he knows, wearing a wire, arranging deals, and trying to set other people up.

> Hi Cam,
>
> So what have you been up to lately? (bad joke) Thank you for your letter and apology. Your whole family's heart goes out to you. We're not embarrassed, we love you, just feel it's a hard road you've chosen. You've got a lot of support out there Cameron. I can't tell you the number of calls from friends I received, all wishing you the best, and all speaking of what a great guy you are; smart, funny, considerate, brave, and just pray you get your shit together. I haven't told the kids, and I think it's better that way. We are all back in the city for much of the fall.

Dad says he's filling out the necessary forms so he can visit me. He updates me on Carys and Dylan, and on his work.

> Just know, Cameron, I say a prayer every day for you, and I do love you. Thinking of you.
> Dad

After three weeks in the SHU, I'm moved to 11S. It's a large open dorm with more than a hundred inmates. I have the top of a bunk bed I share with a Puerto Rican kid named Pete. His charges carry a five-year minimum sentence, mine a ten-year minimum. We tease each other about how old each of us will be when we're released.

Even in gen pop, being at MCC is like being on the moon. We're always indoors, except for one hour, three times a week, when we're let out on the roof. There's no chow hall; meals are brought to the unit, where we line up to get our trays of barely edible food. Every day, inmates head off to court to learn what the future holds for them, only to return with their lives shattered. We're all under extreme stress, and a smothering darkness settles on me like a blanket.

"If I get ten years," I tell Pete, "I'm either going to try to escape or kill myself."

The physical agony of detoxing has faded, but the mental symptoms persist. At night, I lie in bed with what addicts call "crazy legs": I constantly feel like I need to move them. I toss. I turn. I sit up. I can't get comfortable. I can't get a good night's sleep.

I have an unshakable sense of anxiety. For years, heroin was my crutch to function normally. Sometimes just to make a phone call, I'd do a shot. Without it, and at the very moment when I'm having to navigate a new and much scarier environment, my social discomfort returns. Having strangers make assumptions about me is always unsettling, but here it could be dangerous too.

There are lifers on my unit. In my second week on 11S, I'm watching a kid get a haircut when another kid comes up behind him and stoves his head in with a mop wringer. The metal gears get caught in his face, and there's skin hanging off, and a lot of blood.

An alarm sounds, and guards come running. I'm stunned, kind of in shock, and for a moment I just stand there. This is the first real violence I've seen here. I don't know what's going to happen next. Is the fighting going to spread? Then I snap out of it and, like the other inmates nearby, move away from the scene. Moments later, I see the attacker being dragged away in handcuffs, and the victim being carried out on a stretcher. I never see him again. It's one of the bizarro facts of prison life that victims are treated the same as or worse than predators: they're taken care of medically, but then they're the ones who are seen as a risk by prison guards, a pain in the ass, and get involuntarily relocated to a different unit or different prison. People think: *What did you do to get yourself so fucked up like that?* I'm frightened. What *did* he do to provoke that? Could the same thing happen to me?

Outwardly I'm able to maintain my composure, but I start getting stress rashes. Dr. Millman, who specializes in drug and alcohol treatment, is visiting me once a week, and we're trying to get a prescription filled. The Federal Bureau of Prisons (BOP) routinely prescribes anti-anxiety meds and narcotics, including Klonopin and OxyContin, but when Dr. Millman prescribes me Xanax and Suboxone, the BOP won't give them to me. We bring the request before the judge in my case, and he instructs us to hire a specialist to make a diagnosis. I do this, but the BOP still won't give me the medication. We can't figure out whether I'm the target of a sadistic bureaucrat or of a prosecutor striving to keep me on edge as a point of leverage.

Dad's been out of town, and I haven't seen him since my arrest, but in early October he comes for a visit. He's focused and encouraging, and there's a feeling of optimism between us, like we're going to work this thing out.

Afterward, I meet with my lawyers. I've learned, far too late, that Nick has never defended a drug case of this magnitude, and Dad has hired a second law firm to join our team. One of the new attorneys, an associate named Meg Salib, floats the idea that I could be eligible for something called "the safety valve," a legal mechanism that exempts first-time nonviolent drug offenders from mandatory minimum sentences. Over the past twenty-five years, she explains, a sentencing reform movement, spurred by the unduly harsh sentences often meted out to low-level drug offenders, has gained steam in the U.S., and the safety valve was created as part of this movement.

It gives you an out without your having to fully cooperate. You have to debrief—revealing what you did, how you did it, and who you did it with—but you don't have to wear a wire or testify against anyone. There's some question as to whether I qualify, because of my DUI from 2005, but it turns out that the DUI is actually due to be expunged this month, so the safety valve would have been an option for me. But at this point, it's moot; I've already agreed to much more than I would have needed to, including a complicated bail package that my addiction made inevitable I would violate, leading to the added heroin-possession charge.

In our meetings with prosecutors, the outlines of a plea agreement have begun to take shape. Erin and I haven't been allowed to speak. And I still haven't heard from Jay. I've been trying to keep both Erin and Jay out of my accounting of my crimes. I have so much buyer's remorse about this deal with the prosecutors that I'm trying to be slick, oblivious to the reality that they've sat across from thousands of bullshitters before and can see right through me. When I'm withholding information or making stuff up, they say things like, "We'll go pick up your friend Jay right now and add him to the indictment," and I acquiesce.

Nick tells me he's concerned about my level of transparency with the prosecutors. The next week, I get another letter from Dad. He and Nick have clearly been talking.

> *As you know we are trying to do everything we can from the outside, but a lot of it depends on your cooperation. You have to remember that you don't know what evidence they have; taped conversations, video tapes, witnesses, etc. I know the meeting THEY had with you after we met didn't go great. If they feel they can't trust you, reduced sentences will be more difficult. The legal fees, etc., are no small amount, let's try to make it worthwhile . . . PLEASE UNDERSTAND THE REPERCUSSIONS IF YOU DON'T COOPERATE.*

In this moment of crisis I really value Dad's opinion. But I'm a mess inside. Every day that goes by, I'm more anxious and angry and frustrated with the advice I've received and with my own missteps. However much I've let myself and my family down, until now I've taken comfort from a bedrock belief: if nothing else, I'm brave, and I don't flinch from danger. But here I am, committing what feels like an act of ultimate cowardice.

After three months on 11S, I'm moved to another unit, whose manager has taken a maternal interest in me. On 5N, I'm in a cell on a two-tier range surrounding a dayroom. The cell, which I share with another inmate, is a little bigger than my SHU cell; there's a desk with a chair, and each of us has a locker and a separate storage bin. This is a working unit, meaning many of the inmates on 5N have jobs, most of them in the kitchen. That makes 5N a hub for wheeler-dealers earning money by channeling contraband from the kitchen to inmates on other units. The cluster of Italians on the unit is ruled by Jackie "Nose" D'Amico, a seventy-year-old Gambino street boss who was John Gotti Sr.'s right hand. Norman Hsu, a Hillary Clinton fund-raiser charged with running a Ponzi scheme, is here, as is Mahmoud Banki, a Princeton Ph.D. holder who has been indicted for using the illegal hawala money-transfer system to receive money from Iran.

Soon after I'm moved here, I'm approached by a huge guy known as Ohio. He says he was one of the inmate observers on my suicide watch, the night I was brought to MCC. "You were one fucked-up motherfucker," Ohio says. He hands me a letter from Alex, who I'm pissed at. I've spent a lot of time thinking about who helped the DEA against me. I know now, from reading discovery documents, that Alex is CW-3, the person who got me linked into the investigation in the first place; he'd had me on a recorded phone call, though I didn't say anything incriminating during that conversation. Alex's letter doesn't mention his involvement in my arrest, or that he was released from prison on the same day I was brought in. He just says he heard what happened, he's upset about it, and he tried to get word to me about the investigation. I feel like I've been good to Alex, and I'm hurt by his betrayal, but I understand that he did what most people who find themselves in his situation do.

My cellie, George, is a dope fiend in his forties who's doing time for a marijuana distribution case and is connected to the Bonanno crime family. He has a heavy Bronx accent, has been in and out of prison his whole life, and looks like Bugs Bunny, because his only remaining teeth are the two upper front ones. He's been waiting for months for dentures, but he has such a good attitude about it, and he's always friendly and full of jokes.

I find myself spending most of my time with three other guys. Mark Clancy has long gray hair and a handlebar mustache and is in his seventies, but he has a youthful face and is in great shape for his age. Clancy's a tough career criminal who was convicted of armed robbery and aggravated kidnapping in the late 1960s, and was released from prison after forty years. He's here now, doing an eighteen-month bit, because after being released he was a no-show at his halfway house and got picked up again.

Clancy has endless war stories. He claims that a friend of his cut off another inmate's head and ran around the cellblock holding it. His real trademark, though, is that he's an escape guy. In 1966, armed with a gun smuggled in by his girlfriend, Clancy and three other inmates broke out of Cook County Jail in Chicago. He also claims to have been part of a notorious attempted helicopter escape in 1981 from the rooftop right here at MCC.

Eddie Callegari has been in prison for fourteen years. He's solidly built and heavily tatted, with a head Bic-razored clean. His street names were Crazy Eddie and Eddie Wrecker, and the government alleges that as a member of a Queens crew called the Ozone Park Boys, he served as a Gambino family enforcer who took part in strong-arm robberies. He was also a suspect in three murders in South Florida. Eddie's at MCC to testify on behalf of John Gotti Jr. He's missing a front tooth, which makes him seem like a big kid, and I know him as friendly and boisterous. In here, he's like Dennis the Menace. He makes terrible booze and pro-grade knives with rubber handles, and one time he steals an overhead speaker from the chapel to use in his cell.

The guy I become closest to, Dave Hattersley, is thirty-five, has dirty blond hair with a touch of ginger, is lean and muscular, and walks with a strut, swinging from side to side. He's a vicious heroin addict who went to prison for robbing banks. He's constantly shadowboxing, has a short temper, and is quick to violence. His father, who was a Vietnam vet, has always been disappointed in him, which Dave is angry about. Despite our differences, I see some of myself in him: the severe addiction, the willingness to be crazy, the disappointed father. Like me, he was a fuck-up teenager.

As I'll learn, he also has a swastika tattooed on his chest, and he claims ties to the East Coast Aryan Brotherhood, which started in New Jersey prisons and despite its name has no connection to the original Aryan Brotherhood. It's difficult to explain how race plays out in prison. It's very different than out in the world. As I learned in juvie, and in county jail, race lines are starkly drawn. You break bread with "your own kind." It sounds terrible, but that's just how it works.

Despite his swastika and gang affiliation, Dave isn't necessarily racist, and I'll eventually conclude that that's true for a lot of white gang members in prison. It seems to me that many of them click up and band together for camaraderie and survival, rather than from any ideology, and wear their big swastika tattoos as symbols of intimidation rather than signs of any personal belief system.

Dave and I work out together in the dayroom. We play handball on the roof. We sit on the stairs that lead from the dayroom to the upper tier, shooting the shit. Much of the time, we're buzzed on Clancy's hooch, which we call wine or, in code, "pear." Clancy makes it from sugar, water, mushed-up spoiled fruit from the chow hall, yeast from the kitchen, and grape juice, which he has access to because he works in the chaplain's office. He usually has a new batch ready each Thursday, just in time for the weekend. It's good stuff, unlike his white lightning, which he makes by running a live electrical cord into a bucket of the hooch to boil it, then capturing the condensation in a plastic bag. The result is 110 proof and tastes like gasoline. Alcohol has never been my preferred poison, but sipping Clancy's wine gets me through a day or two a week here. The stuff is potent, and I brush my teeth before leaving my cell and try not to talk to anyone.

Having friends here keeps me from getting too lonely and also helps to muffle the insecurity I feel. A friend is one less person who's an enemy. There's safety in having allies. And, though I don't realize it yet, this period is helpful in training me to relate to people without the aid of heroin. Being forced to make idle chitchat with people I don't entirely know or trust, I'm getting more comfortable with myself. I go through the prison ritual of "exchanging information" with other inmates, writing down our names and register numbers on slips of paper for each other. This is part practicality, in case you want to stay in touch with someone, and part symbolism, a kind of handshake confirming you have no issues with each other. You do it sooner than later, after meeting, since anyone can be moved at any time without notice.

Eddie's been sent here from a high-security penitentiary, and Dave is on his way to one. They make knives and extort people. I'm on my way to a minimum-security. But my friendships with these guys boost my confidence. I look up to them. They know how to navigate this world I'm now in. I learn from them just by watching how they do it, seeing how they handle situations, inferring the unwritten code of life here just from what they do and don't do. I see that the closer you adhere to the code, the better off you'll be.

I romanticize my situation—the seriousness of my charges, of the convicts around me, of the place where I am, and of the amount of time I'm facing. I feel like I'm making moves. When George leaves, I take over the football pool he was running. My heroin detox was involuntary; I still like the idea of having a drug habit in prison, like I've seen in movies, and we try various scams to source heroin. They mostly don't pan out. The couple of times we do get it, I snort it.

Do I want to better myself? Yes. Do I want to be sober? No. Life in here is so miserable, and I'm under so much stress, that if I have an opportunity to take the edge off, I'll take it. And the opportunities here are few and far between, so I'm not really worried about overdoing it.

One day, Eddie says to me: "I can't believe you're just coming into the system. I'll tell you right now, you'll make it at any high-security prison." I don't know if I believe him, but as crazy as this might seem later, it feels good to hear.

I'm becoming more focused on self-improvement. My first time in the exercise area, I go to the pull-up bar, thinking I'll bang out ten—in the past, I've been able to do ten with one arm—and I can't even do two. This isn't acceptable. I need to make this prison time work for me. I need to find myself again. After a few months, I'm noticeably stronger. I do 1,500 push-ups every morning, in sets of twenty that alternate between regular, incline, and decline, using a chair for elevation.

I keep a journal and carry it around with me. It makes me feel more intellectual than everyone else, and I get a lot of "Ernest Hemingway over here"–type comments. I find myself praying to God. I know I'm in a lot of trouble, and I can't think who else to appeal to for the amount of help that I think I need. I'm thirsting at least for some sign that I matter, that God, or the universe, is aware of me and my situation. I have long, searching conversations with a guy on the unit named Eddie Boyle, a Gambino-affiliated Irish American bank robber whose Boyle Crew knocked over night-deposit boxes. In his late forties, Eddie has ice-blue eyes and an intelligence and reserve that stand out among the bullshitters and gum-flappers who make up most of MCC's population. He doesn't have a drug habit. He's been in prison for six years, and he spends a lot of time working on his appeal, which has brought him back to MCC. He's arguing that the government improperly applied the RICO Act to his case; his argument will end up before the U.S. Supreme Court (which won't see it his way).

We spend hours hanging out in each other's cells, talking about purpose and suffering and the likelihood of intelligent life elsewhere in the universe. Eddie introduces me to James Allen, a poet, philosopher, and motivational speaker born in the late nineteenth century who died in his forties, and to his essay "As a Man Thinketh," about the power of the mind. It makes an impression on me. It lines up with my own innate understanding of how things work:

> *Man is made or unmade by himself; in the armory of thought he forges the weapons by which he destroys himself. He also fashions the tools with which he builds for himself heavenly mansions of joy and strength and peace. By the right choice and true application of thought, man ascends to the Divine Perfection; by the abuse and*

wrong application of thought, he descends below the level of the
beast. Between these two extremes are all the grades of character,
and man is their maker and master.

To read what I already believe on an intuitive level, clarified in his
words and with his authority, feels somehow vindicating. I get a heavy
paperback compilation of all of Allen's works, which I annotate and
underline and highlight and read cover-to-cover several times.

Erin is in the all-female wing of MCC. I miss her a lot. I'm also worried she will tell the prosecutors things they don't already know, either
because she thinks it will help me or because she thinks it's the right
thing to do.

Finally, in November, on a day when we both have hearings, I see
her in a holding cell behind the courtroom. We're in cages across
from each other. We agree to write to each other, passing our messages through her friends who work in the commissary and leaving
letters behind a pad on the wall of the rec cage on the roof. I implore
her to tell the prosecutors that she really doesn't know anything, that
I did my business when she wasn't around. Another day, I'm visiting
the library on the second floor, where Erin is, and we see each other.
I scream, "I love you." She screams, "I love you." The guards are really
pissed, and we get written up for it.

My proffer sessions are becoming more fraught. The prosecutors
tell Nick they may add a cocaine conspiracy charge to my indictment.
In December, Erin tells them about our guns, and that I sometimes
carried one with me on drug buys. I can't believe it. What was she
thinking? The presence of a firearm during the commission of a crime
could double my sentencing range, and the prosecutors exploit their
new piece of leverage, saying they'll add a gun charge to my indictment unless I play ball. I don't have a chance to confront Erin about
this. I'm angry and frustrated, but I know she wouldn't have done it
with any bad intention toward me. She's just in over her head, and has
no business being here, and the prosecutors know what they're doing.

For a time, my hopes are focused on getting bail again. The prosecutors are opposed to the idea. My lawyers think I can get it. But then I don't get it. The upside of not getting out of here is that any time at MCC will count against my eventual sentence. The downside is that I get no relief from my stress and fear. Some of the fear is physical: Am I going to be stabbed? A lot of the stress is emotional: I obsess minutely over my agreement with the government, beating myself up for letting myself get ensnared by it. I worry about what this environment will do to me.

My cooperation doesn't pose only an emotional struggle or ethical quandary or psychological conflict. It creates real problems for me in a place where the prevailing attitude is *Snitches get stitches*. People want to dislike someone like me, with a famous last name and a rich family, right off the bat. I'm consumed with anxiety, and itchy red welts break out all over my body.

Every new hearing in my case yields fresh articles in the press, and after a closed bail hearing in January, reporters speculate that I'm "cooperating." I'm in my cell and a big Spanish guy I've never spoken to comes in, gets right up in my face and says, "You're a fucking rat. You're gonna give me money, or I'ma beat you off this unit."

It's a crucial turning point in my life behind bars.

23

2010: Acquired Situational Narcissism

Y ou're a fucking rat," says my would-be extortionist at MCC. Without thinking, I head-butt him. I strike with the crown of my forehead, just above the hairline, and aim for the bridge of his nose. When someone's too close to punch, it's very effective, temporarily disorienting to the recipient and giving you a moment to do what you're going to do. But I'm surprised by just how well it works this time. The guy drops to his knees, and I hit him in the face with a flurry of blows, laying him out flat. He doesn't say anything, just gathers himself up and skulks out of my cell. I worry that I'll get in trouble, because his face is bruised and cut, but I don't. He never talks to me or looks at me again. I begin to build a prison reputation as someone who doesn't roll over. I feel triumphant.

I'm having more contact with Mom and Dad than I've had in years. They're happy to see me off of drugs. We're all focused on my case. After so many years of distance, it finally feels like we're working together.

Around my birthday, Dad and Pappy visit. The administrator who's been kind to me arranges for us to have an hour in an empty visiting room where there are a couple of vending machines, and we pull a few chairs together to talk.

I'm so impressed by Pappy, and touched. He's ninety-three, and he's come all the way from California to see me. He's wearing shades and doesn't take them off the whole time we're together.

"You been getting in any fights?" Pappy asks.

"I have," I say.

"Have you been winning or losing?"

"Winning," I say.

"That's my boy," Pappy says.

I tell him I'm ashamed for him to see me like this.

"Do what you need to do, Cameron, and make your way home."

Meg Salib, one of the lawyers from the second firm we hired, visits me every day. She's on the short side, with shoulder-length brown hair, and she's buxom. She looks very professional in her skirt suits; she's my lawyer and I'm in prison, but the first time I met her, from the moment I walked into the visiting room, I had an inkling that something might happen between us. She's thirty-four to my thirty-one. She's warm and kind. For a lawyer dealing with a client, she seems overly concerned with me, but in my situation that feels incredibly good. I'm pitying myself, so the fact that she pities me too is a welcome sentiment.

She started coming to see me every few days, then more frequently. We talk about my case, but feelings are developing. Back on the unit, there are whispers about us, because Meg is attractive and constantly visiting, all eyes are on me to begin with, and that's what guys in prison do: gossip. They read and watch everything and are remarkably up-to-date on current events and what's going on within the institution. I start getting nudges and winks from other inmates, and guards make leering remarks to Meg.

My anxiety spikes in response to the periodic violence around me. There are people here who don't know the protocols you learn at higher-security places and unwittingly breach them, leading to swift reactions. I watch a kid named Chino, a member of MS-13, get choked out by Face, a shot-caller for the Bloods, then come back the next day with three padlocks attached to shoelaces: he windmills them, striking Face's head again and again until there's blood everywhere and Face's face is a pulp. I never see Face again.

In late January, when I formally plead guilty, another burst of articles appears ("Michael Douglas's Son Admits Drug Dealing"—*People*), and again I get hostile, menacing looks from the other inmates on my unit. I have a fresh breakout of hives, which I can't stop scratching. The BOP medical staff still won't give me anything other than non-narcotic meds with unpleasant side effects.

In February, I have another bail hearing. At this one, Dr. Millman testifies about what he calls my "feelings of lack of self-esteem . . . On the one hand, *I am this guy who is so important*—but he is not. And on the other hand, he is nothing, and he couldn't even graduate from high school. So I think that he was self-medicating from a really early age and doing things that endangered his life . . . And he really needs to be rebuilt. I hate to say it, but he needs to be rebuilt."

The fuck? Millman wears his star-fuckery on his sleeve. He treated Keith Richards and coined a psychiatric diagnosis, Acquired Situational Narcissism, to describe celebrities whose fame makes them go nuts. I'm embarrassed and ashamed that I've gotten myself in a position where I have to prostrate myself to get sympathy. That I have to pay someone to basically say I'm worthless.

Then Millman says that I'm "an informant." I look at my lawyers, and they look at me, in disbelief. It's both untrue and the worst possible thing he could say in open court. To a civilian, "cooperating witness" versus "informant" might sound like semantic hairsplitting, but it's a significant distinction in prison. The judge agrees to strike Millman's words from the record, but there are reporters in the courtroom who heard what Millman said.

The next morning, when I come out of my cell, even my friends, Dave and Eddie and Clancy, are looking at me askance. Everyone in prison reads the newspapers, and the *New York Post* seems to hope I'll get killed. Their headlines about me are gleeful in a way that seems optimized to ensure that something terrible will happen to me, which they can then describe with another sadistic headline. Today's is:

"'SINGING' ROLE FOR CAMERON."

The BOP puts me in protective custody. When Meg Salib visits, I've broken out in hives again. But I convince the BOP to put me back in gen pop. At this point, it's become a matter of pride not to hide out in the SHU. And I'm anxious to clear the air with my friends.

When I get back to the unit, Dave starts getting loud. Maybe he's been drinking. "Fuck you, you fucking rat." I go up to him, get in his face, and call his bluff. I'm standing right in front of him, like I'm prepared to do something, but I don't think I really am prepared to do something. Which I know isn't the way to do things. If you're going to posture, you'd better be ready to deliver. And he unloads on me, hitting me with a series of punches and dropping me to the ground.

"What the fuck?" I say. "That guy didn't know what the fuck he was talking about. They *asked* me to be an informant, and I refused."

I'm kind of shocked. I thought we were friends. It becomes more real to me what world I'm now in.

Hattersley and Clancy demand that I show them my paperwork to prove what I'm saying. "Paperwork" means the minutes from my court hearings, plus the pre-sentencing report issued by the probation department, which I don't yet have. Hattersley calls Meg directly to demand the documents.

Meg brings them with her on her next visit, Hattersley and Clancy are placated, and we make up. But Millman blabbing in court, and the resulting press coverage, makes me very unpopular at MCC and sets the tone for the duration of my prison bit. I've fucked myself two ways. My uncooperative cooperation has cost me the goodwill of the prosecutors, while the fact that I have the agreement with them at all has tarnished my name with inmates. Most of them will never know the nuances of my unenthusiastic dealings with the government, such as my efforts to keep my accomplices out of it and to provide useless or unreliable information. They just see the newspaper headlines about "cooperation" in return for a shorter sentence.

I can tell that Dad's angry with me. He has spent a ton of money on my lawyers. He has publicly criticized his own parenting of me. He has visited me a lot. I'm grateful, but I'm also still immature—romanticizing crime and drugs—and probably not acting sufficiently reformed. And my gratitude, tinged as it is with years of accumulated pain and resentment, may not be as robust as he'd like.

When he visits again, not long before my sentencing, he suggests I may have to work as a coffee boy in the entertainment industry when I get out of prison. I'm not a snob, and this could be true, though I hope not. Because there was a time when everything did come to me, maybe I feel like I'm more important than I am, or that my talent is more special than it is. I guess there's a level of entitlement in me. But "You can shovel shit when you get out" is not what I'm looking for right now. I'm wanting something else from Dad. A sign that he hasn't given up on me, some reassurance that he still believes in me, a reason to live and a goal to work for. I'm not sure that he does believe in me, and I'm not sure that he should. When you need someone else's belief in you to validate that there still is anything worth believing in, you know you're at a low point. That's a dangerous place to be.

In a *Vanity Fair* article that comes out in early March, Dad compares our upbringings, suggesting they're similar. I shake my head, reading it. Yes, we both grew up in the shadow of a famous father. But otherwise, the idea is laughable. He had a rock-solid nuclear family, and Granny and Uncle Billy raised him in Westport, Connecticut, away from the craziness of Hollywood. They had a wonderful marriage and were a loving, constant presence in his childhood.

Maybe Dad will never entirely forgive me for decisions I've made in my life. I feel like I've been very forgiving of the decisions he's made, but maybe deep down I also harbor things I can never entirely let go of. Maybe that's how it's always going to be.

———

At this point in my stay at MCC, my stress levels are through the roof. I've still been unable to get the prescriptions Dr. Millman wrote for me, and Meg worries about me. The attorney visiting rooms line a corridor and have glass walls, but other than an occasional check by the officer who sits at the end, we have privacy. I can tell that Meg is starting to fall in love with me. Every day, she stays for the entire hours-long window permitted for lawyers' visits. She says that she can't picture me going through whatever I'm going through in prison, and she wants to be here for me, to give me attention and support. She knows I have a hard time being alone. I'm starting to develop feelings too.

Erin, who has been at MCC for seven months, is sentenced to time served and released. Meg tries to get me to say my relationship with Erin is over, but I tell her that I love Erin and care about her, because she's always been there for me. At the same time, I know that what's developing with Meg would hurt Erin if she knew about it, but in my mind, the two situations are unrelated. And the harshness of prison has a way of awakening the most selfish instincts: all you want to do is try to maneuver things so that you have your needs met to the best of your abilities. The ethics of civilian life take a back seat to surviving.

Meg has been outraged, on my behalf, by the BOP's refusal to fill my prescriptions for psychiatric drugs. One day in March, she agrees to bring me Xanax. The next day, when it's time to see her, I go into my cell, put my finger in a tub of commissary moisturizer, and smear a dab of it behind my ear.

When I see Meg in the visiting room, she walks over to buy a bag of vending-machine chips. Then she sits down across from me at the table and reaches into her bra. She pulls out a lumpy balloon and puts it in the potato chip bag, which she passes to me like she's sharing her snack. I palm the balloon, surreptitiously lubricate it, reach into my pants, and press it inside me. Meg seems into being gangsta. She tells me she listened to Biggie Smalls while she was ballooning up the Xanax and some loose tobacco. I swear to her that I won't share the pills with anyone.

Back in my cell, after pushing the balloon out and emptying it, I take a Xanax suppository-style. It's the next best thing to injecting a drug. I'm still in my isn't-federal-prison-romantic phase—Clancy was recently released, and I took over his hooch production—and I take vain pleasure in having this connect, in having my *lawyer* doing the smuggling no less. I'm making moves, making things happen. I want the respect of people like Dave Hattersley, and I share the pills with him and a few others.

In the months leading up to my sentencing, several dozen friends and family members (from Pappy to my ex Amanda to my first-grade teacher to Pat Riley) write long letters on my behalf to the judge, Richard Berman, and I'm grateful for their love and support. But in their efforts to make me sympathetic, and to try to mitigate my responsibility, the letters add up to an excavation of my parents' divorce. Many of them fault Mom or Dad or both of them in harsh terms. Mom and Dad, in their own letters to Judge Berman, seek to put me in the best light, and one of the ways they do this is by alternating between blaming themselves and blaming each other. Dad acknowledges his substance abuse and careerism, but he also notes that Mom was "a young mother without any parenting skills handed down from her own parents." Mom talks about her "scarred childhood" and youth and immaturity when I was growing up, but also about Dad's "mercurial behavior," "conditional" love, and parenting decisions she believes were motivated by guilt.

Though it's standard for letters like these to be part of a public court file, several of the people Meg Salib solicits a letter from are left with the impression that it will be read only by the judge. When the letters are made part of the public record and are quoted in newspaper articles, a number of people, including Amanda and my friend John, are mortified and find themselves apologizing to Mom or Dad for various comments.

The focus is now on my sentencing and ultimate designation. Mom picks out a suit for me to wear in court, and I read up on different prisons, trying to figure out which one to request. Nick has told me that he's hoping to get me less than five years.

On the day of my sentencing, Nick brings the suit to me in the bull pen before I go into the courtroom. There's an overflow crowd that also fills a second room with a closed-circuit TV showing the proceedings. Mom and Dad have momentarily set aside their differences and arrive together. This—me, my problems—is really all they have left to talk about with each other. It's been a catalyst for them to be in contact, and I don't think Mom ever stopped loving Dad. She was so young when they met, and he was formative, the first strong male figure in her life.

"Therapeutically," Judge Berman tells the courtroom, "we all need to get over the theme that Cameron Douglas is a victim." He faults my lawyers' submissions, and the letters from my family and friends, for not acknowledging the impact on the community of my drug dealing. He says, "I think this case and this sentencing may well be his last chance to make it."

When I'm given a chance to speak, I apologize to my family and loved ones "for putting them through this nightmare of my making—and for my behaviors that have caused a rift between us in the past." I apologize to the judge. I talk about how I've let so many opportunities go to waste.

Then Judge Berman imposes a sentence of sixty months—fifty months for the meth and coke conspiracy count, and ten months for possession of the heroin that Erin smuggled in for me—followed by five years of supervised release, 450 hours of community service, a $25,000 fine, forfeiture of $300,000, and weekly drug testing.

Nick seems pleased with the sentence. The attitudes of Mom and Dad seem closer to *five years is better than ten, but it's still a long time.* I feel detached from what's happening. My mind is all over the place. I'm overwhelmed and confused. I feel like these things are happening to me and are beyond my control. I'm angry. Of course, I know exactly why I'm here. Of course, my choices have caused it. But my introduction to the system, my experience with my lawyers and the stress of it all, made me feel so powerless initially, like I was being pulled along by an overpowering current. And in my gut and heart, I feel guilty and ashamed about my cooperation deal.

When I arrive back on the unit, everyone has heard about my sentence on the news. They clap and offer congratulations. I was facing the possibility of eleven years, or worse, and I got five.

A place like MCC tends not to allow people with criminal records to visit, so Erin can't visit me. But Meg's still coming to see me every day, and sometimes we're assigned to the visiting room farthest from the guard's station. In her final visit before I'm transferred out, Meg brings one last balloon full of Xanax. This one is big and loosely tied, like a beanbag, and when I try to push it inside me, it won't go in. I start sweating from the struggle. The guard hasn't checked on us in a while, and could come back at any moment, and finally Meg says, "Give it back to me."

"No, I'm not giving it back."

"Do you have any idea how wide the human sphincter can dilate? Get it up there."

And so I do.

It has been a revelation to me just how much contraband the lower bowel can accommodate. I know guys who've traveled from joint to joint with two cell phones or a knife fully concealed inside their body. But in May 2010, when I leave the Manhattan Correctional Center for Lewisburg, the federal prison where I've been designated, I'm muling only a small payload: a pinky-sized roll of Xanax tablets, wrapped in cellophane and tied in a balloon.

24

2010: Camp

Nick requested Lewisburg LEC because it's the minimum-security camp closest to my family and friends, and the judge approved it, but my journey there takes a few days. This is my introduction to so-called diesel therapy, the infamous use of extended transit as a disciplinary tactic by the Bureau of Prisons. We're in uncomfortable restraints, poorly fed, and left to wait in bland rooms for indeterminate lengths of time, bored and anxious, in limbo, with no routine. You lose weight on these trips.

I leave MCC at 4 a.m., in shackles: handcuffs and ankle cuffs, both attached to a belly chain. In the predawn light, our bus speeds north and west for a few hours until we reach Waymart, Pennsylvania, home to United States Penitentiary Canaan, which serves as a transport hub for the BOP's northeast region. At Canaan, we're split up by custody level. Those of us bound for minimum- and low-security prisons are funneled into one holding cell, while people heading to Mediums and Highs are put in a separate cell. Both have large windows and face each other, and I take a good look at the men in the other cell. The guys next to me for the most part look like civilians who made a mistake. The guys across from us are visibly in a different category. They have more aggressively placed tattoos, more scarred faces, warier eyes, more worked-out bodies, and above all an intense, animal alertness. I briefly picture myself among them and feel lucky that I'm not.

When I'm eventually moved to a unit at Canaan, after several hours of standing around, there's no clock, no phones, no computer access, no books. I don't know if I'll be here for two days or two months. It's dislocating. When I go to take a shower, I'm overpowered by the stench: someone has taken a shit in one of the shower stalls.

After the months of worry and uncertainty building to my sentencing, I feel some relief. I was hoping for less than the five years the judge gave me, but it could have been so much worse. Now, with time off for good conduct, another year off for taking part in a nine-month Residential Drug Abuse Program (RDAP) at Lewisburg, plus the ten months I've already served at MCC, I'm facing just another two years and some change. And despite what the press has reported, I feel like I've managed my situation without jeopardizing anyone else. But the old anxiety has been replaced with fresh apprehension. A new place means new people. I know I'm going to have to readjust, which is always difficult.

———

USP Lewisburg.

Lewisburg is only 115 miles away, but I spend two nights at Canaan. Early on the third morning, a guard calls my name, and soon I'm on a bus, sitting next to an Irish kid from Queens who's coming from a Low, where he was doing time for his involvement in a marijuana ring. There are only five convicts on the bus, but the two of us sit together to ensure that no weirdo sits next to us, and only once we're on the road do we separate to spread out. After a couple of hours, the bus stops at FCI Allenwood, a Low, where a couple of inmates get off. Then we drive on, passing a truck full of chickens and a horse-drawn buggy carrying an Amish family. We're surrounded by the cheap, remote, unpopulous farmland that has made Central Pennsylvania a favorite of the people who choose where to locate prisons.

Twenty minutes later, we pass through improbably grand black gates, topped with gilt finials and bearing gilt letters that spell USP LEWIS-BURG. On the left is a cluster of pretty guards' houses. The road straightens out and for half a mile slopes gently upward between tall-grass fields. Then it widens into a parking lot and dead-ends at an ominous brick building. A thirty-foot-high wall extends from both sides and terminates in huge gun towers. Behind it is the Big House, a supermax penitentiary. A con's name is called, and he shuffles off the bus in his chains.

I feel a grudging admiration for his higher security level as well as a ripple of gratitude that this isn't where I'm going. The Big House, opened in 1932, is one of four penitentiaries built in that era to cage a generation of rum-runners and bootleggers. It's a beautiful structure, with Gothic arches and terra-cotta battlements: When the prison opened, the uplifting architecture was meant to embody the institution's progressive ideas about rehabilitation. Over time, it has held the likes of Al Capone, Whitey Bulger, and John Gotti, as well as Jimmy Hoffa, Philip and Daniel Berrigan, and Alger Hiss. But the year before my arrival, the prison was converted into one of three Special Management Units, or SMUs, in the country, created to house the most violent and hard-to-control inmates in the federal system.

Our bus continues along a service road and a few minutes later pulls up outside the administration building for the minimum-security camp, which stands on the penitentiary grounds but is outside the walls of the Big House. The BOP locates its camps to provide cheap labor for the maintenance of its higher-security facilities. A guard calls out two names, including mine, and we shimmy out of the vehicle.

A motley crowd of inmates, some in regulation khakis, some in after-work sweats and shorts, stand watching. They've heard I'm coming, and in the monotonous blur of prison life, the arrival of an inmate with my last name qualifies as a welcome break from routine. It's a bit of a spectacle, and it makes me uncomfortable. A corrections officer takes off our shackles and tells us to go into the building. Just walking those ten yards is pleasant: this is the first time in nine months that I've been outside without handcuffs or chains.

We've missed dinner, and inside, a C.O. with a big gut, gradient-lens sunglasses, and an unlit cigar in his mouth hands us each a foam clamshell with a still-hot serving of spaghetti. It's better than anything I've eaten in a long time. Then he gives us our bunk assignments and hands us some basics we'll need—including a bedroll, sheets, blanket, towels, socks, and underwear—and turns us loose to find our own way to our assigned bunks. This feels like freedom. The compound is . . . beautiful. It's big. There's grass.

The camp has three residential buildings: L-shaped, two-story Units 1 and 2, and the rectangular RDAP. I'm assigned to Unit 1. I enter a dayroom where some men sit at tables playing cards, while others watch TV in rooms to the side, behind a glass wall. I can feel eyes on me as I pass through another door onto my range, one of eight in the building. It's a long corridor lined with five-by-nine cinder block cubicles with five-foot-high walls.

My two cubies are waiting in mine, which has a bunk bed and a third bed. "I'm Gavin, from Boston," the bigger one says, shaking my hand. "This is your knucklehead other cellie from New England."

"Oh, yeah," the smaller one says. "I'm a fuckin' knucklehead, fuck you." He offers me a hand. "I'm Renato," he says.

This is the uncomfortable stage when you're new to a place, but my cubies are both really friendly. Gavin is an outspoken roughneck who ran a local for the Tunnel Workers Union in Massachusetts and was convicted of stealing from it. He's finishing up a seven-year bit. "We heard you were coming," Gavin says, "and we cleared out that locker for you."

Renato, Portuguese and goofy and in on a low-level drug charge, offers to show me around, and I throw my stuff on the vacant top bunk and follow him out. He starts with the bathroom on our range, which has four showers and three toilets in stalls with doors. Outside, Renato leads the way to a little pond, and past that to a pair of volleyball courts. Next to them are some pull-up and dip bars, and a softball diamond with a track around it. A couple of guys are hanging out next to a shed near third base.

"Look at fuckin' Renato," one of them says. "He thinks he's a fuckin' tour guide."

"Fuck off," Renato says.

The other one offers me a cigarette, and we move behind the shed to smoke unseen.

Then Renato continues his tour. There are two football fields and a 6,000-square-foot gym with free weights, StairMasters, and cable machines.

"What's that?" I ask, nodding toward a small domed structure in the distance, which looks like the bones of a tent, minus the fabric.

"That's for the Indian ceremony," he says.

"Huh?"

Renato explains that a group of inmates has a weekly Native American gathering, which they're Constitutionally entitled to do. "It's pretty sweet," he says. "They smoke a peace pipe and everything."

Maybe this is going to be okay.

Before I go to sleep, I go into a toilet stall and push out the Xanax. They'll help with the stress of getting adjusted.

Before I can be assigned a job at the camp, I have to go through an orientation, and the next one won't be for another ten days, so for a week and a half, when everyone else goes off to work each morning, I sleep late and take advantage of the feature that most starkly separates Lewisburg from MCC: it's an outdoor compound.

At MCC, I was indoors twenty-four hours a day except for three hour-long trips each week to the caged-in roof. Lewisburg, by comparison, is paradise. There are no fences. Unlike higher-security prisons, where there are controlled movements—ten-minute windows after the bell rings each hour to get from one place to another—here you can go pretty much wherever you please. The pond has turtles and ducks and benches alongside it. There are birds and skunks and stray cats. There's a garden, tended by inmates, which in summer produces fresh tomatoes and watermelons for both the camp and the penitentiary.

At MCC, I was surrounded by human wreckage and devastation, which infused every waking moment with heaviness and fear. At Lewisburg, we all have fewer than ten years left in our sentences. To be at a camp, you can't have violence on your record, or be a full-fledged gang member, or have committed a sex crime. So the population combines doctors and lawyers and judges who have committed white-collar crimes, and low-level drug dealers. We're all going home, and that's the prevailing attitude.

The first few days, a lot of people come up to me, inviting me to join various teams, and at this point I'm a joiner, signing up for softball and volleyball. There's an openness and inclusiveness here that I won't fully appreciate until later. The press coverage about my cooperation has preceded me here, and some people give me the cold shoulder, but if you're at a camp, the overwhelming odds are that you cooperated, and most people are friendly.

My routine starts to take shape. When I wake up, I bring a handful of commissary-bought groceries to the dayroom, where I use the 190-degree hot water tap to make coffee and a bowl of oatmeal with peanut butter, powdered milk, and honey.

My job assignment, when it comes, is an inside sanitation detail, working 7:30 a.m. to 2:30 p.m., five days a week, mopping floors, emptying trash, cleaning toilets, wiping down tables and microwave ovens, and vacuuming in and around Warden Bledsoe's office, for $11 a month.

Other inmates work for Unicorp, which makes license plates, wires, cables, and lingerie. It's slave labor that affects the economy on the street. Inmates earn pennies, while the BOP takes contracts that would otherwise go to wage-paying factories out in the world. And Unicorp jobs are considered the good ones. They pay better than non-Unicorp jobs and are in demand.

As I come to understand how relatively benign this place is, I begin to feel more confident and to find my niche. I work out twice a day with another recent arrival, Sebastian, a painter and sculptor from Philly who graduated from Rutgers and got seventy months for marijuana distribution. He's Jewish, grew up in Spain, and is more intellectual than I am but equally confident and unafraid. We've traveled in some of the same circles. He's been to parties I've played at. A month in, I get permission to move to Unit 2, where Sebastian lives, and we become cubies.

I'm feeling optimistic. Nine months after kicking my heroin addiction, my body has normalized, and I'm finally sleeping well. I'm looking forward to getting into RDAP and then going home. I like looking at the expiration dates on my commissary *picante* sauce and granola bars and Yoo-hoo soda and thinking: *I'll be out before this goes bad.* (When I'm feeling blue, I look at the dates on other items and think: *Shit, this will go bad before I get out of here.*) When I do get out, my family and friends keep telling me, I can do whatever I put my mind to.

Erin is back living with her parents in their Pennsylvania hometown, not far from Lewisburg, waitressing at a local restaurant and getting an online master's degree in entertainment business from Full Sail University. My trust is helping support her financially, and Erin continues to be my lifeline to the outside world. She writes to me every day, updating me on her life, asking about mine, providing news about mutual friends, including some of my fellow inmate friends, with whom she's struck up independent correspondences. She sends me books and magazines and articles about my family and other topics she thinks I'd be interested in. She's taking care of our dogs, and she spends a good chunk of every letter updating me on their health, moods, and foibles, often enclosing a stack of photos of them. We talk about the future: maybe we'll get a Winnebago and drive around the country.

One evening during a softball game, I'm sitting next to my teammate Matt, a kid from Detroit with a Vandyke beard, and he tells me about the Inipi ceremony, a Lakota Sioux ritual he takes part in. I've always had a lightweight fascination with Native American culture. I have a pair of war feathers tattooed on my lower arm, and I wear a bear-bone necklace my friend Santos gave me. Matt invites me to a sweat lodge the coming weekend.

On Saturday morning, I walk out to the Inipi area. It's ringed by low hedges, and at the center of it is the structure I saw from a distance on my first night at Lewisburg. It's now covered with canvas tarps. Ten paces to the east, a bonfire blazes. There are seven other guys. Pud, a well-liked fat dude with long hair that's shaved on the sides, is an actual Mohawk from a reservation. Most of us are white, including the kid I sat next to on the bus from Canaan. Our leader is Tomás, who looks white but is from a native tribe in Puerto Rico.

Tomás steps inside the tent and offers prayers to the six directions— north, south, east, west, Mother Earth, Father Sky—while the rest of us stand around outside saying, "A-ho!" after each prayer. Then one by one we bow low and enter the tent from the east side, giving thanks and taking a seat around a mound where hot rocks are already giving off steam. There's a fragrant smell of sweet grass. We're sitting in a circle now, as Tomás sprinkles water on the rocks, and the air becomes scorchingly hot.

The last time I was in a sweat lodge, five years ago, was at the rehab clinic in Sedona. Halfway through, I spent a weekend in Scottsdale with Erin and her cousin, drinking heavily. When I got back to the clinic and did a sweat lodge the next day, my face puffed up, maybe because of the toxins I'd put into my body. I was afraid I'd get kicked out but managed to complete the 30-day program.

At Lewisburg we sit cross-legged for four hours, sweating in darkness over the hot stones. Periodically, we pass a pipe filled with the traditional kinnikinnick, a mixture of tobacco and other leaves, and offer prayers in the six directions, breaking after each one to open a flap and let light and air in. Then a designated helper replenishes the hot rocks and reloads the pipe, and the next round begins. We thank the north for its purifying winds and the cleansing snow, and the south as the origin and end of all life, where ancestors' spirits reside. We thank the east as the source of the rising sun and of wisdom, heralding new beginnings and life, and the west for its cleansing rains. We thank the heavens above us and the providing earth below. We sing songs.

> Lay-u-ha chey-wank-e-yea lo . . .
> Kola-lay-chay-say ik-cho-wo . . .

The heat is punishing, and it's not easy to go the six rounds. But the ritual appeals to me with its simplicity and lack of dogma. I like the philosophy of atonement through endurance, of giving something to gain something, of seeing the divine in the natural world, of praying while sacrificing. For a moment, I feel outside the prison.

Walking back to the unit, Matt explains that the summer solstice is coming up, and if I want to take part, I need to formally list my religious preference with the prison as Native American. I do, and next Sunday I join the group for this annual event. The Inipi frame stays up year-round, but once a year, at the start of summer, we are allowed to gather new rocks for the fire. A couple of the guys have licenses to drive on the compound, and they take us in pickup trucks to a creek on the outskirts of the property that is normally off-limits to inmates. We gather new stones. We cut saplings, pliable but strong, to rebuild both our Inipi and the one behind the wall. We carve our initials on an old wooden bridge that spans the creek, just beyond the perimeter. We swim in the water, splashing each other. It feels like summer camp, and for a moment we can forget where we are.

I'm starting to rebuild myself. Part of my bond with Sebastian is a shared anguish about our predicament and thirst for some measure of peace. Beyond the weekly Inipi, I open myself to other traditions, reading theosophical tracts and Eckhart Tolle, whose insights have the ring of deep truth, resounding because I recognize them as things I already somehow innately know. I write down a quote from Francis Bacon, the Renaissance philosopher, and hold it close to me: "Seek not to have life happen the way that you choose, but rather choose that it happens as it does, and you shall live prosperously."

I meditate briefly every morning. I do an active meditation, where I recite a mantra and visualize traits I want to embody, and a passive meditation where I clear my head and watch my breath. Sebastian, who's asking himself similar questions, carries a laminated list of the twelve archangels in his shoes, so that, as he likes to say, he's "walking with the angels." At Sebastian's urging, I read *Shantaram*, the 936-page cult novel about the fugitive years of an Australian escaped prisoner who establishes himself in the Bombay underworld and battles in Afghanistan alongside the mujahideen. It's strewn with philosophical jewels, and I read it with a highlighter. At this moment in my life, this book speaks to me. Sebastian and I spend many evenings talking about *Shantaram* and its exploration of guilt and redemption and right and wrong. The book talks about an ethics based on the universe's progression toward complexity, positing that anything that helps this progression is good, and anything that hinders it is evil.

My workouts are further toughening my body. I've been getting stronger and leaner, and now I begin to add definition, too. When friends and family visit, they comment on my healthy appearance, suggesting prison has been good for me. For them, coming to a bucolic minimum-security camp in the Allegheny Mountains is almost a joy, compared with MCC. The visiting room here is relaxed and informal.

Mom has moved to New York, where she lives with her boyfriend Paolo and Imara, and shares joint custody of Hawk and Hudson with their father. She visits me regularly with my young half sister and -brothers, one time surprising me with a visit when I'm in the middle of a softball game. Dad visits with Dylan and Carys, and another time with Catherine, and another time with Jojo and Granny. She looks older but is still elegant and sharp. Her letters to me have been unfailingly encouraging. She has always supported my acting, and in nearly every letter she makes a remark about it. She's worried about me but full of love, and in my lowest moments her words buoy me. *"Keep on with it"*—my journal-keeping—*"even if you find it boring,"* she writes in one letter. *"This is a good time to probe your inner feelings, and reexamine some convictions to see if they still apply. Be totally honest as to how you feel NOW—it'll be interesting for you to read years later."*

Mom's fragile détente with Dad has come to an end. Two months after my sentencing, she sued him over the profits from *Wall Street: Money Never Sleeps.* Though her lawyer had advised her she was entitled to the money under the terms of their divorce settlement, and Mom had recently lost a lot of money investing with two different Ponzi schemers—Kenneth I. Starr and Bernard Madoff—Dad's lawyer has painted her as greedy, and that's the storyline the tabloids run with.

In my phone calls with Meg, my lawyer with benefits, she insists that we have graphically explicit phone sex. This makes me uncomfortable, since the institutional phones are all recorded, as she knows. The officials who monitor prison calls hear this kind of thing all the time, but she's a lawyer. She's *my* lawyer. I'm surprised by how gung-ho she is, but she seems to get turned on by it. I figure that if she feels comfortable doing it, I'll go along with it. Mostly I just listen, throwing in a couple of encouraging words here or there. She's the one getting off in private.

In early July, she visits. We kiss, then sit at a picnic table in a fenced-in area outside, holding hands.

"I have something to tell you," she says. "Carlos and Gabriel were arrested."

They were busted in California on the same day I arrived at Lewisburg. "They're going to be indicted in the next few days."

This is terrible news. I thought I'd never have to testify against them, because they'd fled to Mexico and would never be caught, much less indicted.

"You'll have to testify if there's a trial," Meg says, "but it's very unlikely there will be one."

"You really think it's unlikely?" I ask.

"I do," she says. "They'd be crazy not to plead out."

I really don't want to be a witness against them.

Though I've embraced self-improvement to a degree, I still have a foot in the past. One consequence of the relaxed vibe at Lewisburg is that an enormous volume of contraband floods into the camp. Since the duties of the grounds crew require them to cut grass out to the distant fringes of the compound, they're in a position to pick up packages left there, and they control much of the camp economy.

I can get lobster if I want. Big steaks come in. Everyone has a cell phone. From my first day at the camp I've been offered cigarettes, vodka, and drugs. Commissary mackerel is the currency of choice in minimum-security federal prisons, and a pack of cigarettes costs seven pouches (or $21, the price of a single cigarette in a higher-security prison). A small water bottle full of vodka goes for $40.

I'd made my limited supply of smuggled Xanax last by breaking them into pieces, but eventually I'd run out, and the old familiar unease that has always dogged me began to creep back. Heroin is readily available in the camp, but I resisted its pull for a while. Of course, I worried about getting re-addicted. My withdrawal symptoms had only recently, finally, abated. It had felt good to be able to say, truthfully, that I was clean, and for my parents' belief in my sobriety to have a basis in reality for once. Heroin was the thing that had led me to this place. Was I really going to toss away my painfully earned freedom from addiction and go back to the sorry state I'd been in when I was arrested? But I figured I'd deal with that issue later. *Right now, it's going to be great and feel really good. I deserve it. Look at everything I've gone through. The Garcia case has me extremely stressed, and the heroin will help with my anxiety. I'm going to finish up my time at Lewisburg with nine months of drug treatment anyway, so what does it matter if in the meantime I use something to take the edge off? I've only used heroin to right a chemical imbalance in my brain, to medicate away my intense social anxiety, and now I'm expected to spend years in a hostile, captive environment with nothing to ease my discomfort? If the BOP is going to refuse to fill my legal prescription, then it's only prudent for me to take care of myself with the medicine that is available. I'll be judicious about how much I use. Anyway, I've become so disciplined in so many ways, it's okay if I backslide in this one area. I'll make sure I don't let it get out of control, so it won't be hard to quit.*

Eventually this thinking ate through my resolve like acid. So now, every afternoon when I finish my workout, I head to the bathroom, where I get high. Truth is, I'm not that conflicted about it. I'd known, in my bones, that I wasn't done with heroin.

One day I'm sweeping the Inipi area when I hear "Douglas." I look over and see Mr. Johnson, the cigar-chomping cop who I've developed a rapport with, standing outside the hedge ring at a respectful remove from the ceremonial area. He motions for me to come over.

"Douglas, you know you burned that test the other day." I'd had to give a urine sample. "It came up hot for opiates."

I make up something about my medications.

"Here's what I'm going to tell you," he says. "It may be your lucky day, 'cause it turns out the SIS guy is out of town"—SIS is the Bureau of Prisons' version of Internal Affairs—"and I don't think it's going to be something he'll worry about when he gets back." He's telling me, without telling me, that he's giving me a break this time.

25

2010: Cancer

Two weekends after her last visit, Meg drives down again from New York. She tells me she just received a call from the MCC administrator who was kind to my family, giving her a heads-up that the BOP has started an investigation into her visits with me.

Meg is laughing as she tells the story. In the past, I've reassured her that I told no one about her bringing in Xanax for me, despite my having shared some of the pills with Dave and Eddie. Now I tell her that my cellmate must have seen me with the Xanax and informed on me.

My heart is in my stomach, but I also know the prosecutors have nothing, and if Meg denies everything, we'll be fine. "I swallowed the only physical evidence they could have, Meg. That means all they have is stool pigeons looking to try to get time cut off their sentences. That's not going to hold up against your word. So you have to stick to the script."

"Of course," she says, "of course." But she's smiling. She seems to be taking the whole thing lightly. She's smart, a graduate of Columbia Law School employed by a prestigious firm, and has sat in rooms with federal agents and prosecutors. She should know the system through and through. But she comes from a strict Middle Eastern family, grew up sheltered, and is naive. She's never been in the government's crosshairs, which is a whole other ballgame. And something about our relationship makes her leave her wits at the door.

"Listen, Meg, if they come at you, they're going to try to scare you. You have to deny it. I'm going to deny it on my end."

The next evening, I call her and ask about her drive home. She interrupts: "I actually can't talk to you." She won't say why. I keep asking. Finally she says, "I thought maybe you already knew that I couldn't talk to you."

What? How would I know? I'm getting upset. "Who told you that?"

"My lawyer," she says. She starts sobbing, quietly at first, and then the sobs become a jagged, hysterical weeping.

"It's going to be okay," I say. "Meg, I promise it's going to be okay."

At the fifteen-minute mark, the call automatically disconnects.

It's not going to be okay. When federal agents get you in a room and start laying out a limited menu of options, where one choice leads to prison time and another doesn't, few people can withstand the pressure and not tell them whatever they want to know. I have little reason to think Meg won't buckle, which means that prosecutors will have new leverage to get me to testify against the Garcia brothers.

I'll soon learn that early on the morning of July 26, the day after my last visit from Meg, FBI agents knocked on the door of her apartment in Chelsea and handed her a target letter. Prosecutors then played for her the recordings of our phone sex, including her thunderous orgasms. Within days, she told them everything. As a result of her cooperation, she won't be charged criminally, and she'll get to hold on to her law license.

Back in my cube, I open my locker and pull a can off a six-pack of Coke. Prison contraband is the art of hiding things in plain sight. Since Sebastian works in the metal shop, he has modified a couple of soda cans so that the tops screw on and off. We keep them in the six-pack tabs they came in, and they look like they've never been opened. I unscrew the lid from one and pull out a plastic bag with a few items in it, then grab a cigarette lighter attached with a magnet to the underside of my bed frame and head for a bathroom stall.

There, I balance my makeshift works on my lap: a small square of foil cut from a larger sheet from the kitchen, a short length of hard plastic tube razored from a ballpoint pen, and the pen's cap. I carefully unfold a bindle of heroin and dip the pen cap into the powder, then tap it out onto the square of foil. Putting the plastic straw between my lips, I ignite the lighter under the foil, and as the heroin vaporizes I suck it all into my lungs, holding it long enough that by the time I release my breath, nothing remains to give off an odor.

There's no way I'll have to testify. No way. Right?

A few weeks later, as I head back to my job after lunch, a guy from my softball team comes up to me. "Hey, Cam," he says, "I'm really sorry about your father."

"What are you talking about?"

"His throat."

"What?"

"Maybe I'm wrong, sorry," he says, raising his hands and backing away.

When I reach the administration building, I see my work over-seer, a Queens native who introduces himself to people as Turbo but is universally known as Shmedium, in honor of the too-tight, small/medium T-shirt he was wearing when he self-surrendered.

"Cameron," Shmedium says, "I'm really sorry about your father's cancer."

"What?"

As soon as my shift ends, I go to my bunk, open one of the Coke cans, and pull out the burner flip-phone Sebastian and I share.

I call Dad, but he doesn't answer.

I call Erin. She answers on the first ring.

"I'm so sorry about your father," she says.

"What the fuck is going on?"

"He has Stage Four throat cancer. He didn't tell you?"

"No!"

"It's on *People*'s website."

I try Dad several more times. Later in the day, he finally answers.

Dad, Dylan, and Carys visiting me at Lewisburg.

"Hey Cam, how's it going, buddy?"

"Were you going to tell me?"

There's a pause.

"I was going to," he says. "I'm sorry, the press found out before I expected them to. I didn't want to worry you."

I'm really scared. His cancer is far along, and though he says he's been told he has an 80 percent chance of recovery, the other 20 percent is what I fixate on. I've seen other inmates whiling away their sentences as the people they love most die on the outside. Often the relationships are fraught and unresolved, and they never get the chance to make things right. I'm scared that will be my story too. I already know that when I get out of prison, and have another chance,

I'm going to live my life differently. But I'm worried that Dad will die thinking of me as the failure who didn't live up to expectations.

In the evening, I'm talking to Sebastian about the news when he says, "Dude, have you cried about it?"

"I haven't cried since I was arrested," I say. "About anything."

"For real? I cried for two hours yesterday about, like, missing my mom's pork chops."

"Yeah, no, it's disturbing. I want to cry. I know I should cry. I'm pretty sentimental. I used to have no problem crying. I'd get choked up watching a puppy chow commercial. I don't know what's going on."

There's no shame in crying in prison. There's a lot to cry about, and it's not looked down upon. But it's like my tear ducts have stopped working.

"You know I love you, bro," Sebastian says, punching me in the arm, "but I didn't realize how fucked up you are."

When softball season ends, in late summer, flag football season begins. We all receive a copy of the game regulations, which dictate no body contact, but flag football at Lewisburg is basically tackle football. Players hit, and hit hard. With the huge weight room here, some inmates are enormous, and most of them seem to have signed up for the league. When I tell Sebastian and our friends Dash and Black that I'm going to play, Dash says, "Are you crazy?" Black says, "Bro, they're going to be gunning for you twice as hard."

I'm the token white guy on my six-man team, and my teammates address me as Hollywood. I play wide receiver and cornerback, and opposing teams take to tossing the ball to the huge running backs on sweeps in my direction. Once in the open field, they put their heads down and charge, but I stand my ground, digging in and making the hit, sometimes clinging to them as they drag me down the field. I'm not trying to hurt anyone, just trying to establish myself as a kid who isn't a pussy. Often I grab the flag. Sometimes I get run over. My friends are right. Nearly every game, someone breaks something or gets a concussion. I'm really lucky I don't get hurt.

One day, I'm emptying trash in the administration building when a C.O. who's been talking up the warden's secretary gestures out the window. A busful of penitentiary-bound convicts is rolling past. The C.O. says, "See those guys? You guys are all right. Those are the bad guys."

I think about the "bad guys" all the time. Almost daily, we hear flash-bang grenades detonate behind the wall of the penitentiary

Flag football at Lewisburg.

when a couple of inmates start fighting in a rec cage. I think about what makes me different from a bad guy. Does being a "good guy" mean being a coward?

I saw how my cubie Gavin garnered a certain level of respect because he'd come from a low-security. One afternoon after a softball game, I'm griping about the hardships of doing time. An old-timer named John, who's in on a drug beef and is always shuffling around doing David Blaine–style card tricks, says, "Have you ever been in a Low, Cameron?"

He rasps this, actually, because he drinks a lot of vodka and smokes like a fucking stack, though on the softball diamond he gives the ball a good whack and makes an effort to run the bases, and supposedly back in the day he was an amazing baseball player.

"Have you ever been in a Low, Cameron?"

"No."

"Yeah, you're not in prison right now. You're never going to be in prison. You're at this camp. And that's where you belong."

I can feel my face burning red. But is he right?

For all my work toward bettering myself, I'm still somewhat enamored of the prison lifestyle and haven't come fully to terms with what's going on and where I am—or what the ramifications of all this will be, and the taint it may leave on my family and on me, for the rest of my life. I haven't evolved that far.

A few weeks after Dad's cancer made the news, I get a letter from Alex, my old trainer and friend who was an informant in my case. His letter is a mix of self-justification and apology. I'm torn about what he did. I understand his reasoning, but it's hard to fully absolve someone who had a direct hand in putting me in prison. And what Alex did to me was a lot worse than my unreliable and minimal cooperation. Right?

Every day, I rue my decision to cooperate. It was the pragmatic option, the path counseled by family and my lawyers. It may even have been, in the eyes of conventional morality, the correct route. But it required me to violate some of my most strongly held convictions, about loyalty and friendship and the taking of responsibility, and my decision has tortured me ever since. I don't expect everyone to under-stand, but I believe a person should bear the consequences of his own decisions and mistakes, and shouldn't be the cause of someone else getting punished.

I have a nagging dread, informed by occasional calls from Nick De Feis, that the Garcias, against all legal advice, are going to take their case to trial. If I have to testify against them, it will overturn my entire calculus for my plea deal, which was that I could enjoy the sentenc-ing benefits of cooperation without having to deliver the goods. I've already paid a price for the deal, since my supposedly confidential agreement was broadcast in the media. But what if I just refuse to testify?

Mom is having a rough go of it. A magazine runs an article about her titled "Portrait of a Hollywood Momster." It's a terrible thing, and she's understandably devastated. I tell her I can empathize, having had my own experience with press distortions, and remind her that the peo-ple who are close to her know who she really is—a great mother and a lovely, smart, inspirational woman.

Dad calls my cell phone a few times to talk, breaking down every so often. It seems like he doesn't have anyone to do that with, and as frustrated and guilty as I feel that I can't be with him, I'm glad he feels comfortable opening up to me in this way. He visits with Dylan and Carys right before he starts treatment for his cancer, and then again in late October when his treatment is done. I've never seen a body change so dramatically in such a short time. It looks like a gust of wind could blow him over. For the first time, I feel like I have some understanding of what cancer survivors go through, of the will to sur-vive required to get through the ordeal of radiation and chemo.

26

2010–2011: Night Runner

I'm settling into my life at Lewisburg. Unit 2, being farther from the administration building and closer to the fields that unfurl toward the compound's perimeter, is the camp's Khyber Pass, the point of entry for smuggling operations. The grounds crew isn't the only group bringing stuff in. Unit 2 is also the starting block for a reckless sprint off campus, which a handful of inmates make from time to time.

It's rare for an inmate simply to run away on these trips, because everyone at the camp is going home soon enough, so the incentive to escape is low. But some guys who make the night run go to hotels. They always carry a cell phone, so if they're found missing back on the cellblock, they can get a warning call. If that happens, some guys just don't come back. Inevitably, they are caught. But the success–fail ratio of the runners is favorable enough that to me it's worth the gamble. One night, I join them.

I put on dark green army fatigues normally reserved for the work cadre behind the penitentiary wall, which I've borrowed from a friend who works in the prison laundry, and lie in my bunk under the covers until midnight count is done. As soon as the cops leave the unit, I speedwalk to the back door, where there's a fire escape, and where an inmate named David, who has dark black skin and is a veteran of these missions, is waiting for me.

Though the camp has no fences, a guard truck makes regular circuits of the perimeter, and the penitentiary's front tower spotlights include the fields we'll cross in their sweep. We have to time our run carefully. It's a good mile to the nearest point with car access, and we bound across the softball diamond to the low outfield fence, jump it, then duck and wait for the truck to pass. The grass is tall this time of year, so we have good cover as we make the sprint to the tree line. The wind blowing in my long hair is exhilarating, a small sip of freedom.

While I'm running, Sebastian is on the phone with Erin, who has been waiting at a nearby Weis Market, and giving her turn-by-turn directions to our rendezvous spot. When we reach the last field's edge, David leads the way through a stand of trees to a barn near the road. Suddenly, there she is.

Erin is sitting in our BMW with the lights off. I haven't seen her in more than a year. It's so good to see her, and we have sex in the back seat. It's quick, because we don't have a lot of time, but it's loving, and amazing, probably the best sex we've ever had. I love her for having gone through with this whole plan and showing up; it's very risky, and not a lot of people would do it, and it shows me she really cares and is willing to go the distance for me. She hands me the bag of goodies she's brought me, which include a new pair of white Chucks, as well as deli meats and bread for sandwiches. We kiss goodbye, and then I begin the mile dash back to my unit.

Every prison sells different sneakers, so you can get away with wearing brands that aren't sold by the commissary at the place you're at. Some guys push it, wearing $200 Air Maxes, but the next day I proudly wear my fresh $30 Chucks around the compound, together with socks pulled to my knees, West Coast style. They feel like home and get me some compliments. "Nice kicks, Hollywood," I hear often.

On birthdays, we do what we can to make friends feel special. Everyone in prison has a hustle to make money. There are guys on the compound who make cheesecake using commissary ingredients—every maker has his own slightly different technique—and others who make

Dad and me.

pizza that's really good, by prison standards. When I turn thirty-two in December 2010, Sebastian arranges a cheesecake and pizza to celebrate. But his big gift to me is a chair he designed in the metal shop. I'm always leaning back in my chair, tipping it up on the hind legs and lifting the front legs off the ground, so Sebastian has made me a chair with an extended back and legs that stretch forward. Kind of a customized foldout chair. It's pretty cool.

For Christmas I send Dad a miniature rocking chair, with a picture frame for a back, that I buy from one of the art hustlers–in–residence. *"The amazing thing,"* I write to Dad, *"is what it's made of and how it's made . . . these are all chip bags from commissary fitted together tastefully and held together with dental floss."*

The greatest present I could receive comes in January, when Dad learns that his tumor is gone. He seems to have licked cancer. And he has gained back the thirty-two pounds he lost during treatment.

Sure enough, eight months into my time at Lewisburg, Nick calls and says I have to come to New York to testify. I'm angry, given his repeated assurances that this turn of events was all but impossible, but I have a new clarity about what I'm willing to do and not do going forward. Nick, my parents, my friends—none of them has to do my time. I have to do it. And I'll have to live with my actions for the rest of my life.

"Nick," I say. "I'm not going to testify."

There's a pause on Nick's end of the line.

"This is what you agreed to, Cameron."

"No, you told me all I had to do was talk about my role. You said I'd only have to say what I did and how I did it, and that would be enough." This is substantively true (there are so many people I never said a word about) and technically untrue (I signed papers agreeing to testify), but right now I'm more interested in focusing on Nick's deficiencies than in recognizing that I rolled the dice and lost.

"Cameron, you can't back out of this deal. You agreed to it. And my reputation is on the line here." He'd convinced the D.A.'s office, in an unusual arrangement, to give me the deal before I'd really cooperated.

"Fuck your reputation, Nick. You put yourself in this situation. I know what you told me."

"You have to do this, Cameron. They'll cancel your cooperation agreement, and you'll get ten years at least."

"Goodbye, Nick."

Dad calls. "Just come to New York and meet with the prosecutors," he says. It's not like I have a choice. Prosecutors have the power to move me, whether I agree or don't. I could go kicking and screaming in five-point restraints, but I'd still have to go. Two days before Christmas (not a coincidence, I'm sure), I'm put in transit from Lewisburg. I spend New Year's Eve in a transitional cell at Canaan and arrive in Manhattan in January.

A few days after returning to MCC, I'm taken to the courthouse for a hearing. When I'm led into the bull pen, a holding room with more than a dozen orange-suited, shackled inmates waiting to be called to testify in various proceedings, I immediately see Gabriel and Carlos, my former friends and suppliers and the defendants I'm here, supposedly, to testify against as an adverse witness. It's a major BOP fuckup to have put us in the same bullpen. We warily exchange greetings.

"Look," I tell them, "from what I understand, they're going to give you a plea bargain of five years. Take it. Don't put me in a position where I have to testify, because I will."

I won't. Or at least, I won't testify to what I said in my initial confession. But I need them to believe that I will, because I want them to see that taking the deal is their only real choice. If they take the deal, I can avoid having to refuse to testify, which would almost certainly add years to my sentence.

We speak for forty-five minutes. It's a weight off my shoulders and heart to see them face-to-face and to explain myself. They're disappointed and angry, but I believe they also understand. They're as surprised as I am that they're here, given the seemingly minimal evidence the government has against them. I think that's also why, against all reason, they're determined to go to trial. They don't understand what they're up against, just like I didn't in the beginning. They haven't accepted that there's a reason why 97 percent of federal drug defendants plead guilty.

On January 15, the *New York Post* runs a story headlined "Douglas Son Set to Sing." My cellie is a Dominican general who's been here for years cooperating in a major cocaine-smuggling case, so I'm not worried about him, but other inmates could be a problem. Once again, I wrestle with extreme anxiety, worried about whether I'm doing the right thing. I don't have the highest respect for my own decision making, given some of the choices I've made, yet here I am going against what the people who love me are telling me to do, and what the expensive professionals they've hired are telling me to do. It's scary. But I find some relief in the stubborn resolve of the decision I'm making. The alternative, doing what everyone else wants me to do, is simply unbearable to me.

After I tell the prosecutors that I won't testify, Nick and Dad start riding me hard about it. Then I get a reprieve: the trial is adjourned, because Gabriel's own lawyer, citing the irrationality of his refusal to take a plea deal, has asked the court to order a psychological evaluation. I'm sent back to Lewisburg.

In certain ways, daily life improves. After months of trying to get a different job, I'm finally switched to the grounds crew; we mow grass and whack weeds, but at least I'm outside all day, and I can work when I want as long as I keep my assigned area in good shape. And my status has perceptibly shifted. Guys on my unit who'd kept their distance until now seem reassured by my return, since it means I must not have testified. If I had, they'd surely have read about it.

I take solace in my decision, but the prosecutors ratchet up their pressure, threatening to indict me on new charges over the Xanax that

With Sebastian, Black, and Dash at Lewisburg.

Meg Salib brought me. As my stress level rises, I start letting myself do a bump of heroin a littler earlier in the day. It feels nice to do one at two o'clock and another at six. It's only temporary, I tell myself, during this particularly anxious period. After a while, I add a third little bump right after we break down the sweat lodge and before the four o'clock stand-up count.

Inspired by Sebastian's laminated list of archangels, I pay an inmate named Pat, who has a contraband tattoo gun and real tattoo ink, to inscribe thirteen of their names on my ribcage. I also have him ink a teardrop on each of my index fingers, in honor of my continuing inability to shed them.

One night, when I'm complaining about my lawyers and the Garcias' stupid choices and the judge who sentenced me and the prosecutors who are pressuring me, I crook my index fingers around my eyes, so that the tears are visible to Sebastian, and say, "Wah, poor me."

Sebastian laughs, then laughs harder.

"Dude," he says, "you know those are backward, right?"

"What?"

I look down and study the teardrops closely for the first time. Instead of being shaped like commas, they look like Cs. *Motherfucker.*

The next day, I make Pat start inking a second set of tears on my middle fingers, facing the right way.

My recklessness increases. If there's a correlation between my stress level and my willingness to take risks, it's not conscious. Some people follow all the major rules in prison, then get out and can't follow the rules of society. I may break some of the rules in prison, but I know that when I get out I'm going to really make the best of it and not fuck up. The rules I do break in here are mainly to establish myself. In prison, you want people to think you're a little crazy, a little aggressive.

Ramón, a kid from Elizabeth, New Jersey, who sells me my heroin, has a friend with an escort service and arranges for us to bring a prostitute into the camp. Her name is Adriana, and Ramón says she's "a pretty li'l redbone." Right after the 9:30 p.m. count one night, David and I and a third guy make the run to get her.

Her driver gets lost finding the barn. Finally Adriana arrives, with bags of contraband we're also bringing in. She's wearing a sweatsuit and a beanie. By the time we start back with her toward the unit, it's dangerously close to midnight, when the next count will start. As we run, carrying the bags, she struggles to keep up. Just as we approach the back of the unit, we see cops coming down the path in front.

I think I'm done for. We hug the outside wall, with Adriana and the bags of stuff. She's obviously terrified as we walk through the darkened unit, where the other inmates, who can hardly believe what they're seeing, stand on tiptoes and stare. "I ain't fuckin' with y'all niggas," she says to them as we lead her to the bathroom, where we hide her in a stall with her feet up on the toilet. I race back to my cube, toss the bags under the bunk bed, and jump under the covers just as a cop comes by with his flashlight.

After count finishes and the cops leave, Ramón is with Adriana first. Then I go to be with her. But I'm having trouble getting hard. In the bags we ran back tonight, there's a good little knot of heroin for me, and this is how I know how sick I am: I am more excited about that than about sex with this hooker.

She's sweet and tries to help me. "Here, Papi, let's try something else," she says, taking me by the hand into a bathroom stall. But all I want to do is get back to my cube to get the dope. After we're done, David runs her back to her ride near the perimeter, and I finally get high.

In late August, Nick calls again. The Garcia brothers' trials are really happening. I've been subpoenaed as a witness, and I have to testify or risk being indicted on new charges.

I'm bussed back to New York. I don't know how I'm going to navigate this. My whole life, I've been able to land on my feet, talk my way out of situations, play this side and that side, *make it work*. This time, I know I'm fucked. I just don't realize yet quite how fucked.

27

2011: Badge of Courage

On my latest return to MCC, I've brought provisions: Suboxone, OxyContin, and Percocet, all plastic-wrapped and double-bagged and lodged in my lower bowel. "Nice to meet you, bro," I tell my new cellie. "I need to take a shit, okay?" It's a funny way to make a first impression, but he nods and steps out onto the range. I string my bedsheet to the top of the bunk, erecting a privacy curtain between the toilet and the rest of the cell, and settle in for the big push.

Even with layers of packaging, drugs often end up smelling like shit, and a lot of effort and thinking goes into transporting drugs between prisons while minimizing stank. If you show up on a yard with drugs that smell like ass, you won't be able to get as good a price for them. No one wants the aroma of your shit on the bump of heroin in their throat. The best outer packaging is latex, which you can only get from a cop. Even then, some guys just make the stinkiest shits, and their drugs still smell bad. It's a real problem. If you're smoking a joint, and every time you take a rip you taste that shit, it totally takes away from this small piece of enjoyment you're trying to eke out for yourself in a miserable environment.

I have to be stealthy about using my drugs. I don't know anything about my new cellie, and I wait until he's on the top bunk, and I'm on the bottom, before swallowing a pill. This time at MCC, I'm celled on the cadre unit, on the fifth floor, which does all the maintenance work. It's easier for people to visit me here, and it's good to see my family and friends. But the days are awkward and uncomfortable. At least during my first stay here I could say I was awaiting trial; this time around there's no reason for me to be here except to cooperate, and everyone knows it. Half or more of them are doing the same thing, but they have the luxury of being able to tell whatever bullshit story they want, because their cases don't get reported on in the *New York Post*.

I sleep a lot. I work out a bunch of times with a sweet Albanian kid named Emil, who's cooperating in a major case, which he admits to me. But I'm starting to keep more to myself. I cell with a guy who works in the kitchen and has a hustle fulfilling orders from the supplies there, including eggs that he lowers on a string into the ducting, through a vent in our cell, to deliver to his customers.

During the run-up to the Garcia brothers' trials, the prosecutors tell me they already have a new criminal complaint drafted, indicting me on charges of receiving contraband from Meg Salib and distributing it. They're going to file it unless I go forward with testifying against Gabriel and Carlos.

I'm dug in about not testifying, and Mom and Dad are freaking out. At this point they think that whatever the government is saying, and whatever Nick is saying, must be right. Dad sends Ben Brafman, who represented me years ago, to see me. Ben says, "Listen, Cameron, you're going to get ten years. If you stick with your cooperation agreement, you'll be out of here in a year. You don't want to be the guy watching your release date disappear behind you and you're still in prison."

I grab a book off the MCC book cart one day—Stephen Crane's *The Red Badge of Courage*—and am deeply affected. I relate to deserter–turned–flag bearer Henry Fleming's inner struggle, his fear of his own fear and his need to prove himself in battle.

After Nick negotiates an immunity agreement barring the prosecutors from using anything that comes up in my testimony against me, I reluctantly agree to get on the stand.

Carlos Garcia's trial comes first, on October 3. Carlos's lawyer, antici-
pating my testimony, spends part of his opening statement discredit-
ing me. "Once upon a time there was a child born to a well-known
family . . . Cameron Douglas is a manipulator . . . one of the most
cunning, wily individuals" the jury will ever encounter. He notes the
unusual nature of my deal with prosecutors, where I was sentenced
before my cooperation was completed, implying that I received special treatment. When I'm called to the stand, he grills me about the
agreement.

He tries to paint me as a callous sociopath who was indifferent to
the potential repercussions for Meg Salib when she brought me the
Xanax. I say that my feelings for Meg were real, and that while it was
my idea for her to bring me the Xanax, I didn't press her to do it.

Meg was only bringing me anxiety medication that I'd been legally
prescribed and improperly denied; she was very upset on my behalf,
and angry at the Bureau of Prisons. Erin was only bringing me heroin
for the same reason. But to hear myself described as a manipulative
master sociopath, to know that I've sunk so low that this is how some
people might view me, is sobering. It feels like the lawyer is talking
about somebody else. In a way, he is. Addiction *is* sociopathic. Prison,
too, encourages survival behavior more than empathy. Could I have
encouraged Meg, or Erin, or both of them, not to take such a risk?
Sure, but from where I was sitting, and with everything I was going
through, I wasn't about to turn away someone's help. The goal of any
convict is to get what you can get, to get what you need, to open those
pathways to the outside world.

I know what the lawyer is doing, and when he tries to impeach my
original statement to the DEA, I seize the chance to distance myself
from it. He asks whether, when the DEA arrested me, they told me I
could face life imprisonment, and I acknowledge that they did. I say
that Carlos didn't supply any of the serious quantities of drugs I talked
about in my original statement to the DEA. If I said otherwise right
after my arrest, well, I was detoxing from heroin at the time.

I see Erin for ten minutes in the courtroom. After I'm taken out, she'll testify that she only learned this morning, from the *New York Post*, about me and Meg Salib and the Xanax. She's humiliated and heartbroken, and I feel like shit.

Gabriel's trial is next, but after testifying as unhelpfully as possible against Carlos, I've made up my mind that I won't go back on the stand. This is my opportunity to get right with myself. I feel too guilty about implicating them. I'm responsible for my situation. I'm ashamed by my early cooperation. At least I can start to climb out of the reputation hole I've dug for myself. I meet with the prosecutor and Nick, and I tell them flat-out that I won't testify against Gabriel. They leave angry, but I feel only relief. Now that I've made my decision, a weight has lifted.

My heroin habit, at this point, is three or four times a day, but I'm doing much smaller amounts than when I was on the street. Six weeks after my arrival from Lewisburg, the stash of contraband opiates I brought with me is running low, but MCC is flooded with heroin. It now seems bizarre to me that during my first stint here we were so unsuccessful at obtaining it. On a Saturday, Manuel, an ex-boxer from the Bronx, brings me some bindles.

The next day, in the early afternoon, I'm sitting at the table in my cell, finishing off the dope. I've hung a towel over the small window in the door, just as I would if I were using the toilet. Guards tend to respect that, but one suddenly enters my cell. I try sliding my left hand into my sweat pants, rubbing the heroin residue out of the bindle, but the cop notices the movement.

"What's in your left hand?"

"Nothing."

"Stand up and put your hands on the wall."

Fucking Manuel tipped them off about the heroin he sold me, to gain the favor of his own prosecutors. This is the kind of shady shit that happens in here all the time.

The guard gives me a pat-down. In my left pocket he finds the small piece of paper, inside a piece of plastic. "What's this?" I don't say anything. He starts looking around the cell more carefully. In a bag of Q-tips near the table he finds an orange speck, the last of my Suboxone, one-eighth of a pill.

He field-tests the Suboxone and it turns purple, falsely indicating that it's heroin. There's no powder left on the paper, but he field-tests it anyway, and it turns blue-pink, falsely indicating that it's cocaine. I'm arrested. The guard says I have to give a urine sample, and at 2:17 p.m. he takes me to a bathroom, hands me a cup, and stands there while I do my business. They find traces of opiates in my urine. Then I'm transferred to the SHU.

When a guard comes to give me my personal property a few days later, I ask for my bottle of vitamin B, which immediately makes the cop suspicious. He takes the bottle and looks it over, unscrewing the cap and shaking up the pills inside. I breathe an inaudible sigh of relief when he puts the cap back on and hands me the bottle. There are four OxyContin pills in there, but fortunately they're the same color as the vitamin B tablets.

The Oxies cushion my withdrawal, and the best way to do hole time is with drugs like that. When you're spending twenty-three or twenty-four hours a day, seven days a week, in a tiny cell, trying to manage an extraordinary amount of stress, an OxyContin or Percocet feels awfully nice.

When I get the write-up for the "shot," as violations of prison regulations are called, I say that the orange stuff is Suboxone, which I got at Lewisburg, and that there's no way the white powder on the paper was cocaine. They assume it was heroin. I improvise a mutating story about where it came from. I got it in the television room. I got it during a church service. I found it on the floor.

Three days after the arrest, I go before Judge Berman to plead guilty to a new count of possession of a narcotic. "We're having a little too much drama here, Mr. Douglas." He asks the prosecutor to tell him what's happening. "So what does this mean?" Judge Berman asks. "You know, maybe I am naive. When I send somebody to the MCC or the MDC"—the Metropolitan Detention Center, in Brooklyn—"or Lewisburg, I have an expectation that those places are well managed, safe, that this kind of unlawful behavior doesn't go on. Is that wrong or are you all doing some investigation?"

The prosecutor says that the BOP turned the matter over to the FBI yesterday.

Judge Berman says that he's sending me to MDC, and directs that I be subjected to random urine testing.

"God knows I am sorry," I say.

My sentencing on the new charge is scheduled for December 21.

Gabriel's trial date is postponed.

At MDC, I'm put in administrative segregation, aka the SHU, pending a Unit Discipline Committee hearing for a 112—drug use—and a Disciplinary Hearing Officer (DHO) hearing for a 113—possession of drugs. I'm despondent. Next month, November, is when I was going to become eligible for the RDAP program. "You were almost to the rehab part of your incarceration and you blew it," Patsy Webb, our old family friend, writes me in a letter. As the mother of seven kids, she has never minced words. "I know that is the nature of addiction—but we have to change your mindset." She shares a list of ten affirmations for me to use for directed meditation.

My last four Oxies are gone now, and I can feel the familiar junk sickness creeping back, my third time kicking heroin. It's more bearable than the first two times, since my habit now involves much smaller quantities.

Typically, the BOP's response to my latest infraction would be negligible. At a medium- or higher-security, you might not even do hole time for it. But DHOs have an enormous amount of discretion, and I happen to draw a hard-ass.

My BOP sanctions for this bust are a version of double jeopardy. For "use of drugs," I'm sanctioned to a forty-day loss of good time credit, four months of disciplinary segregation, a one-year loss of family visits and commissary usage, and a two-year loss of all other "social" visits. Then, for "possession of drugs," I'm sanctioned to an additional forty-day loss of good time credit, an additional seven months of disciplinary segregation, an additional year's loss of family visits, and an additional loss of other social visits for another two years. I'm now looking at eleven months' solitary confinement, two years' loss of family visits, four years' loss of other visits, one year's loss of commissary, and ten months' loss of phone privileges. This is unheard of, even if you have multiple shots, and these are only my first major shots.

A lot of people are disappointed in me. A lot of people are pissed off at me. The judge is angry about Meg Salib and the Xanax. The cops are mad because I lied to them about where I got the heroin, and because of the extra heat they're now getting. I haven't heard from Dad since my bust.

If anyone's happy about this latest development, it may be the prosecutors. They were already furious over my refusal to testify against Gabriel. They couldn't undo my original sentence, and my immunity deal blocked them from pursuing the contraband charges, but the Suboxone bust, and my refusal to help with the heroin investigation, has provided them with a way to give me at least some of my time back.

Nick reaches a deal with the prosecutors. In return for my pleading guilty to possessing prohibited objects, they agree not to further prosecute me for possession of either Suboxone or heroin. The sentencing guidelines call for another twelve to twenty-four months to be added to my time. The prosecutors reveal in a court filing that they no longer plan to call me as a witness at Gabriel's trial, because now that I'm no longer cooperating with the government, I'm a "problematic witness."

For a month and a half in cell 208, in MDC's solitary unit, I have no cellmate and am allowed contact with no other prisoners. I've been deemed a danger to inmates and civilians alike; even with my lawyers, I'm allowed to talk to them only through glass.

I'm enjoying being alone, but this place is grim. There's a guy here who shits and pisses all over his cell and tries to throw it under his door at the cops. The food is terrible. Liver is in heavy rotation. I've never liked liver under the best of circumstances, and the liver here is the worst. It's inedible. I won't touch it. I ask a cop for extra bread. One morning, the portion of rice at breakfast is tiny and not fully cooked, and at lunchtime the whole range refuses to eat, screaming and cursing.

I'm in my cell early one evening when I hear scuffling sounds.

"You don't fuck with me"—hitting sounds—"I fuck *you*."

Another voice: "Get off me, what the fuck are you doing?"

"Shut the fuck up, taste my fucking dick."

More sounds. Lots of banging around, really violent.

"I fucked you."

Then a lot of quiet, heavy breathing.

It's a fight that turned into a rape.

This is the bleakest moment in the bleakest stint of all my time in prison. I think of a line from *Shantaram*: "The worst things that people do always strike at that part of us that wants to love the world." MDC is a terrible place. I'm angry at my lawyers. I'm at odds with the prosecutors, with the BOP, with the judge. I'm at odds with my parents. And I know I'm getting more prison time. A really dark feeling is sinking deep into my bones, and the rape compounds it. It's sickening, and unsettling, and feels like a harbinger of things to come. I'm not worried I'll be raped, but it's like: *This is so ugly, and it's my life right now. How did I get here?*

I can communicate with Mom and Dad only by mail. Considering what I've put them through, they are humblingly supportive.

Dad writes to me a month after my Suboxone bust.

Dear Cameron,

I must admit, I haven't written because I didn't know what to say to you. Not wanting to make you feel worse, yet at the same time unable to comprehend your actions. You were so close, yet so self-destructive. I hope through whatever counseling you can get,

and a stronger belief in a higher power, you will understand why
you continue to undermine yourself. The serenity prayer. Please.

I'm starting to numb a bit. A pervasive anger is settling in. I'm feeling the evolution that a lot of prisoners experience. It's the transformation from everyday Joe with a drug problem to convict with violent
tendencies. I'm going through the things that twist the mind and fuck
with your heart and soul. Some people break, and lose their hair and
shrivel up and look like the homeless person on the street corner.
The prison system isn't set up to provide hope or push real reform
or rehabilitation. It's built to test you and try to break your will. A lot
of my anger is self-directed, and what Dad wrote is what I'm already
thinking about myself. But I'm kind of past the Serenity Prayer at this
point. I don't have faith in God or anything else. I'm looking inward
rather than outward for strength to get through this. In that sense,
this is an important time for me. I'm developing the resolve I'll need
to endure what lies ahead.

Mom writes too:

Hawk has been talking about his big brother to his teacher at
school, they told me. Hawk said you were in trouble for having
drunk some water, without following the rules, and that he loved
and missed you very much . . . Something I was thinking about
yesterday—I was very young when I married your father. For 20
or more years, I felt as if I was always operating, or trying to at
least, in your dad's shadow. Because wherever I went that was how
I was identified, I really must admit I really hated it— It really
haunted me. I felt I was a prisoner of his name. Then one day after
being haunted by this feeling for decades and being really angry
about it, it suddenly dawned on me—what if I could let go of my
"EGO," which is false anyway, because all EGOS ARE FALSE and
NOT the true nature of who we really are! What if I could really let
go of my "Ego" and embrace the gifts that did come along with that
name and all that life entailed—the good and the bad. Nothing in
the world is all bad or all good, so I decided to focus on the good
(the gifts of the situation) and to let go of the feelings of limitation,

expectations, anger, frustration, my feelings of lack of self esteem, etc etc. Because my own emotions were holding me captive, and I was becoming my own victim of the situation. Well, life is far too short for that. Now I am building my own life—sometimes bigger steps, sometimes really small steps. However, the direction I am committed to moving is forward. PS I keep all your letters in the drawer by my bed so I can be closer to you.

Mom has always been insightful, and even wise, and the desire to form my own distinct identity, to be known for who I am rather than for my last name, is something I have in common with her. But the knowledge is the easy part. The hard part is to heal, to use the knowledge to fix yourself. I know how hard and frustrating it must be for her to keep reaching out and supporting someone who's so self-destructive. I've started noticing that when I look at my reflection in the dented pieces of glossy metal attached to my sink and toilet, I only take quick peeks. I'm not sure why, and I tell myself: "It's okay, you can stand there and stare yourself in the eyes." So I do. I stare at my features and I ask: "Is that face, or that person, capable of being loved?" I guess the answer to that is what I am afraid will be revealed if I hold my reflection for too long.

This SHU time at MDC is something of a turning point for me. It's now, when I have little else to fill the hours, that I assign myself a formalized curriculum in earnest. Every day, I write—journaling at first. Every day, I do thirty to forty-five minutes of meditation. Taking advantage of my single cell, I become almost scientific in my masturbation practices. Afraid that the next several years of disuse will destroy my libido, I jerk off twice daily, without fail.

My reading becomes more systematized, so that I always have three books going at once: a beach read, a self-help book, and a literary classic. Erin, who seems to have forgiven me, sends me *Chicken Soup for the Prisoner's Soul*. Dad sends me a book of Stephen Crane's stories. Mom sends me the *Odyssey* and two books of Crane's poetry.

I've always been kind of put off by poetry, because it has never really clicked with me. Now I start reading the Crane books and I'm touched and inspired, and finally I get it: So this is what poetry can do to people. This is why historically poetry was such a big deal, why in the past poets were the rock stars of their time, why poetry is taught in school. Lines as simple as *"A slant of sun on dull brown walls / A forgotten sky of bashful blue,"* from a Crane poem, stir me. I start playing around with writing poems of my own, increasingly using my journaling time to write verse. I content myself with the tiny marvels of everyday life: When I go to the hot tap with my packet of coffee, and the water is slightly warmer than usual, I enjoy my cup of coffee that much more.

The guards put someone in the cell with me, and we have a disagreement over I don't remember what, and one day he asks to be moved, and then I'm alone again. I won't take another cellie. The cops come to my door and say, "Cuff up!" and I refuse. MDC is getting increasingly crowded, but I continue to buck, saying I won't share my cell. Then one day, a cop I have a rapport with says, "Hey, will you trust me on something? We have a kid we want to put with you. He's quiet, he reads a lot, he's mellow, it would really help me out. If it doesn't work, we'll take him out."

"Okay," I say.

Aracelio is nice and gay and Dominican and likes to read, and we have a good rapport. He has a little crush on me, and he gives me the first massage I've had in a long time.

With my resentencing coming up, Mom and Dad once again come together for my sake, cosigning a letter to the judge: *". . . We love him dearly with all our hearts and feel in part responsible for the terrible situation he now finds himself in."*

It's now November 2011. If the Suboxone bust hadn't happened, and I hadn't refused to testify against Gabriel, I'd almost certainly have made it into RDAP after returning to Lewisburg, which would have meant I'd be released to a halfway house in August 2012, with supervised release ending February 2013. Now, if I don't win my BOP appeals, I'll be in solitary until October 2012. And even if I get a time-served sentence, I'll be in prison until February 24, 2014. And that's a real "if."

My legal team and doctors argue to the judge that my heroin addiction, and the BOP's refusal to fill valid drug prescriptions for me, should be taken into account in my sentencing, as should the sanctions already handed down by the BOP. They note, too, that the length of my SHU time has made me ineligible for RDAP. They point out that only 4 percent of the 3,500 drug misconduct charges handled by the BOP each year result in investigations, much less prosecutions, and that the 4 percent tends to be very serious cases.

The probation department is recommending a sentence of 366 days, the low end of the guidelines range. The prosecutors—unhappy with my refusal to testify against Gabriel, and citing inmate and cooperating-witness reports that I was "seen snorting substances" during my first stint at MCC, and claiming that more recently I "misled the government" about how I obtained heroin—are asking for a sentence of twenty-four months, the upper limit of the guidelines range.

The only silver lining of this disaster is that the prosecution has now documented my withdrawal from cooperating with them.

On December 13, 2011, I turn thirty-three. Happy fucking birthday to me.

On December 20, the night before my resentencing, I meditate over the blue, prison-issue shirt I'm going to wear, willing good vibes into it.

When I enter the courtroom the next morning, I see Mom sitting with Tiffany, her goddaughter who lived with us for a year when I was growing up. Dad isn't here. Maybe he's not in New York. I know he's angry and frustrated and disappointed with me, and upset at the whole situation. My biggest fear has been that he'll give up on me, and I can't help wondering: Is this it? Is this the end of our relationship?

Shortly after 10 a.m., the proceedings begin. I plead guilty to one count of "possession of prohibited objects while an inmate of a federal prison." The government says that it won't be calling me as a witness at Gabriel's trial. I address Judge Berman, talking about my addiction struggle, my lapses. I throw myself on his mercy, asking for medical help instead of punishment. "I feel ashamed," I say. "I feel defeated." I guess Nick is trying to win me some sympathy points, but it doesn't feel great to hear my own lawyer say, "We are dealing with a very damaged individual." I've never thought of myself as very damaged, or even mildly damaged. I'm reckless. I've been viciously addicted to drugs. I have never felt that I'm a piece of bruised fruit.

"What is really important," Berman interjects, "is not to get warm and fuzzy."

I don't know whether Judge Berman dislikes me personally, or the Meg Salib thing has pushed him over the edge, or he feels like a chump for giving me a short sentence the first time, or he wants to demonstrate that he won't go easy on someone with a famous last name, or what, but he is pissed. He tells the courtroom: "Mr. Douglas . . . not to oversimplify, seems to have blown the biggest opportunity of his life." He says I obstructed justice.

Even the prosecutors have argued that any obstruction is mitigated by the "responsibility credit" I should receive in a sentence calculation, because of my immediate guilty plea to the latest offense. But Judge Berman rejects the responsibility credit. He's angry that the government and defense "swept under the rug" the Salib episode, in his view. He says of me, "He never, as I understand it, testified against his suppliers pursuant to a cooperation agreement; rather, he testified against [Carlos Garcia] . . . pursuant to an immunity compulsion order."

Judge Berman has presided over the trials of terrorists and child abusers. But he declares now that he has never "encountered a defendant who has so recklessly and wantonly and flagrantly and criminally acted in as destructive and . . . manipulative a fashion as Cameron Douglas has." As he says these things, I find them hard to believe. It's like he's talking about someone else. *Really, I'm the worst you've ever encountered? This is insane.*

Then he hands down my sentence. He's departing upward from the guidelines range and adding fifty-four months to my existing time—four years and six months—essentially giving me back all the time he lopped off my original sentence. Plus another three years of supervised release. He does recommend that the BOP immediately lift restrictions on family visits, and that I be placed somewhere where I can receive drug and dental treatment, and that I be put in an RDAP program.

As I leave the courtroom, I look over at Mom and Tiff and smile and wink to let them know I'm okay and am going to be okay. But Mom is about to cry, and in fact I'm devastated. I didn't see this coming. Outside the courtroom, I sit in a holding cell trying to digest what's happened. I'm in shock. My lawyers are in shock.

The sentence is so draconian that the *New York Times* will later call it "one of the harshest ever handed down by a federal judge for drug possession for an incarcerated prisoner," and two dozen drug-addiction groups and doctors will file an appellate brief on my behalf, arguing that I'm a classic case of "someone suffering from untreated opioid dependence." One of the signers tells the *Times,* "What the judge has imposed has zero benefits for the community and has staggering consequences for society."

It seems like it takes forever to get back to my cell at MDC. After waiting in the holding cell next to Judge Berman's courtroom, I'm shuffled in handcuffs through a glaringly lit concrete tunnel under the courthouse to a set of larger holding cells across the street, the bull pens. There are more inmates here. I lie down on a bench and pull my top over my head. I'm almost dizzy as I try to process what's happened. My sentence was just doubled from five to ten years. Overwhelmed, I pass out.

———

Eventually it's time to get on a bus to Brooklyn, and we roll past store-fronts gaily decorated for Christmas. At the MDC in Sunset Park, I go through another two hours of being strip-searched and processed and trading-out my blue court outfit for a bright orange jumpsuit before I get back to my cell.

When I step onto the range, there's water everywhere. Inmates with mops are wading through inches of water. Other inmates are screaming and banging on doors. A bunch of guys have been "bucking," clogging their toilets to flood their cells, as happens from time to time in the SHU. I'm confident that Aracelio is dealing with the flood. There are no drawers or shelves in our cell, so I keep my books, letters, photographs, writing, and legal paperwork under the bed, on the ground. I'm sure that Aracelio will have plugged the crack under the door and elevated our belongings above the waterline.

When we reach my cell, I see through the slit of window that Aracelio is lying on the top bunk, passed out. I glance down and see water everywhere. My books and legal papers and my own writing are still on the floor, ruined. So are my photos and magazines. Aracelio is in such a deep sleep that the cops have to bang on the door a few times before he hears them and jumps down, clearly surprised by the water.

When I enter the cell, I'm enraged. I'm feeling unstable and am scared by the violent thoughts I'm having toward Aracelio. But I also know he genuinely slept through the mini-riot. He sleeps with ear-plugs. This whole mess isn't his fault. It's just one more time when, to my self-pitying way of seeing things, the shitstorm that follows me has covered me in shit.

Aracelio immediately starts tearing up a bedsheet into strips for clotheslines, and hanging my pictures and papers on them to try to salvage something. As he does that, I lay down on my rack. I feel like something's breaking apart inside of me. In the eighteen months since my arrest, I've never cried. Now I come very close.

Last night, I lay here in a spiritual frame of mind, meditating on the mundane and appealing to some higher power, almost talking to God. Now I say to myself: *That's the last time I'm reaching out to anyone or anything to ask for help.*

28

2012: One of the Bad Guys

While I wait to be designated to my next prison, I spend another Christmas behind bars. The BOP hands out big bags of candy. Inmates try to stave off depression and forget that they're not with their families by getting together to cook meals and conjure some version of merriment.

I kill the time by reading Charles Dickens's *A Tale of Two Cities,* which is partly about the fallout from a man's eighteen-year prison sentence. With books, the fatter the better. I have nothing but time on my hands, and when I'm enjoying what I'm reading, I want it to go on and on.

MDC is so poorly heated that I'm cold even on relatively warm days. On New Year's Eve, the cell is so freezing that my hands are shades of white and blue. I think about my family, together and celebrating. Mom is with Hawk and Hudson and Imara. Dad and Catherine are spending Christmas in Panama, celebrating Johnny Pigozzi's sixtieth birthday on his private island. Erin and our dogs are in Connecticut, visiting her sister's family. Picturing them all lifts my spirits. At least the people I love are happy.

Aracelio and I jam sheets under our cell door. In the box, on New Year's, there are always inmates "popping bottles"—setting off sprinklers for shits and giggles—and the rise of cell phones in prison has only encouraged this trend. Inmates like to text pictures to their friends on the street, showing that they're doing big things inside.

I'm in a foul mood, preoccupied with the doubling of my sentence and the harsh BOP sanctions, and not thinking straight. There's a cop here, a short, fat, Hispanic woman in her thirties, who's always flirting with the black inmates. Every time she comes on the unit, someone yells, "Movie's on!" and she bends over suggestively, like she's picking something up. Now I tell Aracelio that I'm just going to ask her if she wants to have sex.

When she makes her rounds, and is walking past our cell, I call out to her through the cell-door window, a vertical slit of shatterproof plastic. "Listen, I don't know you that well, but it's New Year's Eve. Why don't you just pop this door before you leave, take me in back, and let me fuck you."

"What?"

I repeat myself.

"First of all, you're not the right color. Second of all, you're way out of line. Go to sleep."

In the morning, I'm mortified. I think I just wanted a story to tell, or something to remember this New Year's by. I'm pretty sure I didn't offend the cop, but I make a resolution for 2012: *The stunt I pulled last night will be the last stupid and reckless thing I do.*

I doubt I'll get a shot, and as the day turns to dusk, it looks like I'm right—guards have twenty-four hours to write you up—but then a lieutenant comes down to the unit. He walks past my cell, then doubles back and reads out my violation. "Is this right? Is this yours?" Even he is shocked that I'd be getting this shot. I make up an excuse: I'd made a bet with another inmate on the range that I'd do it, and I'm a man of my word. "All right," he says, shaking his head, and walks away. It's a 200-series shot. Medium serious. Better than a 100-series shot, like killing; worse than a 300-series shot, like insolence toward a staff member.

A few days later, I'm bussed back to Lewisburg, but this time to the Big House—the supermax penitentiary behind the ominous wall—

which, during my months in the minimum-security camp beside it, I'd looked up at, thankful not to be there. When the bus turns onto the familiar prison grounds, I think back to the day when I was in the Lewisburg administration building, on sanitation detail, and a bus like the one I'm on now arrived transporting convicts. I remember the cop saying to me, "You guys are all right. Those are the bad guys." Now, one and a half years later, I'm one of those guys. I know I'm not a bad guy. But I know that's how people must be starting to see me now. As a bad guy, one of the dangerous ones. When the bus pulls up outside the wall, my name is called.

I'll only be here for a few days this time, and I'm in the SHU, so I don't interact with the general population. A week later, I'm moved to FCC Allenwood, which is nearby. It's a complex on 640 acres, with a low-security prison, a medium-security prison, and a maximum-security penitentiary. The SHU at Allenwood draws from all the security levels and is in its own building. The budget's bigger here than at MCC and MDC, and the food is better, but otherwise Allenwood is a grimly efficient place.

My shot from New Year's has followed me. The guards are leery, expecting me to be aggressive with female staff. I get no sunlight. It's winter, and most mornings, during my allotted time for the rec cage outside, I pass up the opportunity to freeze while surrounded by high concrete walls, in favor of sleep. The water in the shower has no temperature control, so it's either freezing or scalding. I have to jump in and out of the water to wash. It still burns my scalp. I obsess that my hair may be falling out. I have a series of dreams in which something's wrong with me—I can't move my body freely, as if I'm in a straitjacket, or I can't speak properly because my mouth is too dry, or I'm wearing ill-fitting, ridiculous-looking clothes—and I feel embarrassed that the people around me can see me struggling. One of them is Pop. He doesn't say anything about my condition, and he is loving toward me, but I feel ashamed.

The cops must be really bored, because they start playing games, forcing me into situations likely to entertain them. The best way to do SHU time is by yourself, but the cops here cell me with a black Muslim kid from Philly, a flagrant break from standard practice. The way the prison system has evolved, racial segregation is a fact of life behind bars. It has less to do with any deep racial animus than it has to do with gang affiliation, which breaks down along race lines. As a result, it's unwritten Bureau of Prisons policy not to mix races in cells, purely as a pragmatic way of curbing needless violence.

Other black guys in the SHU call my new cellmate Supermax Sam. He's tall, with a Bic-smoothed head and a small chin beard, and in his late thirties. He tells me right away that he's Nation of Islam, in a tone that suggests he wants nothing to do with me. I'm friendly by nature, and at first I try to be cordial and polite. "Good morning." Crickets. "Hey, you want the rest of these fries?" He gives me a menacing look, then ignores me. He's not particularly friendly with anyone, but my whiteness is clearly a problem for him.

Over the first two weeks, I don't think we say more than two words a day, and they're "Excuse me," as we pass each other in the narrow cell. I start thinking of him as Angry Man. Other than when Angry Man prays to Mecca, he spends all day, every day, lying in his bottom bunk under the covers, with his head under his blanket or else peering out and staring at the bottom of the upper rack. One day, we exchange a few more words. The only ones I remember are his final sentence: "I could kill you in this cell, and I might."

The situation was acutely awkward to begin with, and now I'm scared. He's clearly trying to muscle me out of the cell. Partly out of fear, and partly out of an imperative to leave the cell of my own volition, rather than getting pushed out, I feel I need to take Angry Man out of the equation, to get myself moved by hurting him. You don't want to let yourself get bullied out of a cell; that will follow you and shape your reputation.

He's working out one day, doing push-ups on the ground. I'm wearing the commissary slippers we call Jackie Chans. Angry Man has a long scar, running the length of his stomach, from a gunshot wound, and I consider kicking him there, but think better of it, deciding that a scar isn't the same thing as a weak spot.

Instead, I kick him in the throat. I learned about doing this when

I was a kid and Leo, whom I'd later employ, taught me and his son to spar. I need for Angry Man not to be able to get up after the kick, but I also know it's easy to overdo it. My adrenaline is going crazy, and the kick is harder than I intend. Suddenly, he can't breathe. He's looking at me, eyes blank and wide, and I start worrying that I've killed him, that I caved in his throat and he's going to die.

I hit the duress alarm button. When the cops come, Angry Man, to my relief, is just starting to get his breath back.

"Back away!" a cop says. "Come to the door and cuff up!"

"No!" I don't want to be cuffed if Angry Man suddenly comes to.

"Direct order!" the guard says. "Come here and cuff up."

"No!" I repeat.

The cop tells me to go to the corner of the cell and face it. Then a couple of them come into the cell, cuff Angry Man, and take him out.

I don't try to defend my actions. I just say, "You guys put me in a cell with that dude, when you know he doesn't want me in the cell with him." The next day they move me.

The guards have only just begun fucking with me. My new cellmate, named Bobby Tanner, is a member of the Aryan Brotherhood of Texas, a white prison gang known for committing lots of murders and torturing people. He's well-built and inked up with ABT badges and SS lightning bolts, and he talks about the Brotherhood all the time.

I take little solace from the fact that he's not a gang member in good standing. The ABT has said he can't "walk the yard" in Texas, which is why he got kicked up to Pennsylvania. But the reason his gang ostracized him is his volatility, which is also the reason he's in solitary and why he doesn't already have a cellmate: the BOP hasn't been able to find anyone who can cohabitate peaceably with him.

For a few days, we get along. But Bobby has recently been diagnosed with schizoaffective disorder. He exudes aggression, constantly shadowboxing in our small cell and talking about fights and fighting. And this is when he's taking his lithium. One day, he is suddenly possessed by the belief that the nurse who delivers his meds has been pausing, while making her way to our cell, to administer hand jobs to black prisoners. Bobby immediately stops taking his lithium, and I witness a drastic decline in his mental health.

He begins having regular conversations with Jesus, talking about "hotdogs" and "donkey dicks" and reciting disturbed mantras: "I hope all of them, their children turn to faggots and die in the deepest darkest hells, in Jesus Christ's name, amen."

He also becomes increasingly rude toward me, stomping around loudly during his morning workouts in the cell, when I'm still sleeping. One morning, I'm asleep when the rack suddenly shakes really hard. *What the fuck?* I look over. Bobby is kicking the side of the rack. He tells me he's stretching. For him to do something that disrespectful lets me know that he thinks I'm a chump, which means I could be in real danger. The rest of the day is almost unbearably tense. The true solitude of prison is less about the number of people around you than the knowledge that anyone could be an adversary and nobody's coming to save you. I'm on high alert, and I know the only option is to try to hurt him before he hurts me.

That night, I'm on the top bunk, meditating as I do every night, and Bobby starts going on and on about "the faggots" and "dying" and "kill all the babies."

"Hey, Bobby."

"What?"

"Can you keep that to yourself, 'cause I'm trying to pray up here?"

He jumps up.

"You're trying to pray? Well, you better pray harder."

He begins pacing. He spits on the glass the officers look through. He's completely out of his mind.

Bobby has a lot of time left in his sentence, and if he gets hold of me, I'm thinking he may kill me. This is not paranoia. It's not uncommon to be stabbed or smashed with something in your sleep, and that night I lie awake, fighting sleep until dawn.

At 5 a.m., a guard comes by to let prisoners out for their allotted daily hour in the cage outside. This morning, Bobby goes out.

After he leaves, I tell a guard that he has to get me out of this cell. I say, "If you don't get me out of here, I'm going to get me out of here." The guard ignores me and lumbers off. The cops here have the same mentality as people who like to fight dogs. They know this kid has problems, but they're happy to wait and see what happens between us.

The rest of the day, there's a nerve-wracking tension between me and Bobby. I start my workout around 5 p.m., thinking about what I know I need to do to him. I do a bodyweight circuit of four sets of three exercises: diamond push-ups, squats, lunges. Then I do another four sets of a different group of three exercises. Then another. Then I run in place to let my muscles regenerate. Then I start over at the beginning. The idea is to go nonstop.

What should I do? I have my answer, but I'm hesitant, and I put the question to the universe, which I vocalize silently as *God*. I ask Him to show me a sign, to tell me I need to pull the trigger, right now. I'm doing push-ups when I notice a speck of green glitter on the concrete floor. There is no good explanation, as far as my prison-crazed mind is concerned, for how green glitter ended up in my cell. This can't be an accident, and green means GO to me. I'm carrying on an inner dialogue: *What kind of man are you, Cameron? You asked for a sign, you got one. Now what?* I decide that the next time I have an opportunity to attack Bobby, I will.

When the moment arrives, around 7 p.m., the timing is unfortunate, because I've just finished a solid two-hour workout and my muscles are fatigued, but I know what an influx of adrenaline can overcome. Cell 222 is tiny, with room for a bunk bed, sink, toilet, and not much else. There's a dull sheet of metal instead of a mirror above the sink, which has those buttons that only stay pressed for a second. To make coffee, you have to keep pressing the hot-water button until it gets hot. But with the tension in the cell now excruciating, and me at a diagonal behind Bobby when he approaches the sink, he keeps pressing the button and then walking away. I make my plan of attack. When he has to stand at the sink for a few seconds to fill his Styrofoam cup, that's when I'll get him. I know I can't let him get the upper hand, or it could all be over for me.

As soon as he puts his cup under the tap and presses the button, I throw a good right hook from behind him, making solid contact with his jaw. My plan is next to take his head and smash it on the corner where the sink comes out and the toilet is. And that's about as far as I've thought this through, because if it works, that should be the end of the fight. Unfortunately, when I go to grab his hair, I'm so pumped up on adrenaline that I pull a clump of it out. I quickly improvise a plan B, grabbing him in a headlock and teeing off on his face with a series of uppercuts.

Bobby starts screaming and hollering in a high-pitched voice. "Stop! Stop!"

He probably thinks this is the end of him, and he's trying to get the attention of the police, but this is not what you're supposed to do when you're a tough guy like him. Meanwhile, someone has hit a duress alarm button.

It's lucky for me, because I'm almost out of gas, and if I continue I might just end up doing something that would add years to my sentence. I loosen the headlock, as if I'm showing mercy, just as the cops arrive, yelling at us to separate. The whole thing has taken maybe two minutes. I still have Bobby's head in my armpit, and am not yet ready to let him go completely, when suddenly I can't breathe. The cops have fired pepper-spray bullets into the room. I scramble to get as far away from the door as I can.

Bobby tells investigators that he believes the fight was "set up by the FBI" and that "I feel I was hypnotized." But my plan works. I'm moved to my own cell. More importantly, to me, I've passed a crucial threshold. For the last fifteen years, I've been testing myself, often in self-destructive ways. But now, I know exactly what I'm capable of. I know that I have what it takes—a certain freedom from restraint, even a kind of craziness—not only to survive in prison but to thrive. I'm not a victim. I'm mostly in control. I'm not going to be taken advantage of. Maybe I can finally accept that, and stop being obsessed with proving it.

I get a shot for the Angry Man fight and another one for the Bobby

Tanner fight. Every infraction adds points to your "jacket," or prison file, and between those two incidents and my propositioning of the guard back at MDC, I've turned my eleven months in solitary into twenty-four months and gotten my security level raised to just below medium.

29

2012: Hole Time

The hike in my security level gets me transferred to FCI Loretto, another prison in Central Pennsylvania. Loretto is old and crowded and is what's called a "disciplinary" Low. It's where they put prisoners who are troublemakers but don't qualify for higher-security places, as well as people who do qualify for higher-security places but for some reason, such as a gang conflict, can't be placed there.

When I arrive, a cop in Receiving & Discharge says, "We're not going to have any trouble with you and any of our female staff, are we Douglas?" They've asked me this everywhere, since the MDC proposition. I have another fourteen months of solitary remaining in my sanctions, and I'm taken straight to the SHU, where the cell is even smaller than usual.

Books have become my security blanket. Each time I come to a new place, I'm anxious without them. As long as I have my books, I feel okay. A few days after I arrive at Loretto, a guard tells me that the prison has confiscated some books that arrived in my mail. "We don't let inmates in the SHU receive books from the outside," he explains.

"That's not right," I say.

He shrugs.

"You're telling me I can't try to better myself? You want me to go crazy?"

He says I'll have to wait for the book cart, which comes around once a week, and walks away. This is a disaster. Books have given me purpose and let me feel I'm being productive during this waste of years. When the cart comes, it's all religious tracts and 'hood novels and makes the one back at MCC look like the Great Library of Alexandria on wheels.

I'm lonely in solitary, but not as lonely as when I'm surrounded by sociopaths who exude hostility and dark looks, who shun me, who think they know me and what I've done but don't really, while I know nothing about them. *"I am not so afraid of the dark night / As the friends I do not know."* When I'm surrounded by other inmates, I never know if someone has a weapon and may intend me harm. In solitary, at least I feel relatively safe. I've spent much of my life accompanied by a retinue of friends. Now that solitude has been thrust upon me, I've come to see it as a gift, a thing that I need.

I have a lot of time to ruminate, and I catalogue my grievances. I dream of seeing Nick and slapping him in the face. I feel embarrassed that I gave the DEA my original statement. I regret my decisions.

Hope is the oxygen of captivity. Everyone has a legal submission pending, or a petition for clemency waiting to be heard. When those options are exhausted, people find religion. My lawyers and family say they're confident that my second sentence will be overturned, but I feel my hope slipping away. What's the point of hope, if it gets consistently dashed? There have been so many times when I hoped things would turn out one way, and they turned out another way. I hoped that heroin would save me. I hoped that once I moved to New York from L.A., I'd escape the DEA investigation. I hoped that if I put my trust in my lawyers, everything would turn out all right. I hoped that by backing out of my cooperation agreement, it would automatically remove my deeply felt sense of shame, and change how I was perceived by other inmates. Instead, it's been one serious blow after another.

How did I get here? Is something wrong with me? I'm finally starting to question my romantic notions about prison. For every storybook bank robber like Eddie Boyle, there are a hundred codeless drug fiends who'll do anything for a fix. I'm choked with regret. I regret never giving myself a chance. When I had everything going for me, when all I had to do was jump in the water and go with it, I insisted on tying a boulder to my ankles. I didn't have a belief in myself that was earned. I lacked determination. I read a passage in *Night Soldiers* by Alan Furst that speaks to me: "*Regret will kill you.* A concept he embraced to a point where any thought that represented itself for contemplation had to be inspected for traces of hidden anger or sorrow before he would allow his mind to pursue it."

At the same time, I do take some comfort in how things have unfolded. If Dr. Millman hadn't divulged my cooperation in court, I'd probably have gone along with the deal. I'd be lying about it every day, and just waiting for the truth to be revealed, because in prison people live to dig and to expose. Instead, the revelation of my cooperation, and my decision to stop it, have forced me to become brutally honest with myself and to make some serious choices about what's important to me, what traits I admire, and what I'm willing to do to honor those traits.

Until now, I've prayed every night. I stop praying. Instead of waiting around, whittling off the years, passively hoping for some kind of divine intervention, it's on me to make every day mean something. I want to be industrious.

My feelings of regret and remorse are necessary, if I'm to evolve. I believe that we all contain everything we want to be, and life is the process of making it real. The traits I held in high regard as a child are those of the man I'm becoming. Whatever I may think about the justice system's approach to addicts, it's up to me to change my situation.

I try to forgive myself. There's no escape from where I am. All I can do is make the time work for me. I'm paying a high price for my mistakes, so it's essential that I get what I'm paying for. I need to use hope as a tool. It can keep me inspired and pushing forward toward something better. I just can't let it break me down when it doesn't work out.

It's unnatural being confined to a little box like this, but I try to highlight the positives of solitary. I can use this time to educate my mind and strengthen my spirit. I spend more time writing poetry. I read the shitty cart books. Some other inmates who hear me going back and forth with the guards give me better books. Occasionally a nice cop is on duty when mail arrives, and he lets my books through, including Ernest Hemingway's *For Whom the Bell Tolls* and Alan Furst's *Night Soldiers,* a historical spy thriller partly set in a prison. One line in the Furst book makes me laugh out loud: "Thus, at last, he came upon the prisoner's timeless and universal conclusion: *There is nothing worse than prison.*" In the margin, I make a note: "I hold this truth to be self-evident."

We go outside at 5 a.m. every morning, the crack of dawn, and stay out until 8 a.m. at the latest. The SHU's yard is hemmed in by four high, concrete walls. If I catch any direct sun at all, it's just a sliver at the corner, which I seek out. There's no exercise bar or handball wall, and I do most of my exercising in my cell.

I do a daily calisthenic workout for two and a half, sometimes three, hours. I interval-train, alternating three high-intensity exercises with a sixty-second jog to get my breath back. I run hundreds of miles in place in front of the metal mirror, closing my eyes and imagining I'm out on a road, visualizing it as clearly as possible, then opening my eyes to my real surroundings. I do this so that one day, when I get out, I can do the reverse: close my eyes, imagining I'm back in prison, and then open them.

I'm disciplined about meditating and have an active mantra: "I move fluidly through balance, harmony, awareness, understanding, and intelligence." As I say each word, I try to feel it, to pinpoint a time that day when I used each quality.

My twice-a-day masturbation practice continues—rain or shine, happy or sad. I'm a scientist of self-pleasure. I consider it a dispassionate matter of practicality, a Darwinian imperative to use it or lose it.

A lot of inmates have calendars in their cells, and mark off the passing days like castaways carving notches in tree bark. I just get lost in the time. I often don't know what date it is, or even what day of the week it is. I just focus on my routine.

Once a month, I get to make a fifteen-minute phone call; a phone is wheeled to my cell, and I usually use it to call Erin. Otherwise, my only real connection to the outside world is mail. People live for the mail call in prison, especially in the box, and when it comes to mail, I'm blessed. A lot of the guys around me have nothing and no one to write them. I've been gone, out of sight and mind, for two and a half years, but my letter flow has never dried up. I get more letters than anyone else here, and mail call is the high point of my day. The guards make fun of me. They say, before looking, "You know Douglas has mail." Then it's "Douglas . . . Douglas . . . Douglas . . . Douglas."

Erin continues to write every day. My pal Gabriel's trial finally happened, and she went through the stressful ordeal of being a prosecution witness. I've really been touched, lately, by all her love and support and warmth toward me. She still can't visit me, because of her criminal record, but since my arrest we have talked about the day when I'm released, when she'll come with the dogs to pick me up: Eve, who was too young to mate when I went to prison; Scooby, who now has only three legs; and Junior, the greatest dog I've known. Erin has gotten Junior's sperm frozen, and it's stored in a bank.

Mom writes every day too, enclosing inspiring quotes, articles about solitary, updates on my appeal, and pictures of her new farm. Dad writes me once a week. Pappy writes every two weeks, sending his and Oma's love and words of support and hope, sharing family news, updating me on his progress writing his latest books, *I Am Spartacus!* and *Fragments of Memories,* and doodling cartoon heads. The mailbag also brings daily installments of *This Is Your Life:* I get letters from childhood caretakers, teachers from elementary school and high school, fellow students from Provo Canyon, addicts I was in rehab with. I get letters from people who tell me I changed their life, but whom I don't remember. Twenty-three to twenty-five, my liquid cocaine years, are a blur. I receive letters from unsolicited pen pals, including a young woman named Ashley, a self-taught artist in Connecticut who sends me impressive drawings.

Someone I still haven't heard from since my arrest is Jay. We were best friends from the age of seven. I still have his initials tattooed on my arm. When I was arrested, I protected him, even though he was as involved as Erin and I were in our crimes. But he's also the same guy who left me high and dry in Ireland, who ditched me after fights we were both involved in. I kept overlooking his actions, because I wanted him to be someone he wasn't. I wanted him to feel the same way about me that I felt about him. Even now, when I understand all of that and see it more clearly, I keep expecting to hear from him. I keep believing there was some kernel of genuine friendship there. It still hurts that I haven't received a single letter from him. I'm sure he's told himself all sorts of things to justify his distance. He feels ashamed. He feels guilty. He doesn't want to get roped into the criminal case. But the sad truth is, I think he just doesn't give enough of a shit about me to make the effort to find out where I am, write a letter, and mail it. The only thing he gives a shit about is drugs.

After four months in the SHU, the unit captain comes by my cell and says, "If we let you out into gen pop, are we going to have a problem?"

I'm moved to C1, an underground unit. The surroundings are grim—cement, pipes—and overcrowded with sweating men. I'm in a cube with six beds. It's July, and C1 has no windows, ventilation, or air-conditioning. Loud industrial-size fans blow 24/7, but it's so fucking hot.

After nearly ten months in the hole, when I first step onto the sunny yard, I feel like a Sherpa who lost his goggles and is stricken with snow blindness. I don't have any of my property yet, and I walk laps around the track shirtless, wearing prison-issue work boots. I've spent months pacing my cell in Jackie Chans, and the boots tear up my feet. I get terrible blisters. But it feels great to be outside.

Everyone knows who I am and is trying to size me up. My hair is hippy-length. When you come onto any yard, people check out your tattoos closely. If you have the tattoo of a gang that controls a yard, and you're not in that gang, they'll make you cut it out or cover it up or "check in" to protective custody. I have to explain some of my ink. A pair of stars on my back looks like the logo of Tango Blast, a Texas gang. Two S's, which stand for Safe & Sound, a small record label I founded with my friend Serebe, resemble the mark of the Southsiders, a Mexican gang. The 13 behind my ear could easily be mistaken for the mark of MS-13, the Salvadoran gang. And everyone seems simply confused by the giant monarch butterfly on my chest.

When I was at Lewisburg, I thought I understood what prison was like, but now I see that I didn't have a clue.

A lot of inmates here have violence on their records. One of my cubies is a gay meth head who gave a friend a fatal dope shot and is now doing twenty years. Another is a sharp-looking Cuban hustler—he always has a fresh haircut and shave and a gold chain around his neck—who stabbed someone at a penitentiary and has another sixteen years left in his sentence. While I'm here, there will be a serious riot between Mexicans and blacks. It starts on one unit and spreads to all the units and to the yard, where combatants smash each other in the head with balls from the bocce pit. It's pandemonium, and afterward there's a lockdown for a few days.

People are more guarded here. If you ask someone for something— maybe you want a particular job, and he's an inmate involved in dol- ing them out—he'll say, "I'll have to check with my people." You have to be *vetted*. I think back to my eagerness to join in when I arrived at Lewisburg, and now see that it was a rookie mistake. Only luck kept me from getting hurt in flag football.

Here, instead of trying to find things to belong to and giving anyone the satisfaction of shutting me out, I become more of a loner. No mat- ter how friendly people may be, I know now, you need to give yourself time to understand what's going on before making any moves.

But Loretto has a nice weight pit, and after a week in gen pop, I find some people to work out with. Dimitri, who is my height and well built and has a raspy Jersey accent, became a millionaire at twenty- five by moving truckfuls of weed from the West Coast to the East

Coast, and he invested the profits into building successful contracting and snowplowing businesses. Kenny is older. He's in on a crystal meth case and has had a tough life; he has Hep C, and was in a terrible car accident where his arm almost got torn off. Jerry Woo, a black kid from Harlem who was attached to a famous criminal named the Priest and robbed and killed drug dealers, has been in prison for at least a dozen years and worked his way down to this Low. Jack, an Albanian who everyone likes, was a truck driver who ferried illegal immigrants on their first leg after crossing the border. He really doesn't belong in prison.

I learn that I can pay to have a no-show job. Each unit has a head orderly, an inmate who can go to the cops and say, "I want this person on my team," and the cop will sign off on it. The crew mops bathrooms, scrubs toilets, empties the trash, cleans the TV room. To get out of the work, you have to bribe the orderly. I buy him a pair of Nike Air Force 1s from the commissary, and in return he gets me on his crew, and I don't have to do anything.

While I'm here, the BOP introduces MP3 players. The day it happens is the closest I've seen in prison to Christmas morning when you're a kid. Everyone is so happy, smiling and hugging each other. At these prisons in the boondocks, all people have had is a small plastic radio that doesn't pick up many stations, so to be able to buy your own music is a huge deal. It's also smart business for the BOP, which makes a killing charging a dollar a song or more. MP3s change my prison life. Now I always wear my headphones. They let me tune out.

Prison is drowning in bullshit: made-up, self-glamorizing tales of criminal derring-do, defiance of the Man, and general acts of badassery. No one cooperated. No one committed a sex crime. Everyone, to hear them tell it, is "rock solid."

But increasingly, it's hard for inmates to skate by on their bullshit stories, because of a huge shift that's taken place in the five years since I entered prison. Then, inmates had no access to computers. A year in, computers arrived, and they began to change the game. Besides connecting inmates to a comprehensive online law library, they led to an explosion of other information available to convicts with nothing but time on their hands.

When I first arrived, inmates not routinely covered by the *New York Post* could by and large tell the stories they wanted to about themselves. Fellow convicts, with no easy way to research each other, tended not to bother digging into the facts. Now there are inmates who sit in the law library all day just looking up the names of new arrivals and doing due diligence on them. The Italians, who also have their lawyers out on the street doing research, pay other inmates to sit on the computer and look into everyone. I've seen a lot of people get exposed, including high-ranking gang members being revealed to have worn wires. It turns out that some of the most outspoken alphas and shot callers, having the most highly developed survival instincts, are among the most aggressive cooperators.

The new transparency punctures the absurd myth, prevalent in every prison I've been at, that these places are snitch-free. In reality, nearly a quarter of federal drug defendants cooperate. Everyone has his story, but only some of them hold up under scrutiny.

I meet a guy named Michael who says he's in on a cocaine conspiracy charge, doing ten years after his best friend ratted him out. I can relate, having been betrayed by Alex. Michael and I work out together. He says he's getting a football team together and asks if I want to join it. We're practicing one night, before the season begins, and I go to catch a pass, and the ball hits my left middle finger. It's bad. The bone pushes through the skin at the base of my cuticle. A physician's assistant named Ms. Golden tells me "there's nothing we can do." That's the end of football for me, but after the finger heals a bit, I resume lifting weights with Michael.

Then someone asks me, "Why are you fucking lifting weights with a pedophile?"

"What are you talking about?"

"That guy is a chomo." That's what they call child molesters in prison.

I ask Michael about it, and his story is that she was sixteen and was flirting with him, and he didn't realize how young she was, and he got lured in, and da-da-da-da-da. He's a nice guy, and I feel bad for him, and I'm not interested in making his life any harder, but I'm also not interested in continuing to hang out with him.

By prison standards, my reaction is mild. Another guy Dimitri and I become pretty good friends with is Danny Doyle, who's doing ten years for what we figure is drugs. Then there's a special on ESPN about Kayla Harrison, the Olympic gold medalist in Judo, and how starting when she was thirteen years old, she was sexually abused by her coach: Daniel Doyle. That's what he's in prison for. He's immediately ostracized. If he were at a higher-security prison, he'd be stabbed, most likely.

I snort heroin a few times at Loretto, to take the edge off. Under normal circumstances, this would obviously be inconsistent with my recent strides toward self-improvement, but these are hardly normal circumstances. I *am* extremely disciplined and motivated, but I'm also motivated to be active in prison, to make money in prison. Part of me is still curious, and I want to know that I'm capable of running with the dudes who are doing things in here. The qualities I'm applying to prison proficiency—drive, motivation, cleverness—are qualities that will help me pursue my goals after prison.

Getting high every once in a while, ironically, gives me confidence that I've licked my addiction. When I'm closer to the door, I'll test myself more rigorously and make sure I really can leave it alone altogether, but right now I don't want to deny myself something that lets me unwind every once in a while. The rigors of prison take their toll. I've given up smoking. I almost never drink. I rarely smoke dope. But every now and then, it's nice to have something to look forward to—kicking back with your cellie, taking a little bump, laying back, playing some cards, watching some sports, letting go of everything for a little while.

The original press coverage of my case continues to make life difficult for me. There's a guy on the compound, Tetley, who's from Buffalo, claims to be half Italian, and is in an Italian "car," as a prison racial group is called, that is an offshoot of the main New York Italian car. He has a hustle printing out the betting sheets for guys who run gambling tickets. He's a thorn in my side, always going up to people I've been talking to, asking them why they were talking to me, and trying to stir up trouble.

Early in my time in gen pop, I'm in my cell when Dimitri comes in and says, "Cameron, get your shit together, we've got to go out to the yard." He was just there, and a crowd of whites and Italians, including Tetley, are up on the hill, conferring about whether to beat me off the yard. No one really knows me here, it's relatively early in my prison sojourn, and they're going to see if they can push me around, get something from me, test me. They asked Dimitri why he hangs out with me, and Dimitri challenged them.

Jerry Woo, who's friendly with us both, asks Dimitri if we want him to take care of these guys. Dimitri says, "No, we got this." I thread a couple of locks onto a belt, and Dimitri and I go outside. There are two of us, and maybe thirty of the whites and Italians. It doesn't hurt that I'm friendly with guys like Jerry, who has a serious reputation. But also, we're ready to go—while none of them will make a move. They're unsure of themselves. This is an important day in establishing myself here.

The next day, in the chow hall, I'm about to sit down at the white table when someone says, "You can sit over there with the chomos."

I say, "Fuck you guys," and sit down at their table.

That night, three white supremacists, probably stirred up by the Italians, come into my cell, while another two stand guard outside it. I'm expecting them. I have a padlock on a couple of shoelaces, and I stand in the corner windmilling it as they come at me. Dimitri pushes his way in past the guards, and it turns into a melee, two against three. I get in a couple of good blows and Dimitri does too, and after a minute, which seems like much longer, the whites take off.

No one's seriously hurt. But this is another important moment, a story that will follow me through prison and help make my reputation as someone who it's not necessarily safe to fuck with.

I don't play a lot of handball here, but I'm playing it one Monday, me and Kenny against two Mexicans, when I swing hard and hear three quick pops. I look down and my foot is stuck in a crack. I black out and wake up on the ground. My kneecap is bent sideways over my leg, like I've dislocated the joint. I try to move, and a wave of pain surges through my leg. Kenny goes to tell a cop, and after maybe forty-five minutes on the ground, I'm rolled to the medical center in a wheelchair.

I tell Ms. Golden, the same physician's assistant who pooh-poohed my finger injury previously, that I've broken bones before, and I can tell this is serious. She tells me to straighten my leg. I say I can't, which annoys her, and she has another nurse straighten it and put an immobilizer on it, which is excruciating and not sound medical practice. Then Ms. Golden hands me crutches and sends me on my way.

"Ms. Golden," I say, "I don't know what you think, but I can't walk on these crutches."

She says, "If I put you in a wheelchair, and I find out you're not in it, it's going to be trouble for you. And you're making me go through all this, now I need to change your bunk assignment." I have a top bunk and will need a bottom bunk.

"I know it's a pain in the ass, but the fact is I can't walk on these crutches, and there's no way I can get into the top bunk."

She gives me a piece of paper with the number for a bunk in a different unit, tells me to go there, and leaves.

It's now a few minutes before the four o'clock count, and I need to roll myself to my new unit. I wheel to the door and can't reach it with my hands, so I have to push it with my foot, which sends an amazing amount of pain through my leg. I have a feeling that my leg is in really bad shape. I finally get to my new cell, where my belongings from my old cell have been dumped on the floor by guards. There's no mattress on my bed, but a couple of friends get me one and put my stuff away. I'm in a four-man cell with some older white guys. I'm lying in my bed. A bone has popped out of my knee, and my leg is ballooning and turning crazy colors. Ms. Golden gave me some ibuprofen.

On Friday, four days after the injury, I'm not on the callout for X-rays. When the warden comes around, doing checks, my friend tells him about me. The warden hadn't heard. I say, "I've got to get to the hospital. This is really serious." The warden, who seems displeased that I haven't been attended to, approves me for an X-ray, and when they take it I can see that there's something wrong. Ms. Golden and another staffer huddle, whispering, until a doctor enters and joins them. Then the doctor wheels me into the office of Ms. Golden, who says, "Have you ever broken your leg before?"

"No."

"Well, it looks like you may have a hairline fracture of your femur. It's up to you, but if you want to get to the hospital sooner than later, I wouldn't call your family, because that will only delay things."

She knows she fucked up, and she's trying to minimize the damage. I'm taken to the hospital, where I'm told that I have a compound break, a 22-inch crack running the length of my femur bone. When the doctor asks how long ago it happened and I tell him four days earlier, he's nervous. He says they need to give me an ultrasound right away to make sure I don't have a blood clot. It turns out I do have a blood clot, and they have to perform emergency surgery to insert a filter where the arteries connect in my abdomen.

Because of the clot, they have to wait to do surgery on my leg, and they put me on blood thinners for a couple of days. Then they operate, inserting a titanium rod from my knee to my hip, with two screws fastening it at each end. While they're at it, they fix my finger, which they say wasn't treated correctly when I injured it. As soon as the operation ends, over the surgeon's objections and before I've had any rehab, the prison guards return me to Loretto.

Back at the prison, I call Dad and tell him about the malpractice of the prison medical staff, and my lawyers start to get involved. The prison knows it fucked up. I feel too vulnerable to sit in the chow hall, immobilized. My friends take care of me, wheeling me around and bringing me food.

It was a freak accident, but the *New York Post* runs a story suggesting the injury is the result of a $100 bounty on my head by "a crime-family captain." The *Los Angeles Times* regurgitates the idea that I was "beaten badly." It's one more lesson in tabloid fakery. Apparently someone in the prison told a reporter this, and maybe made a couple of bucks, and that's all it took. Everyone is convinced that someone broke my leg. The surgeon says, "Tell us what happened, you won't get in trouble." Even my family and friends are skeptical of my story. But that's how it happened.

A few weeks after my leg break, I'm still in agonizing pain, and I ask the prison doctor to continue me on the pain medication I've been on, Percocet. He says he can't.

A week or two later, an SIS lieutenant tells me I need to give a urine sample. This one comes up dirty. I know it's not possible. I know there are no narcotics in my body. This feels like a setup. A dirty urine is a 100-series shot, and in a lot of places you won't even go to the SHU for it. But the SIS guy says: "You're going to a Medium unless you help us." He wants to know how drugs are coming into the prison.

I say, "Hey, I wish I could help you, but I can't, so it's going to be what it's going to be."

I'm not about to start ratting now, though I'd be lying if I said I wasn't extremely apprehensive.

I'm sent back to the SHU for another six months. It's depressing to be back in solitary. Is this karma? It's like I have a dark cloud over me. Everything that could go wrong has gone wrong.

The prison has nothing to offer me, as far as physical therapy goes, but the surgeon said physical therapy is the most important factor in my recovery if I ever want to be active and run and play sports again, and I take his words to heart. I push myself really hard, doing a massive number of squats and lunges every day.

After three months in the SHU, I'm informed that I'm going to be transferred out of Loretto. The latest shot added points to my jacket, allowing the prison to move me to a higher-security facility. My theory is that this is all about my leg: with a lawsuit brewing, the prison wants me out of here.

As I'm leaving, an inmate I don't know hands me a note from Dimitri telling me to check in as soon as I reach the next prison, because he's learned that the whites are waiting for me and are going to come for me and hurt me.

30

2013: Notable Inmates

It's March 2013. I'm on a bus to my next prison, which is—I have no idea. Of all people, Tetley, who was always trying to stir up trouble about me at Loretto, is also on board. His ticket-printing hustle finally caught up with him, his security level was raised, and he's getting transferred too.

We go to Canaan first. My previous times here, I've been put in the cell with other prisoners going to Minimums and Lows. This time, I'm in the cell I used to look at from afar, relieved not to be in it, among the convicts who looked so scary to me. Shit is getting real. Looking across to the Minimum/Low holding cell, I see wide-eyed felons stealing looks at me the way I used to steal looks at the group I've now joined.

An officer has just been stabbed to death at Canaan, and the place is in lockdown. I'm held here for a few weeks. Then it's back on a bus to I-don't-know-where. It starts out full and keeps stopping—at FCI Schuylkill, at USP Lewisburg, at FCC Allenwood. Usually, transit drags on, and you want it to be over as soon as possible, but this time I'm dreading our arrival. Just after 8 p.m., having crossed the border into Maryland, we turn off the road at a sign that says FCI CUMBERLAND.

I've never heard of this place. I'd hoped I was going to Otisville, a

Medium in New York that's known to be relatively tame, and which would have put me closer to my family and friends. It's dark now, and raining. My name is called. So is Tetley's. Just my luck. I was already anxious, in light of Dimitri's warning, and now I know that Tetley is going to cause trouble for me right away.

Intake lasts awhile. The SIS officer photographs my torso, cataloguing my tattoos. I still have three months left in solitary, but she says I've been in solitary long enough, and they're going to let me out on the yard. "Is there any reason you can't be on the compound here?" They ask this of everyone, mainly to weed out gang conflicts, informers, and pedophiles. I think about Dimitri's warning, and about Tetley. For a moment, I consider checking into protective custody.

I say, "No."

Checking in would be waving the white flag, broadcasting that I'm afraid to be out on the yard, that I can't take it there, that I'd rather be isolated and safe. There are people who'll stab someone just to get sent to an SMU, because it will guarantee eighteen months out of gen pop. Even some of the famous rappers check in for their own protection.

That's not an option for me. If I took it, I'd feel terrible about myself.

Cumberland.

I know that someday I'll be out on the street and telling my story, and I don't want it to be about how I spent my time in protective custody because I was afraid to walk the yard at a higher-security.

I sign a piece of paper, as I've done upon arrival at every other place, absolving the BOP of responsibility if I'm killed here. The cop hands me a bedroll and a pair of tiny, goofy-looking pants to replace my transit pants. I'm sent down to my assigned unit, A2, where the guards are just locking prisoners in for the night. When I get there, everyone's already inside, staring through the locked glass door at the end of the unit to where I'm standing. They're waiting to see who the new arrivals are. These moments are exciting for many inmates and scary for others. I still have long hair. As I wait to be let in, a young white kid with a shaved head and tattooed arms runs up to the glass from inside.

"Where are you coming from?"

His tone is more intent than aggressive, but it immediately sets me on my heels. I'm already noticing a different type of inmate here, men with face tattoos and serious white boys.

"I'll see you when you get in here," the kid says, neither friendly nor hostile.

A cop replaces the kid at the door, opens it, and leads me to a two-man cell, which is a pretty good size and has a steel door with a little window in it. An older guy, who introduces himself as Dickie, has the bottom bunk.

Night is my favorite time of day. One more day in the books. It's quiet. It's peaceful. I'm locked in. No one's coming in. I can relax a bit.

I can't believe I'm here. Am I going to make it at a medium-security? Actually, this is a medium-high, a step up in security level from a regular Medium. Will I be killed? People get killed all the time in places like this. I think about the old-timer at Lewisburg who embarrassed me when he asked, "Have you ever been in a Low, Cameron?" I imagine running into him now and asking him, "Have you ever been in a Medium? No?"

When I was at Lewisburg I felt like I was Billy Badass and that when I emerged from prison I'd be a bona fide convict. Now I know that I'd barely even started down that path. And now that I know what the path is about, I want to separate myself as much as possible from the people who are on it.

In the morning, as soon as they pop the doors and I emerge from my cell, I go to the laundry to get towels and other things I'll need. A kid named Buck, who's from Virginia, offers me a bunch of extra items but cautions, "If you're no good, don't take this stuff." He means, if I'm a chomo or don't have acceptable paperwork. I say, "I'll let you be the judge of that when my paperwork gets here."

Reps from the major groups watch who comes in, feeling out who's gang-affiliated. This is when your prison future is determined. Most people in prison are sheep who either belonged to a gang before prison or want the protection of one in prison, or they just want to feel like they're part of something. An emissary from your racial group will come up to you and give you shower shoes and soap. You don't want to be alone. You start hanging out with them. Now you have friends. They give you a job, moving drugs or running gambling tickets. Now you have some income. A month later, if you're white, you're running around shouting Nordic prayers to Odin. And if war comes, you have to go to war. If they ask you to "put in some work" and hurt someone who owes money for cigarettes, and you don't want to do it, you'll be labeled a coward. Your only option will be to check in and tell the cops you're not safe here. But three or four months later, at your new place, you'll get beaten up or stabbed.

There's no welcome wagon for me, and I have no interest in one. I'm an anomaly. Maybe it's because of my family, or because the details of my case have been publicized, or because of the reputation I've developed in prison, but I manage to avoid a gang's embrace.

On the unit, a white shot-caller named Farmer—who is heavyset and tattooed, with a brown goatee, a southern drawl, and a perpetual smirk—says I can sit at the white table in our dayroom until my paperwork arrives. It's standard, when you arrive at a new place, to plunk your paperwork down in the dayroom so that anyone can inspect it. "We ask everyone for their paperwork," Farmer adds. I say it's in my property, which I should get in two or three weeks.

One of the people sitting at the table is the high-energy kid who greeted me last night. His name is Eric, but everyone calls him Easy. Easy gives me the rundown on our block, which has 150 inmates. The white car sits together at two tables. There are also Crip tables, Blood tables, Muslim tables, Tango Blast tables, and Sureño tables, and there are separate TVs for each group.

When I step out onto the yard at Cumberland for the first time, it's like something out of a gnarly prison movie. It's summer, and everyone's shirt is off. People are tattooed head-to-toe. Guys are hanging by the fence, doing furtive business.

Trucks circle the yard, but although there's always some tension on it, there's surprisingly little police presence. The yard is partitioned so that guards can isolate a riot if one starts. There are lots of people working out but no weights: the purchase of new weightlifting equipment by federal prisons was banned in 1996, out of a concern that prisons were creating jacked super-convicts, and weights have been removed from medium- and higher-security prisons.

Every prison is controlled by one or two gangs who, through some combination of numerical dominance and a violent reputation, "hold the keys to the yard." At Cumberland, it's two Mexican gangs: the Sureños, from Southern California; and Tango Blast, from Texas. That means they control a lot of the illicit activity on the compound and have the strongest relationships with the dirty cops, and it means that members of any gangs they're enemies with can't be placed here.

On the yard, different gangs and racial groups have their preferred areas to congregate, but in the chow hall, segregation by car is strict. Each group has its own table or tables: Crip. Blood. Baltimore. Tango Blast. Sureño. Gangster Disciple. Folk. White. Puerto Rican. Ñeta. Muslim. Christian. If you're white, and all the white tables are full but there are three empty Sureño tables, you wait until there's an opening at a white table or someone at another table invites you to sit down. Whites are a minority in higher-security prisons, which is one of the reasons they've developed such a violent reputation: if they aren't feared, they'll be prey.

For years, I've been hearing how deadly these higher-security places are, and given Dimitri's warning, I'm uncertain what's in store for me. Right away, I start running around the track, but I still have a limp, which is unnerving, given that I'm surrounded by predators with hypersensitive antennae for wounded animals. But my diligent exercising will pay off, and eventually I'll regain full use of my injured leg.

Higher-security federal prisons get more money than lower-security ones and are more manicured. Cumberland, being the highest-security facility near D.C., makes a good showpiece when federal brass want to tour a prison, so they keep it looking nice. Loretto was a dump and falling apart; this place has newer paint, and it's the rare higher-security prison with a grove of trees. You're not allowed, as an inmate, to leave the path that wends through the grove, but it makes such a difference to me, to see something other than concrete.

The kitchens at higher-securities have bigger budgets, and the guys who work there, especially the lifers in key positions, are serious about it and take pride in their cooking. The food here is decent, and they give you a good-size tray. There are more activities, and there's more equipment. There are TVs literally anywhere there's an open space. Anything to keep us as pacified as possible. There are more cops here too. Some are hyperaggressive, but in general they're more respectful, because they have to be: there are inmates here—killers, gang members—who are never going home. Before doing population moves, the guards even tend to check with the shot-callers first.

Inmates here are caught all the time doing things like tattooing, gambling, or smoking—any of which could land you serious hole time at my previous prisons—and only have their commissary privileges suspended. Even shots for drug possession or a dirty urine—for which I had five years added to my sentence—might only get you ten days in the SHU, or even zero days, if the cops need the limited number of SHU cells for violent prisoners. A cop might just say he's "putting it on the shelf," essentially giving you a suspended sentence, and if you stay clean, it's never activated.

At the same time, higher-securities are more regulated. I can't move freely around the compound. I can't just walk to someone else's block. Cell phones are much scarcer here. Where maybe one in fifteen inmates at lower-security places has one, here it's more like one in five hundred. The cops here take them much more seriously, because the security of the institution is at stake. At Cumberland, a no-frills flip phone goes for $3,500.

Moving too quickly, when you hit a compound, is called "speeding" and almost invariably ends with a crash. I know this. But it's also my nature to speed, and I'm eager to find allies. Easy and I become friends, hanging and working out together. He's from Rochester, New York, in on drug charges. When he first arrived, he hung out with the other Rochesterians, who happened all to be black, but by the time I met him he'd become increasingly aligned with the white car.

Soon after my arrival, some heroin hits the compound. I'm anxious about adjusting to the most dangerous place I've been in yet, and it sounds good to me. Easy makes alcohol and has connections, and together we buy a decent amount of brown-powder junk, which we hide in plain sight. Easy has a prescription for fluoxetine, generic Prozac, and I empty the capsules and refill them with dope.

We start taking orders for the heroin, shaking it out into papers, each a folded wad of glossy magazine paper containing a Bic pen cap's worth of powder. We sell the papers for three books of stamps each. When heroin's around, people like to do it, and I cut some guys a really good price. I'm trying to settle in, and it ingratiates me to the yard, or at least to some of the white guys.

Easy is wild. He jokes around a lot but also commands respect. We get high together. My involvement with heroin, at this point, is opportunistic: I'm not worried about relapsing—every time I snort it, I'm vigilant about not doing it again for a while, lest I slip back into a habit—but it's helpful for taking the edge off, and it's the drug most readily available here.

Sometimes, when I can get pot, I smoke it instead, though it's a production. I put a towel under my door. I roll a playing card into a tube held together with a piece of tape, and make an incision in one end with a disposable razor blade. I take the metal sleeve from a pencil eraser and put it in the incision, pack a little weed in the makeshift bowl, and run a toilet-paper wick out of that. Then, when the corridor is guard-free, I take a double-A battery, remove the plastic wrapper to expose the naked metal, and bend a thin strip of Hershey-bar foil from the side of the battery to the negative terminal. It sparks, lighting the toilet paper and then the weed. I draw as much smoke into my lungs as they'll hold, then exhale into the ceiling vent.

Uncertain who's an enemy and who isn't, I'm just waiting for something to happen. As usual, everyone knows who I am, while I don't know who anyone else is, but now the stakes are much higher. I'd be a great person for a guy doing life, or a young kid looking to make a name for himself, to put some steel in. The Italians here, led by Vittorio Amuso, the Lucchese crime-family boss, don't like me. The white supremacists don't like me. I never know if the guy approaching me is going to shank me. "In prison, a man rations his smiles, because predatory men see smiling as a weakness, weak men see it as an invitation, and prison guards see it as a provocation to some new torment." From day one, I carry a lock and a belt with me whenever I leave my cell, and after a few weeks I get a knife from Easy. It's a piece of sharpened metal with some rubber from the kitchen on the end for a handle. I dangle it inside my sweatpants, tying it to one of the drawstrings. When I'm going out to the yard, which requires passing through a metal detector, I leave the knife in my cell, in a hidden compartment in my locker, and just bring the belt and lock with me. A good number of the guards seem to recognize the jeopardy

Me with Farmer, Casper, Hafer, and Easy at Cumberland.

I'm in, know I need all the help I can get, and let me enter the yard with those.

Facial hair is one of the few mediums available to express yourself in this place. A lot of it is white supremacists aping Vikings. They get Celtic-knot tattoos, and they grow huge handlebar mustaches and crazy beards. Notably, given the racial inspiration of much of the facial hair, I never see an inmate with a Hitler mustache; even the neo-Nazis must think it looks ridiculous. The white shot-caller on my unit is a guy named Peter Hafer, who has a monster beard that he wears alternately as a giant ZZ Top bush and as a single tail held together by evenly spaced rubber bands.

Hafer is nice to people he likes, but is generally aloof and can get really grouchy. He has minor folk-hero status because of a courtroom video on YouTube, with more than two million views, of him cold-cocking his court-appointed lawyer, the ultimate disgruntled-felon fantasy. When he's walking around the compound, he keeps up his pace so he won't get stopped by anyone to talk. He's one of the white shot-callers mainly because people fear him. He also makes hooch.

My paperwork arrives in a brown envelope. It's an inch-thick sheaf of court minutes—everything said at my various hearings, including my resentencing—plus my pre-sentencing report by the probation department. Most importantly, it documents that at a certain point I refused to cooperate, which contributed to my harsh sentence of an extra five years. My paperwork now accurately reflects the whole truth: when I entered the system, I didn't know what was what, but once I started realizing the score, I had a change of heart. So although my initial cooperation was a strike against me, my ultimate about-face, resulting in the doubling of my sentence, balanced it out.

Hafer has Farmer scrutinize the paperwork. I tell Farmer, "You're going to have to go over everything carefully to get a real idea of what happened. It's not perfect, by any means, but it is what it is." I'm hoping that the details that fucked me with the prosecutors will be what save me with my fellow criminals.

Farmer takes the envelope and spends hours poring over its contents—all the documents, briefs, and minutes. Then a kid named Donny, a sweet country boy with a ponytail and glasses who did something like blow up a police station and runs errands for Farmer and Hafer, comes down to my cell.

"Go to Farmer's cell when you have a chance."

My fate rests on the outcome of this process, and given my luck, I'm not optimistic. If Farmer's an asshole, and decides my paperwork is problematic, he'll tell me to check in with the cops and ask to be transferred into protective custody, or else I'll be hurt. Before going to see Farmer, I make a promise to myself: I'm not going to check in. I walk upstairs to his cell.

"Dude," he says, "I've gone over everything. You're good. I'm going to let everyone on the compound know that you're good." I'm so relieved, and I feel vindicated. Someone has taken the time to see the details of my case and decided that I'm honorable. Farmer is in good status with the whites on the yard, which in turn means that he's in good status with the shot-callers from other races. His approval basically means that I'm good to go.

Ten minutes later, Hafer, who's been keeping his distance, comes up to me and is friendly for the first time. I also show the paperwork to Bob, an older bank robber from Boston I've become friendly with; he spends hours in the library peering at it through his glasses, and reaches the same conclusion Farmer did. After that, it's pretty much smooth sailing for me, and I almost start to enjoy myself for the first time since I've been in prison, ripping and running with Easy and Farmer and Hafer.

With Bob the bank robber and
my beloved Chucks at Cumberland.

31

2013: As a Man Thinketh

Six weeks after my arrival at Cumberland, I come back to my cell and find a bunch of my stuff missing, including a couple of pairs of nice eyeglass frames and a radio. This is how new inmates get tested. Someone wants to see if I can be chumped. If I am, it will mean one kind of future here. Before the day's over, it gets back to me who the culprits are. It's two guys from Baltimore, a black kid and a white kid. This is a loophole in the Byzantine racial codes at Cumberland: it's acceptable for whites from Baltimore to hang out with blacks and run with the predominantly black Baltimore car.

I've been drinking with Easy, and I go into the interracial duo's cell, which is on my unit. They don't try to deny they took my shit. "Fuck you," the black kid says, and I start hitting him. The violence comes easy to me by now. It feels natural, an innate survival skill. It is not just a part of prison life, it is a part of me. But this battle does not go well. The white kid starts hitting me. They get the better of me. Meanwhile, a cop searches my cell and finds a jug of alcohol Easy and I bought from Hafer and hid in our trash can, and sends me to the lieutenant's office. I'm still bleeding, and he Breathalyzes me. I take the rap for the alcohol, so I get one shot for that and another for fighting. I'm going back to the hole, and I think the DHO is going to knock my block off, but when I have my hearing he only gives me two months. I thank him.

———

Cell 136, my new home in the SHU, is only five paces long and extremely narrow. With my arms spanned, there's maybe a foot and a half of clearance on each side. And I have a cellmate, a member of the Pagans motorcycle gang. The BOP wants to move him to gen pop, but despite having another two years in his sentence, he's dead set on staying in the box. He forces them to keep him there by saying that if they move him he'll kill someone.

My first weeks back in the hole, I don't go outside. The rec hour is 5 to 6 a.m., and I'm not willing to sacrifice sleep for fresh air. My mental state is precarious. Just when I'd begun to form alliances, I'm in the SHU again. There's no guarantee that when I get out, someone won't have mounted a slander campaign against me in my absence. Having tasted relative freedom after so long in solitary, I feel like I've taken a major step backward.

One night, I dream that I'm at dinner with my family and closest friends, and I can't shake the feeling that I'll never amount to anything and that they feel the same way. Then I'm having sex with a woman who turns into a demon. Then I'm marrying a woman I've loved since I was a child, and although I know that she has consented to be my wife only out of pity, I'm still willing to go through with the wedding. When I wake up, I'm shaken, but as I lie there I slowly fill with determination. I'll use the images of doom and failure to inspire me to chart a different course for my future. I've had thoughts like this so many times before. Will it stick, this time?

Another night, against all odds I glimpse, through a visual cacophony of steel plates and fencing and razor wire, a full moon. I've always felt a connection to the moon. I've spent hours looking at it and daydreaming. With my return to solitary, I'm thirsting for a sign—something, anything, to remind me of life beyond my monotonous daily feelings of despair and lostness—and this stolen glimpse of nature feels like a moment of grace.

———

A few weeks later, Easy is sent to the hole. This concerns me, for his sake as well as my own. I know he's here because of the heroin, and I figure he might suspect that I ratted him out to try to get out of the box. I want to talk to him to clear the air.

Early the next morning, during rec hour, I go outside and see him in a cage a little ways down.

"What's up?" I shout.

"What's up?" he shouts back, without his usual friendly tone.

I start going out every morning so we can talk, or shout, cage to cage. Eventually I ask the cops to put us in the same cell. Their willingness to cell us together goes a long way toward convincing Easy that I didn't snitch on him, because if I had, the cops would never put us together.

He says the cops went straight for his Prozac bottle; they clearly knew that's where the drugs were. "Then someone else clearly knew," I say. " 'Cause I didn't tell them."

After I was sent to the hole, Easy says, he moved in with Charlie, a tattoo artist on our block who was going to do some work on him. Easy is now convinced that Charlie gave him up to mollify the cops about his illicit ink operation. Easy is nearly homicidal. He knows that for this shot he'll be transferred to a higher-security prison. "When you go back to gen pop," he says, "you need to hurt Charlie for me."

"I don't know," I say. "It doesn't seem like something Charlie would do just so he can tattoo. I'm not going to put my hands on that guy without more proof."

"Well, then, you've got to let people know that this is what I think, and this is what I'm saying."

Easy's racial attitudes are starting to offend me. Increasingly, every second word starts with *n*. It's a word that he, like a lot of prisoners, applies to anyone he doesn't like, including white people. But Easy is becoming over-the-top about it. In the hole, we tear off strips of bedsheet to create bandannas for working out, and Easy puts a swastika on his. When, after a few weeks, he's sent to Big Sandy, a penitentiary in Kentucky, I know he'll fit right in. He's exactly the specimen that the neo-Nazis are looking for: a strong, good-looking soldier with a shaved head who's volatile and energized by his newfound sense of tribal aggrievement.

My hole time ends up being a blessing. It slows me down and lets me take a step back. I see myself losing sight of the future, being digested by the beast. Something awakens inside me. *No, I'm not going to let this happen.* My determination to turn things around is helped by a jolt of reality, when the appeals court affirms the lower-court opinion in my case instead of reversing it.

I resolve, finally, to stop fucking with heroin altogether. Dealing it comes with way too much baggage, and I won't use it again either. I have to be honest with myself. I'm doing all these edifying things, such as studying, but I've also been using the drug that helped get me here. If I'm doing heroin, I'm not doing everything I can do to put myself in the best possible position, when I'm released, to have a real shot at a meaningful life. I just don't want it in my life anymore. It's an obstacle to what I want to achieve.

By now, I have some understanding of the science of my addiction. I know that after years of opioid dependency, my brain can't produce the chemicals it needs, leading to my constant feeling that I need something just to feel okay. It's going to be difficult, but abstaining will be just one more accomplishment, another thing I can power through and overcome. I'm more than halfway through my sentence now, and there's a glimmer at the end of the tunnel.

All that gets me out of the rack in the morning is the imperative to make each day count. To become a little bit better of a person. I become almost militant about practicing my four-pronged self-improvement program of writing, reading, meditating, and exercising—never skipping a day, never deviating from my practice. In the hole, the light stays on at night until you ask a guard to turn it off by slipping a piece of paper out through the slot in the door. I read a lot of books, including a bunch of fat James Michener paperbacks and some volumes of Persian poetry. Once my cell goes dark, I lie awake listening to *Coast to Coast,* a radio show best known for its focus on paranormal phenomena and conspiracy theories. For me, it's just a relaxing ritual. I put on my headphones and tune in so that I can tune out, listening to smart people talking about interesting ideas, like the evidence that heating garlic can destroy its anti-cancer effects. Some are more interesting than others. Sometimes I listen to all four hours of the show, and sometimes to no more than half an hour. But it's a moment of solace, an escape from the narrow confines of my cell, and the relentless, animal physicality of prison, into the sphere of ideas.

I didn't know I had this work ethic in me, because nothing in my past experience suggested that I did. Seeing what I'm capable of, I begin to think that I previously suffered from a deeply ingrained laziness that was almost a spiritual sickness.

When I'm released from solitary in June, the white car is waiting for me. Hafer and a couple of other guys on my block have managed to get most of my stolen stuff back, which is nice. I go to Hafer's cell to debrief everyone. Easy has already had some notes smuggled, by orderlies, from the box to the yard, in which he fingered Charlie the tattoo artist as his betrayer. And a guy who came to Cumberland while I was in the hole, Michael Becraft, arrived as Easy was leaving, and they somehow intersected on the transit bus. Easy told him about me and to look for me, and also told him all about his betrayer, Charlie. He told Becraft to spread the bad news, and Becraft, like a good convict, said that he would. He has already kicked up another level of shit about Charlie, and the yard is now ready to give Charlie an ultimatum—leave or get hurt—but is awaiting my opinion before taking that step.

"What's the deal?" everyone asks. "Did he rat him out or not?"

I choose my words carefully. "Easy is convinced he did," I say. "You're asking my opinion. I don't know. It seems a little farfetched to me."

I'd started working in the recreation department from 8 a.m. until noon. Now I'm able to get a no-show, no-pay job with an orderly on my unit without greasing any palms, because there's more demand for jobs here than supply. This frees me up to focus entirely on my self-imposed curriculum.

I'm still reading three books at a time—a classic lit pick (Jack London, Charles Dickens), a beach read (*Game of Thrones*), and a self-help selection (Eckhart Tolle). After doing my reading, I write poetry. I work out every afternoon, and play handball in the evening. After that, I meditate for as long as an hour and a half. Right now, my mantra is William Ernest Henley's poem "Invictus." I pay a lot of attention to how I carry myself, to being a gentleman, to having manners and being honest and polite, to not conforming to peer pressure, and to being my own man.

My will to make this time meaningful has trumped my will to be as comfortable as possible. Besides giving up heroin, I no longer drink prison alcohol. Now, when I feel discomfort, I find other ways to cope. I do smoke pot occasionally. It relaxes me.

Every day is an exercise, a chance to make this sacrifice count, from the smallest to the most important things. Living this way gives me an inkling of freedom, a sense that under difficult circumstances I'm making the most of each day, and gaining knowledge about the world and myself—what I'm capable of and not capable of, what I can endure and not endure. This feeling and this knowledge are my inspiration, my motivation, and my salvation.

Every day, I'm reminded that I'm fundamentally alone. I have my small group of friends, and I've never been among so many people all the time, but I've never felt so lonely or isolated. I also know that somehow this is an important experience. That my old urge to surround myself with people isn't conducive to pursuing my dreams. To be an actor, to work for success, I need to believe in myself and stand on my own two feet, not need someone to lean on. How else would I learn this lesson if it wasn't forced on me in this way, in this environment?

Solitude, instead of being something that makes me sad, is now something I value. Every day, I have to walk the compound. Cumberland is the hardest time I've served, because of the security level, but also the most significant, and the best other than the minimum-security camp.

I have greater clarity every day: I no longer belong here. For years, I glorified all of this, and for a time I wondered if I was like these people. I almost hoped that I was.

Now I see how much of a fish out of water I am. I go out of my way not to identify with the other inmates. I'm not impressed or inspired by them. The majority, I've come to realize, are defined by prison: it's their identity through and through. There are so many followers and very few leaders. Prison talk is an endless stream of time-killing bullshit, lies, ignorance, bigotry, stupidity, cruelty, and anger.

It's enough to make you not want to talk to anyone, and I wear my headphones and listen to music whenever I'm out of my cell. I now see socializing with other inmates as a distraction, one more thing pulling me away from the things I want to be spending my time on: writing, reading, meditating, exercising.

I'm respected enough to be allowed to do my own thing. Ninety percent of inmates adorn their cells with bikini photos; I hang a world map and *National Geographic* pictures of animals in mine. The decor stands out, and guards seem to think a little better of me because of it. I stop casually exchanging information with other inmates. It's a formality or pleasantry that now strikes me as frivolous. Unless I'm really close to someone, there's no reason to pretend we're going to stay in touch. And my tolerance is less than it was. At Lewisburg, my first cellmate was a snorer. Now, if I'm sent a new cellie, the first thing I ask is, "Do you snore?" If they say yes, I say, "Nothing personal, but you can't live here." The guards here, as at other higher-securities, are pretty good about honoring inmates' celling preferences. Probably some of the other inmates consider me aloof or stuck-up, but I don't want them around me. When I get out, I don't want them around the people I love.

———

Ironically, my newfound confidence and self-respect and comfort with being alone lead to my making real friends here. My trip to the hole has helped my reputation with inmates and also with guards. They understand why I got into that fight and, I believe, respect me for going into that cell to get my stuff back.

I hang out with other "independents," as we're called, and become friendly with the shot-callers in some of the more serious gangs. I'm surprised that this happens, but it feels good to be received this way. I feel like an equal, which makes me feel more confident and relaxed. Even with all of my baggage, I'm carrying it. Everyone in prison is always complaining about something—the judge who railroaded him, the prosecutor who fucked him—but I'm not one of them. Intelligence, strength, and courage are the qualities respected in here, and I have them to a degree. I feel pride that I can keep my head up. It's not easy, it's not the way most people do their time, and it feels like a real victory and achievement. I think about what Eddie Callegari told me when I was just at the start of my prison odyssey: that I could make it at a high-security prison. I didn't really believe him. But he was right. I can.

When Hafer's cellmate leaves, Hafer invites me to live with him. I'm not sure about this, given that he has serious mood swings and a reputation for violence, and that I don't take well to being alpha'd over, but he turns out to be a great cellie. I have mood swings too, and we're both respectful, understanding that none of it's personal, minding each other's boundaries. He likes to tinker with things, but he's not a slob. Sometimes we're just really quiet, which suits us both. I lend him my copy of "As a Man Thinketh," and he reads it with a highlighter in his hand. We live together for much of my time at Cumberland.

I make some real friends. I define a real friend as someone you can count on and trust, and who isn't just a taker. Someone who, even if he isn't a saint, I consider a decent person. Everyone I become close to reflects some side of my character. All are people who, like me, want to better themselves and improve their lives, in their own ways. Peter, my cellie, is a Wiccan, and more often than not he's a voice of reason; he has a kid, and even though he's looking at a lot of time, he makes an effort to put his best foot forward and is focused on trying to hold his family together.

John Willis is a white Catholic kid from Boston who was orphaned at fourteen and improbably became a high-ranking member of the Chinese Triads gang, with the Cantonese nickname Bac Guai John, or White Devil John. He's doing twenty years for his involvement in a South Florida OxyContin ring.

Mike Becraft is six three and good-looking and a tremendous athlete. He was his high school quarterback and a baseball star too, and he's a former minor-league hockey player. He's strong as an ox; in hockey he was the enforcer. He's from D.C., and much of his family is involved with the CIA. He's obviously the black sheep. He's in prison on a local Washington cocaine case, but D.C. convicts are sentenced to federal prison. He projects a self-assured ease that masks what I suspect is a fair amount of internal turmoil, and he's very outspoken, saying the craziest shit to other inmates and getting away with it. He's always reading and making notes and drafting business plans for

With John "White Devil" Willis and Michael Bridge, at Cumberland.

when he gets out. We run around together and work out together and become close in the process.

After Hafer leaves, I have the cell to myself; then Becraft pushes to become my cellmate, and he moves in for a time. I've hit a plateau in my workouts, and Mike is a great workout partner, helping me mix up my routine. He's always reading up on the newest exercise techniques, and we do a lot of handstand push-ups and handstand walking, which is big in CrossFit. Neither of us knows how to do it, and at first we look ridiculous, but a couple of months later we're walking thirty yards on our hands. We take turns doing squats, with the other person on our shoulders. Mike makes amazing dumbbells and barbells out of rolled-up magazines and trash bags filled with water. I do 2,500 push-ups in two hours. I reach a new level of fitness.

Mike also convinces me to get my hair cut and wear it shorter. During my months in the hole, I'd let it grow. He keeps saying, "Dude, just cut it off." So I trim a few inches, then go for it and get most of the rest clipped. It's a new look that fits my new lease on life.

Another guy on my block who I become close to is Talib Shakir. He's a top shot-caller with the Muslim car, which is powerful in the BOP's northeast region, so no one's going to question him for hanging out with a white person.

Talib has been in prison since he was eighteen. He grew up in inner-city D.C., and although he was regarded as studious and well-behaved, according to later newspaper reports, he was a troubled kid who drank alcohol and smoked marijuana, and, when he was seventeen, shot a convenience-store employee during an attempted robbery. He was charged as an adult with felony murder and sentenced to fifteen years to life.

When I meet Talib, he's been in prison for twenty years, and he has completely turned his life around. He's a gentleman and is almost professorial. If you took him out of prison and put him in a tweed jacket with tortoiseshell glasses, you'd never guess he'd done time. He has started a life-coaching program called Reconstruct, helping prisoners with reentry to society; he's become fluent in Spanish and Arabic, teaches English as a Second Language and GED for Spanish-speaking prisoners, and has six months to go until his next parole hearing. (Parole no longer exists for federal prisoners, but D.C. inmates, though held in federal prisons, are still eligible for it.)

Talib is sure he's going home. He has everything set up on the street. Since entering prison, he has married a Montessori schoolteacher who lives in Washington. He's gotten various professional certifications, including as a barber. His record has been flawless. He's done everything he can do to be a model prisoner and someone the parole board will look favorably on.

Having real friends helps take me out of myself. I get caught up in their aspirations and struggles. When Talib goes up for parole, I share his hope. The assistant warden advocates for his release, and the parole hearing examiner recommends that he be paroled. When she is overruled by the U.S. Parole Commission, and Talib is told to try again in five years, I share his devastation.

He really thought he was getting out, and he's also embarrassed, because he told everyone on the street that he was coming home. He's been in prison long enough to know you don't say stuff like that, for just this reason. He had a new life planned. Now it has been taken away, and he will be spending at least another five years locked up.

For a moment, he questions the path he's been on and flirts with despair. I worry about how many more of these reversals he can bear. He could do a lot of good in the community. He could help the government fight homegrown terrorism, as someone who's both a rock-solid convict with unimpeachable prison ethics, and a person willing to work to combat it.

Life here is overwhelmingly bleak. From the moment I wake up, it's a hike and a climb until the moment I go to sleep. I'm still a target. Maybe because Tetley has heard that my paperwork was accepted here, he and I end up having an understanding, and he doesn't create any problems for me at Cumberland. But any number of other people might want to come for me.

I'm just waiting for it. Someone's going to stab me. Why wouldn't they? Maintaining a hypervigilant state, day after day, I worry that too much cortisol is being released for too long and that it's burning out my mind. I obsess about it. It comes in waves. For a month or so, I'll feel my vocabulary is slipping. Then it comes back. There are times I feel I'm losing my mind. But the shiv between my ribs never happens. People may not like me, but I think they respect me. That's why the most valuable thing you can carry with you in prison is your reputation.

In prison, there's a lot of laughter to punctuate the gloom. People are constantly joking, telling stories, and playing little tricks on each other—summer-camp stuff like short-sheeting a bed or putting hot sauce in someone's skin cream—anything to make light of a heavy situation. There are touching moments when you see men just trying to hold it together the best they can. I look over and see Farmer coming down the stairs with a bowl of rice and some ramen noodles, getting ready to make a special meal for a group of people; he has years left on his sentence, but there's a look of contentment on his face, if only for a moment. I see people in the visiting room putting on a face so their families and children won't guess what's really going on inside them or outside that visiting room. I see guys slaving for Unicorp-job pennies to support their families and keep them together. I'll see a guy walking alone, and I can tell something's happened—a family member died, or his wife asked for a divorce, or his child won't speak to him, or he just got diagnosed with cancer—and I'm moved by his dignity in shouldering the news.

A small hobby of mine since entering prison—one of my little efforts to feel like a person in a dehumanizing environment—has been collecting the different colognes sold by commissaries in the various prisons where I've spent time. At the end of a day, after I've come in from my workout and taken a shower, I slap a little on. None of them contains alcohol, so they don't last very long. By now I've amassed around fifteen bottles.

When softball season starts, everyone turns out to watch the opening game. Since I entered prison, men's commissaries have started selling bras and other women's items, and a group of cross-dressers here sing the national anthem. The game is umpired by Jeffrey MacDonald, the army doctor and former Green Beret who was convicted of murdering his pregnant wife and their two daughters, and portrayed in the book and television movie *Fatal Vision*. Everyone in here calls him Doc and goes to him for medical advice.

Guys in prison compete to have the best photo books, little binders ideally filled with pictures of scantily dressed girls. I've put together a pretty decent one over the years, which I take pride in. Even G-rated photos of friends and loved ones make a huge difference to us all.

I've been away so long that I've lost touch with a lot of people. I remember, before my arrest, hearing about an acquaintance being sentenced to ten years in prison, and writing him off in my mind. I feel like people have forgotten me. I'm sure some of them are angry with me, and disappointed, and ashamed. I'm extremely fortunate to have a hardcore group of family and friends who've consistently visited and written and been there for support. That's extremely rare in prison, and a blessing. It makes me feel still relevant.

I get a letter, with some photos, from Hans, one of my old crew from Carpinteria. In the years since our days of teenage mischief, he got heavily into using crystal meth, dealt it small-time, and did a stretch in prison. His reaching out means a lot to me, because so many other people I'd have expected a lot more from have done a lot less: girls I've been involved with, friends I was close to, family friends who've known me well since childhood. Hans is one of a different set: people I'd have expected less from who do more. In prison, you develop a mentality of *I do for you, you do for me; you don't do for me, I don't do for you.* I really appreciate the people who've popped out of the woodwork and made an effort.

Early in my first September at Cumberland, I ask the unit manager for a special visit to see my family, who I haven't seen in two years. He says, "We'll have to ask the warden, but it's not very likely." Three weeks later, as Dad accepts the Emmy for Best Actor for his role as

Mom, Hudson, Imara, and Hawk
visiting me at Cumberland.

Liberace in HBO's *Behind the Candelabra*, he makes an emotional speech: "My oldest son, Cameron, I'm hoping I'll be able and they'll allow me to see him soon."

I learn about it from another inmate. It makes me feel so good to hear that Dad said that. The speech gets a lot of media coverage, and not long after, my unit manager suggests that I put in a request to the warden.

The warden grants me separate visits with Mom and Dad. Dad comes first, flying down to see me. In the visiting room, there's the usual swiveling of heads that happens wherever Dad goes. "Holy shit," Dad says, looking at my muscles and tattoos and short haircut. We're assigned to sit in connected plastic bucket chairs that face in the same direction, so that the two of us are next to each other, with neither of our backs to the guards. We have to twist our upper bodies to talk.

It's a little awkward at first. Over the past two years, we've talked on the phone from time to time, but there was a long period during my solitary months when we didn't speak, because I'd usually use my phone call on Erin. It's hard for anyone to understand what it's like to be in a small cement box twenty-four hours a day, and Erin was my emotional center.

It's really nice to see him. Seeing the seriousness of Cumberland, he's a bit more curious and worried than usual. I've begun to feel like things are finally shifting for me, for the better, and I feel like something has shifted in him, too. There's a level of respect there that wasn't present before. It gives me hope that we can have a solid relationship.

Mom visits the following weekend with Imara, Hawk, and Hudson. Mom has lived on hope for seven and a half years. *We have a new lawyer. Now we're halfway through preparing the document. Now we're submitting it. Now we're going to get it heard. Now we're down to the last twelve months. Now he's going to get out* . . . Finally, something real is happening. We're seeing each other for the first time in two years. It's a joyful day.

Right after that, I put in another request for a special visit. "We're starting something new in the BOP," the associate warden tells me. "If someone's visits have been taken away for an extremely long period of time, and we feel that they have good behavior, and it serves no purpose for them not to see their family, we'll reinstate their family visits. You're the first person we're trying this with, so do a good job."

Mom starts driving to see me every other week, a 600-mile-plus round-trip journey. She calls the visits "prison pilgrimages" and brings the kids with her every time. In the visiting room, we sit in the plastic chairs not facing each other and play gin rummy, checkers, chess, Connect Four, and board games on a little plastic table we set up in front of us. Mom brings coins in a Ziploc bag, for me and the kids to use for vending-machine junk food. It's always the same inmates in the visiting room. Only a handful of prisoners have people who come to see them.

My first December at Cumberland is when I was originally to have been released. As the date passes, I think of Ben Brafman's words about watching it pass me by. It's impossible not to wonder if I made the right choice when I reneged on my cooperation. Until I arrived at Cumberland, I didn't even receive the benefit of that decision, since

Jojo and Dad visiting me at Cumberland.

inmates knew the headlines about me without knowing the details. Here, I've had a different experience. I've finally been rewarded for my decision. I have the friends, and the reputation, and the acceptance of a stand-up convict. I have self-respect. My feeling of vindication blunts the pain of watching another birthday and Christmas behind bars come and go.

32

2014: The Boy with the Nazi Tattoo

Maybe a year after getting to Cumberland, I see a new guy on the yard, noticing him right away. He looks very convict, with a matrix of tattoos that includes swastikas, and a six-inch throat scar that starts at his jugular. He's the kind of hard- and dangerous-looking person I'm particularly alert to, wondering if he's going to cause me problems.

His prison name is Snake, but he introduces himself to me as Michael Bridge. He speaks with a rasp. As I'll learn over time, he's in his mid-forties, has been in prison most of his life, and has a serious jacket. He's affiliated with the Nazi Low Riders, a notoriously violent prison gang that began in the California Youth Authority in the 1980s and does the dirty work for the Aryan Brotherhood. Mike's paperwork comes up to my knees. From a civilian perspective, he's done terrible things. From an inmate's standpoint, he's fucking Rambo. Cumberland is Mike's first non-penitentiary in decades.

He's originally from L.A., too. We become handball partners and sign up for some of the same classes at the education center. He makes me a sticker that reads KILLA CAM to put on my MP3 player. Our biggest bond is poetry. Mike writes a lot of it, and some of his poems really impress me. We have little poetry sessions on the yard, our shirts off, reciting our latest works to each other. In spite of all of our differences, I come to consider him a friend.

Before I went to prison, I'd see guys with full face tattoos and keep my distance, thinking they were crazy and to be avoided. I've gotten to know some of them here, and they're regular guys; they just have tattoos on their faces. A face tattoo doesn't tell me much more than that its bearer is 100 percent dedicated to his gang or lifestyle. Some people with face tattoos are dangerous sociopaths, but a lot of the more aggressively tattooed guys I've met in prison are relatively normal people—certainly by prison standards—who have just chosen to mark themselves as an homage. It may be intimidating to other people, but in prison that's a good thing.

In the real world, though, their tattoos will make a terrible first impression and be severely limiting. Mike Bridge and I talk about it. One day I say to him, "I know your life is in prison, but you're going to get out of here someday, and you can't have swastikas all over you. It's super offensive. You don't even think like that, but you won't be able to explain them away." His mom really wants him to get rid of them too. Between thinking of her, and taking my advice, he gets most of them blacked out. He has a tattoo on his side, of a guy giving a *Sieg heil!* against a Nazi flag backdrop, changed to a guy holding a gun. He's not sure yet how to handle the enormous swastika that covers his chest, but getting rid of some of them is a major step for someone like him. It wasn't easy to earn those tattoos. They're intertwined with his identity. They carry a certain status in prison. But it's like he's having a midlife crisis—for the better.

Talib would never hang out with someone like Mike, but even between them, there's a level of mutual respect. Tattoos like Mike's swastikas are so prevalent in prison that, inside, they have a different meaning than on the street. Out in the world, Mike and Talib would have nothing to do with each other, but in prison you have to deal with everyone, walk past them, do business with people holding extremely different worldviews. Mike's not running around screaming Nordic chants. I can't say he's not a racist—anyone who's been in prison as long as he has, with the kind of anger that fuels, is prone to using race as the easiest outlet for it—but he's not extreme about race. And since everyone's guilty of racism, they tend to be able to cohabitate peacefully in spite of it, unless someone's specifically trying to offend someone.

It's at Cumberland that I get most of my tattoos. I'm lucky to be on a cellblock with one of the compound's best artists, Charlie, the same guy who Easy believed ratted him out. Though tattooing is technically against the rules, in higher-security places like this, where the administration's main concerns are drugs and weapons, cops tend to overlook it.

Charlie works on me in his cell in four-hour sessions. Prison tattoo guns tend to be a MacGyvered combination of a motor from beard-trimming clippers and a battery pack with a variable number of batteries, depending on the desired speed—four for really fast, three for medium fast, three shitty ones for slow. A typical needle is a piece of sharpened guitar string. Charlie has fancier three- and five-prong needles he's had soldered together.

I buy my own set of needles from him, taking them with me after each session to wash in my sink. I also bring my own ink, which I buy from Hafer. Hafer doesn't have a single tattoo of his own, but making pigment is one of his hustles. He cuts a can in half, pours baby oil into it, puts a wick into it, and burns it in a three-foot-high box made from taping twelve cardboard soda six-pack holders together. The box captures the black soot, which Hafer shakes out and sells. Every tattoo artist has his own recipe for the best, darkest ink, mixing the soot with mouthwash or shampoo, or adding coffee grounds.

When I get an idea for a new tattoo, Erin does Google Images searches and mails me printouts of photographs and illustrations. I probably spend 160 hours getting tattooed by Charlie. On my left bicep, I get a half-sleeve still life with an unspooling cassette tape marked THIS IS MY LIFE, musical notes, a key, a broken heart, a hammer and sickle, and a woman holding an umbrella. In the center of my chest, over the butterfly, I get a compass. To one side of it, I get NY and the Washington Square Park arch and a leaf; to the other, I get LA and some palm trees. On my stomach, I get a pyramid with an all-seeing eye, which many inmates insist must mean I'm connected to the Illuminati. On one shoulder, I get a hammer, and on the other an anvil. Across my clavicle, I get TAKE THE LONG WAY HOME. On my right side, I get a Kodiak bear coming out of the water with a salmon in its mouth. I don't like to explain my tattoos. The whole point of inking images on your body is to let them speak for themselves. If there was simple verbal reasoning behind one, I wouldn't bother distilling it into a picture on my skin.

Mom is not a tattoo fan, and on one visit, when she sees all the work I've had done, she says: "If you really want to be an actor, don't typecast yourself. They can cover up the ones you have with makeup, but don't get any more. You'll get pigeonholed." I've already paid for a whole right-arm T-shirt sleeve, but she makes me promise not to get it.

My most significant tattoo, which I get across my abs, is a pair of portraits depicting Dad and Pappy. I've never been able to overcome

With Mo at Cumberland.

With Mike Becraft at Cumberland.

my conflicting feelings about my last name, my pride in it and at the same time my discomfort with having it define how other people see me and assess me.

But Dad has really made an effort to come and visit me at Cumberland. As we've started to spend time together more often, I've felt something rekindle inside of him, like he's changed his view of the prospects for my life, and for me, and for our relationship. It feels like he hasn't given up on me entirely, that he sort of believes in me. That's an important feeling for me. I've always had so much respect for him and Pappy, and maybe because of the self-respect I've gained in prison, I'm able to acknowledge to myself that they are a huge part of who I am. When I get their faces tattooed on my body, I feel ready, finally, to show an uncomplicated pride in them.

When I show the tattoo to Dad, he seems embarrassed.

A year into my time at Cumberland, Erin tells me in a phone call that Junior has cancer. I'm devastated. She'd mentioned that Junior had been acting lethargic, and I'd told her to take him to the vet. All those times I asked her to have his symptoms checked out, she hadn't, until he passed out, bleeding from his nose, and she couldn't ignore it any longer. Now it's too late. His body is riddled with tumors.

She coordinates for me to call her on a borrowed cell phone when she takes him to the vet, so that I can listen; but the vet says there's nothing he can do. The cancer is so far along that it's inoperable. Erin takes Junior home with her to die. I make Erin promise to have the vet extract some of his cells so we can clone his DNA later. For the next couple of weeks, I call every day, and Erin puts me on speaker, and I talk to Junior. One morning, Erin says she had to have Junior put down in the middle of the night.

I've been wrestling with my feelings about Erin for a while now, and Junior's death pierces me. Nothing has so painfully made me face my powerlessness. I've been counting on Erin for a few things, one of them being to take care of our dogs. She knew how important Junior was to me. She's had her struggles these past few years, but Junior didn't have to die as soon as he did. I resent her flakiness, and I suspect she may have fallen back on old habits. It causes a rift inside of me, as far as my feelings toward Erin go, my confidence in her priorities, and my belief in her.

Around this time, I get a letter from Viviane, a woman I knew well before I went to prison. I first met her at a fashion show in L.A. a decade ago. I was out there shooting *Adam & Eve*. Viviane was a model from Brazil, and she was wearing a huge blue Afro as part of her costume. We were chatting backstage and I told her, "I'm trying to take you seriously, but your hair is making it difficult." Over the next several years, we had an intermittent romantic entanglement. I knew she had strong feelings for me then. But we were both partying at the time, I was living with Erin, and then I got lost in my heroin pit. I last saw Viviane a couple of weeks before my arrest at the Gansevoort, when I ran into her at a club in the Meatpacking District.

Viviane has written to me several times in prison, but this letter feels different. She has gone through a lot since I last saw her, switching paths from the one she was on—working in nightclubs and staying out late partying—to a much more spiritual, thoughtful one. She has stopped using drugs and has gotten into yoga and spirituality. She has spent a lot of time in India and has just returned to New York from her latest trip there. She tells me that she was recently at dinner with a friend, talking about love, and her friend asked if she'd ever

Viviane visiting me at Cumberland.

met someone she felt was her soul mate. Viviane named me. Using the Bureau of Prisons' online Inmate Locator, she found my latest address.

Now I get to know her in a whole new way. We're both very different people than when we last spoke. I know the strength it takes to make the decision to change, and then to take the necessary steps to actually do it through sheer willpower. I don't think I'd have had the strength to do it outside of prison, and really respect that she was able to. I think that's what initially draws me to her.

I still don't have friend-visitation privileges, and at first we write letters and e-mails back and forth, until we're e-mailing every day using the inmate e-mail system, TRULINCS. When my phone privileges are finally restored—three hundred minutes a month—we start talking almost every day. I send her photographs of me out on the yard with my inmate friends, who she cuts out of the pictures.

We're becoming reacquainted; it's an important time for us.

In the spring of 2014, the U.S. Sentencing Commission changes its guidelines: The amendment, called Drugs Minus Two, lops time off of the sentences of many offenders imprisoned for nonviolent drug crimes. My lawyers are sure I'm going to qualify for it. While I'm waiting for confirmation, in August I enter the RDAP program, the nine-month residential drug treatment program that trims a year off your sentence. With RDAP, you want to time it so that you finish as close as possible to your release date, because if you come out of RDAP and get a serious shot, the BOP can add the year back to your sentence. Assuming I qualify for Drugs Minus Two, I'll get out of prison just when my RDAP stint ends.

My cellie in the RDAP unit is Mo, who's tan, tall, and fully tattooed and has a Bic-razored head. He's half Libyan but is from Florida and speaks with a little bit of a southern twang. He's twelve years into a fourteen-year sentence for wholesaling meth, and he's a gang-affiliated convict who's been in a bunch of penitentiaries. We become business partners.

The four biggest moneymakers in prison are drugs, gambling, cigarettes, and weapons. The people who administer higher-security prisons are mainly worried about drugs and knives, leaving the entrepreneurial inmate a relative degree of safety in running a gambling ticket or selling cigarettes. Cigarettes probably carry the lowest risk and bring the highest reward, but it's a closed business. Cops on the take bring in the cartons, and the inmates with those relationships can sell a single filter cigarette for two or three books of stamps ($14 or $21), depending on supply and demand. Some guys buy one filter cigarette, break it down, and reroll five more, which they sell. Some guys hoard cigarettes, wait until the yard is dry, and then charge crazy prices. There's a separate hand-rolled cigarette business, but it's controlled by the gangs whose job it is to take care of "hot trash," as the cops' trash bins are called; they sift through it for guards' spent plugs of chewing tobacco, dry them out, and roll smokes that they sell for a book of stamps each. I meet guys who are taking care of their entire family, out on the street, with cigarette profits. I started smoking when I was fourteen, but the cigarette prices in prison cured me of that addiction.

Mo and I start a gambling ticket with a third guy, named Loco. I put up half the money. Loco, a physically imposing, half-Cuban, half–Puerto Rican avid gambler, puts up the other half. Mo calculates odds and runs the operation. Ours is one of maybe a half dozen tickets on the compound, and Loco's job is to place big bets on other inmates' tickets in the hope of bankrupting them and removing a competitor. He's not very successful at this.

Every day, we create a new ticket, a piece of paper listing all the important pro and college games happening that day. Mondays and Wednesdays we try to come up with specials for our Four Picks, enticing offers that usually pay out 14-to-1. For the Super Bowl, we offer more specific bets: Will the coin toss be heads or tails? Will Tom Brady throw fewer than three touchdowns, or three or more?

A guy we know who has a job in the education department, and whose hustle is making photocopies, runs off a few hundred copies of the ticket for us. We have a runner for each unit, and they go out with the tickets in the morning and through the day, distributing them;

later, they retrieve the filled-out tickets and the accompanying wagers, paid in $7-book-of-stamps units—or in wire transfers between external bank accounts. We record all bets on a master sheet.

To guys who want to bet larger amounts, and who we know are good for the money, we might extend a $500 marker. If they hit that limit, they have to have someone on the street wire money to my commissary account. One guy has a $10,000 marker. But we always get paid. Our head runner is Knee-High, a Mexican kid from Austin who's a high-ranking member of Tango Blast, and that affiliation instills enough fear that no one tries withholding payment. We always want a minimum of five hundred books of stamps—Forever Stamps—in our bank, and any profits go first to maintaining that reserve. After that, we divvy up the profits three ways: 25 percent to Mo, with the remaining 75 percent split equally between me and Loco. I net $1,000 to $1,500 a week.

Everyone doing any kind of business has stash spots. For our gambling ticket, we need places to squirrel away our books of stamps and our lists of odds and wagers and debts. Hiding contraband is more elaborate here than at Lewisburg. We have close friends on the maintenance crew, and I pay one to loosen a tile in my cell and drill out a couple of inches of cement beneath it, where I can hide a little box. For a second space, I have the same guy install a false back in my locker. And for my personal use, like the knife I carry whenever I leave my cell, I burrow a couple of shallow holes in the soft core of the cheap wooden table in my cell: one behind a drawer handle, the other behind the rubber lining of the edge of the tabletop.

Running the ticket adds to my confidence. I'm making money and doing most of the things that qualify as success in prison.

Before I went into RDAP, Talib and I talked all the time. Now that I'm in a different unit, we make a point every Sunday evening, rain or shine, of walking the track together for two or three hours. We inspire each other, push each other, have the kind of conversations where you feel smarter afterward.

We talk about Talib's conviction that prisons are radicalizing susceptible kids through exposure to actual terrorists like Cumberland inmate Masoud Khan, who once headed a network of Virginia-based jihadists. Many of the guards are ex-military, setting up a hostile dynamic and turning prisons into breeding grounds for homegrown terrorism. We talk about energy vampires and the importance of conserving our limited time and energy for the people we love. We watch *Ant-Man* together, and Talib, who has met Dad during his visits, comments on the father-son dynamic between Dad's character and his protégé, wondering if Dad had me in mind.

Word comes that Judge Berman has rejected my petition for Drugs Minus Two leniency, ruling that I'm disqualified by my second sentence for heroin possession in prison. Since I'm already in RDAP, which will take a year off my sentence, I stick with the program.

When I get out of RDAP, my plan is to cell with a guy named Captain. His story is that he's been in prison for more than twenty years, twelve of them at Administrative Maximum Facility (ADX) Florence, in Colorado. He was Special Forces in the military, was over in Iraq during the first Gulf War, and began shipping weapons back to the U.S. for the mob. Later, he became a mob hit man. Eventually it caught up with him, ending in a gunfight with police that left cops dead. This had made Captain a convict hero. In person, he is quiet and humble and friendly, and before I went into RDAP I'd often see him up in the education center.

One day when we were on the yard, it came up that right before Captain arrived at Cumberland, he was at Coleman in Florida. That's where my old friend from MCC, Dave Hattersley, was, and I asked if he knew him.

"From New Jersey?"

"Yeah."

"He's dead, dude."

"What?"

"Yeah, he was killed."

With Mo, Sebo, and some other fellas at Cumberland.

While I've been in RDAP, a book has been published, written by Meg Salib. Early in my time at Cumberland, I received a letter from her, seeking my permission to write a book about her experience. She assured me that it wouldn't delve into my family or my case, and I gave her my blessing. I said, "If you want to write a book about your experience, I can't tell you not to do that," and I did want the best for her. She'd suffered from our relationship; although she'd kept her right to practice law, she had lost her job.

I haven't read the book, a memoir, but I've heard things about it— that it goes into considerable detail about my case, including my early, quickly regretted cooperation, as well as talking about my family at some length. She wasn't honest with me about the content, and I feel betrayed. It's pretty slimy for a lawyer to write a book about her client.

When I return to gen pop, I immediately experience the book's impact. Captain, who I was supposed to move in with, and who'd told me he was holding a cell open for me, now claims a former cellie of his is just coming out of the hole, so he has to give him the slot.

As I walk away, a kid named Josh comes up to me.

"I saw you talking to that dude Captain. Do you know what his story is?"

"I think so," I say. I run through the facts I know: his tour in Iraq, his weapons shipping, his mob killings, his cop killings.

"I don't think so, man," Josh says. He shows me an article about Captain that he found online, and the facts laid out there, using Captain's real name, are very different: Captain and a partner hijacked a seventy-year-old truck driver and killed him, then rang the doorbell at a house, asking to use the bathroom. When a woman answered and said no, Captain and his partner killed her, raped and kidnapped her daughter, and then, in a gunfight with police, killed a cop. He also later killed a cop in prison with his bare hands. This story is a death

With Talib Shakir at Cumberland.

sentence in prison. Even here, killing or hurting innocent people isn't considered acceptable.

It turns out that Captain's biography isn't the only thing he's full of shit about. Dave Hattersley is alive.

Two years after my family-visitation privileges were restored—and four years since I lost my other visitation privileges—I'm allowed to see friends again, and Erin is finally approved to visit me. Everyone in here has relatives with prison records, and the higher security of higher-securities makes the officials more relaxed about who can visit.

I haven't seen Erin in five years. It feels bittersweet to see her. All these years, she has been my go-to. In certain ways, Erin has been there for me like no one else. But she has also been inconsistent, and I can see that she's still struggling with addiction. I've lost faith in our relationship, and I increasingly believe that one of the things I'm paying for is a fresh start.

With two and a half years left to the door, I tell Erin I don't plan on living with her when I get out. I want to surround myself with people who are on the same wavelength as I am. I've now been completely free of heroin for two years. She's upset but also understands.

One of the many things I'm looking forward to when I get out of prison is seeing a dentist. In prison, you're supposed to be able to get one teeth-cleaning a year, but you have to sign up for an appointment, and there's a long waiting list; it can take up to eighteen months to happen. If you haven't been at a compound for eighteen months and you're moved to a new one, the clock resets to zero. My first cleaning in my whole prison bit has been at Cumberland, and it was pretty rudimentary.

At least partly because it's such a hassle, a lot of people in prison neglect their teeth. I've seen more than a few guys who have none. If a tooth goes bad, a lot of guys just get it pulled, and it's never replaced. Men lose their dentures and wait weeks or months for a replacement set; in the meantime, with few gummable food options, they struggle to eat nutritiously.

Around a year after Viviane sent her first letter to me at Cumberland, we make a plan for her to come and see me. During a phone call, as the date of Viviane's visit approaches, I say, "Listen, I'm sort of self-conscious about this, but I only have five real teeth left in my mouth, I hope you don't mind."

There's a short silence on Viviane's end, then she says gamely, "What do you mean?"

"Well, I have one in the center, and two on each side."

Viviane is sweet about it, but I can tell she's having complex feelings processing this news.

"Just kidding," I say, and we share a laugh.

It's good to see Viviane in person, and after our first visit she's extremely loyal and present and solid and attentive. She and Mom hit it off and become friends. Sometimes Viviane spends weekends with her and the kids at Mom's farm in Millbrook.

I'm watching the clock, counting down the days and hours until my release, which is eighteen months out. My routine is pretty fixed. I sleep as late as possible, getting up at ten or eleven. I have a bowl of oatmeal and a cup of coffee. During the 1:30 p.m. move, I go to the yard, where I work out for two hours. At 3:30, when we all go back to our blocks for the four o'clock stand-up count, I take a shower and eat something. Then I go outside again and play handball for a couple of hours. Maybe I smoke a little weed first to make the handball more fun or the mundane conversations more palatable. I usually play through chow and cook a meal with my friends later. In the evening, I might watch a little TV.

I was never much of a TV watcher, and in prison I've mainly avoided it, other than football games. Now, maybe because I've hit my stride and become more sure of myself, I have a couple of series I watch—*Vikings* and *The Strain*—and always make sure I have a seat in the TV room. I also watch movies when the prison shows them.

Then I go back to my cell for my evening ritual of reading, writing poetry, and meditating. I'm beginning to let myself imagine a future beyond these walls. I spend a lot of time paging through a coffee-table book about India. Before I went to Brazil, years ago, I'd felt an almost mystical gravitation toward it; and now I'm starting to get that same feeling about India.

Even though I carved out my place at Cumberland and secured others' respect before I went into RDAP, there are now a lot of new faces. Meg Salib's book has gotten people who don't know me riled up.

Tex, a younger Aryan Brotherhood kid, tries to kick up some dust. And I have an issue with another white, a militant kid named Shawn who came from USP Victorville while I was gone. There's a tension that feels like it could erupt into a stabbing. Tex and his cronies are talking shit about me. But I have only another six weeks at Cumberland. I turned thirty-six while I was in RDAP, and, according to the BOP's inmate-classification tables, at thirty-six a male prisoner becomes less of a risk. My security level dropped, and I put in for a transfer. While I wait for it, I try to avoid getting caught up in the whites' drama.

Adding to the whites' discontentment with me, I've moved into a cell with Talib, a devout black Muslim—a living arrangement that is an extreme rarity in higher-security places. Even now that we live together, when we enter the chow hall we still split up. He sits at a black table, and I sit at a white table. If one line is much shorter than the other, we still go to our respective lines. That's how segregated it is in the chow hall.

At night, Talib goes to sleep early. I stay up reading. Our first night celling together, Talib all of a sudden yells, "Ah, ah, ah!" and starts screaming and kicking and trying to grab something. Then he relaxes. I'm like, "Dude, what the fuck?" He says, "I'm okay," and goes back to sleep. Forty-five minutes later: "Ah, ah, ah!" and all the rest. Talib is in such a panic, as if there's some terror inside him. This happens a third time. In the morning I say, "Dude, what's that about? You have night-mares?" He says, "No, I just wake up with this feeling that I'm falling." It happens several times every night, but I leave it alone and don't pry. To me, it seems like a response to something extremely traumatizing, like he's reliving over and over something that he manages to success-fully set aside when he's awake. It's disturbing, and I feel for him.

Shortly before I leave Cumberland, Talib's father, who has been ill, dies. He's been a regular visitor during Talib's decades inside, and his rock. They were really good friends. Since I've known Talib, he'd been looking forward to getting out and spending time with his dad. I think he wanted to get out there and be the son his father wanted him to be, a feeling I can relate to on many levels. With Talib's father's death, that possibility has been taken away.

33

2015: Orange Isn't the New Black

I'm being transferred to my next prison. From Cumberland, Maryland, I'm driven to Harrisburg, Pennsylvania, another northeast hub of the BOP transit system. Buses from the regional divisions, and planes from all over the country, converge here to pick up and drop off inmates. After waiting on the tarmac for several hours, a few of us are transferred to a plane with nearly two hundred prisoners on it, which soon rises into the air.

I'm wearing handcuffs attached to a belly chain attached to ankle cuffs. A few convicts on the plane who are considered particularly dangerous have black lockboxes covering their handcuffs. My ankles are cuffed too tight and are raw and bleeding. I have a window seat, and I pass the time trying to read the landscape below for clues to our direction and destination. There's not a lot of conversation among the passengers.

Six years ago, the last time I was on a plane, I was flying back to New York from L.A., having just made the deal that would lead to my arrest. Since then, I've watched planes pass overhead, trailing their white exhaust, and wondered about their routes and their passengers. I've pictured the next time I'd be on a plane, free at last, looking down at guys like me. This is definitely not what I had in mind. Instead, I'm just headed to another prison.

I don't know where I'm going but am guessing FCI Danbury, in Connecticut, because it's a northeast Low and my case manager at Cumberland thought I'd be going there. When we land after several hours and are taxiing down the runway, I see the words ATLANTA INTERNATIONAL AIRPORT. Our plane veers away from the terminal and stops in a remote section of the field. A cop starts reading off names, and the summoned cons disembark.

We sit on the tarmac for hours, then the plane takes off again. This time it looks like we're aiming west. The mountains are higher, the rivers become red and muddy and winding, and the land is more arid. Maybe my case manager didn't know what he was talking about. We land at an airport in Oklahoma City, another BOP transit hub. The plane pulls right up to a terminal. This time, my name is called.

The terminal houses a federal prison, and I spend two nights here. Then I'm put back on a plane. I ask a cop if he knows where I'm going, and he says Danbury. The plane flies for hours before beginning its descent. I assume we're in Pennsylvania, where I'll get on a bus for another five hours, but I notice the houses below us are huge and have pools and manicured lawns. This is definitely not Harrisburg. We land at a little airport near Millbrook, New York, not far from Mom's farm. From there, it's a fifty-minute bus ride to the prison where I'll be living, its name confirmed only when we finally pass through its gates: FCI Danbury.

Danbury is closer to my family, and it isn't as bad as my last Low, Loretto, but it's pretty run-down. Before being converted to a men's prison two years ago, Danbury housed only women. *Orange Is the New Black* is based on the thirteen months the author was incarcerated in the minimum-security satellite camp here. Maybe because of that history, Danbury has the most female officers of any of the prisons I've been in.

After three years in a cell, I'm back in a cube setup. My bunkmate, who everyone calls Lou the Jew, is a slick-talking degenerate gambler from L.A. who's eight years into a fourteen-year sentence for selling tickets to ridiculous-sounding, nonexistent concerts, such as a "Beatles Revival."

I know, from when I was new to the system, that I'll be given some space here, since I'm coming from a higher-security. At lower-securities, there are more guys trying to act some way they're not, and they put guys from more serious places on a pedestal.

When I went to my first compound, Lewisburg, I was still a child—addicted to heroin, recklessly leaving the grounds and smuggling in a prostitute, enamored of the criminal lifestyle. The last time I was at a Low, Loretto, I was at my bleakest—in despair from my newly doubled sentence and harsh sanctions, and still using heroin. I didn't understand yet that you can do prison time in different ways. You can make it hard on yourself, or you can make it easy.

Now I'm repelled by the false romance of prison life. I have clarity and focus. As soon as I arrive at Danbury, I go directly to the administration and ask for a no-show, no-pay job, and they give it to me. I contract with a guy in the kitchen to smuggle me four or five milks a day, at a cost of four stamps per bottle. I spend my time reading, writing, meditating, exercising, and running a small gambling ticket to pass time and make some change. I continue to masturbate in the shower twice a day like it's my job. Some guys here have a hustle selling laminated nude photos that cling to the shower walls, five stamps for three front-and-back pictures. The shower floors are disgusting, and I'm not without blame for that. As a result, cleaning the showers, which happens at least twice a day, is a very important job: the crews assigned to do it are paid well, and inmates expect them to be on point.

I feel safer here. A few weeks after my arrival, I notice that a real weight has lifted. I literally feel lighter, which makes me aware of just how heavy I've been feeling for years.

It's June 2015. I'm twelve months from the door now, which is tantalizingly close, but there are still painful reminders that I'm not yet free.

Me with Granny.

Granny is ninety-two and has cancer. Though I haven't seen her since she visited me at Lewisburg, she writes all the time. Shortly before my arrival at Danbury, she was moved to the Motion Picture & Television Country House and Hospital's palliative care unit. As soon as I get to Danbury, I drop a letter to her in the mailbox next to the officers' bubble, the enclosure on the unit that serves as their command center. I don't hear back from her, and then, on July 3, Dad calls from the hospital to say Granny has only hours to live. I ask him to put the phone next to her. She can't speak, but I hear her breathing, and I tell her what I want to say to her. A few hours later, she passes away. It kills me that I can't be there for her funeral, and my disappointment and frustration are compounded when I find out that the prison doesn't use the mailbox where I put my last letter to Granny; she never received it, because it's still sitting in that unused box labeled MAILBOX. I'm more angry than sad. I want to lash out at someone, but I don't know who to blame.

———

Danbury has a weight room, and after years of calisthenic workouts, I'm curious to see how strong I've gotten. I start hitting the weights again, and I bulk up. Being back in a cube, after years in a cell, I find it harder to read in peace here, though I do pick up a James Clavell doorstop or two. With my headphones to tune out the surrounding noise, I write more, and I begin writing notes for this book. I know I'll be going home relatively soon, and I have a story I want to tell. Dad has suggested that it would be a good idea to tell it sooner than later. This is something productive that I can focus my energy on. It's also a forced march down memory lane, which is sometimes frustrating, sometimes painful, sometimes funny.

This is the easiest time I'll do—I'm more seasoned, and the end is in sight. Early on, I'm offered K2, a not-yet-illegal "synthetic marijuana," which I think is probably bullshit, but which is not yet detectable by urine testing. I smoke it and feel like I'm coming unglued. I'm unable to talk. I see words vaporing out of my head.

I won't touch the stuff again, but I see other people who use it vomiting and crying. One guy screams that people are trying to kill him and frantically punches a window to escape until his hands are shredded. Another night, a guy who's an Army Ranger, ex-boxer, trained killer, extreme calisthenics practitioner, and one of the angriest people I've encountered in prison smokes K2 and goes into attack mode. He breaks everything in sight, including someone's nose, and hurts two inmates who try to hold him down. The only thing that prevents additional damage is that these K2 freak-outs wear off after ten to fifteen minutes, and his rage begins to taper. He's lucky, because there aren't any cops on the unit when it happens; had there been, he probably would have hurt them, which would have led to a lot more time for him in prison.

Though I'm keeping to myself more than in the past, I do make a few friends at Danbury. On one of my first days here, I'm talking with some guys when a short, chubby man with a yarmulke and wire-frame glasses approaches. "Cameron, I'm Avi Gersten, welcome to Danbury." I can tell by the way the guys I'm talking to regard him that he has respect.

Avi becomes a friend. He's an Orthodox Jew who grew up poor in Brooklyn, became a used-car dealer, and went into real estate. He's here for allegedly committing various frauds.

He's a gambler, and like a lot of white-collar defendants, he turned down a plea bargain of five years, thinking it was too long and that he'd take his chances. But at trial he ended up with a twenty-two-year sentence. He's now desperately trying to get some time back on appeal. Prosecutors would say that Avi's rejection of the plea bargain resulted in the waste of government resources and taxpayer dollars. But it's hard not to see vindictiveness as a driving force in the justice system. How could those same prosecutors think that it was appropriate for Avi to serve five years and also appropriate for him to serve twenty-two years?

Avi has five adoring kids who visit him pretty much every weekend with his wife. I'll be in the visiting room, and one of his kids will come over bearing a gift of really good pastrami or lox or a bagel. How they brought it in, I don't ask. I gravitate toward Avi because he's smart and open-minded, and he's generous with me. When I need to make a call, it's usually his cell phone that I use. At one point he pays for Viviane to go round-trip to India, first class. I write some poems for Avi.

We partner on a gambling ticket, and it does well for most of football season. But when basketball season starts, the ticket nosedives, and then we get killed on the Super Bowl between Carolina and Denver. We shaved the odds to make people want to take Denver, because we thought Carolina was going to destroy them, so we got all the Denver money on the compound. Then Carolina shit the bed. We call it Black Sunday. We also have problems collecting, which is an issue at lower-security places where there aren't the same repercussions non-payment would bring at a higher-security place.

Then I lose my partner. At a place like Danbury, which is over-flowing with drugs and cell phones, you're lulled into complacency. If you've never been caught, your survival instincts haven't been honed.

And Avi, only two years into his bit, is flagrant about his cell phone use. One day he's on someone else's bunk, a blanket hanging down to make a tent, one of his legs sticking out, jawboning on the phone with someone. He has a lookout, but when a cop approaches and the kid says "Avi, Avi," he is so engrossed in his conversation that the cop walks right up and catches him red-handed.

Avi is transferred to Loretto, my old terrible prison.

I think about the future constantly, and meditate about it. My relationship with Viviane is strong. We're talking about being together after prison, though I want to have some time to myself, to live alone, right when I get out. With freedom in sight, I let myself feel twinges of excitement. I feel good that I've done the best for myself during my prison bit. I've made steady progress, and I continue to make it. I really didn't know if I was capable of this kind of discipline, and it's been heartening to see that I am, though I'm nervous about whether it will carry over to the street.

My relationship with Mom was pretty nonexistent when I entered prison. Now it's solid, and I'm grateful to her for giving me a chance to get to know my little brothers and sister. Dad sends me packages filled with real-estate brochures and information about different apartment buildings in Manhattan. I love getting them and visualizing life after prison, and my friends gather around and look at them with me. Catherine visits with Carys. When I last saw Carys, I was at Lewisburg, and she was seven years old. Now she's almost thirteen, a mature little lady.

Meg Salib's book is in heavy circulation here. Early on, some people say they have an issue with me sitting at the white table. I tell them I'll sit wherever I want, and that's the end of that. Otherwise, the few people who bring it up—"Dude, I was just reading this thing you were in"—do so more for conversation than provocation. At this point in my bit, I'm not looking to make new friends.

Meg comes to visit. I'm upset about the book, based on what I've heard about it, though probably not as upset as some people around me expect me to be. It probably helps that I didn't read her book, so I don't have specific phrases or opinions rattling around my head and fueling my anger. And I want to ask her to advise my friend Sebastian on his case. The visit goes weirdly. We don't even talk about the book. It's clear she still has strong feelings for me. She kisses me. I just stand there, kind of disgusted, which is saying a lot when you're in prison, desperate for a woman's touch. She tries coming back in for more kisses, and I bob and weave, avoiding her lips, and say it's time for me to leave. She ends up not helping my friend.

I feel more at peace. At lower-securities, a gay man is frowned on until someone who's respected talks to him. By this point in my journey, I seem to be seen that way, because shortly before I'm to leave Danbury, an obviously gay man moves in across from me. He's a great guy, and I speak with him openly, and pretty soon a couple of other guys talk to him openly, and soon he's accepted on the block.

34

2016: Kashi Vanilla Pepita

"And so you arise from the mud . . . And you cleanse your eyes in a great brightness, and thrust your shoulders among the stars, doing what all life has done, letting the 'ape and tiger die' and wresting highest heritage from all powers that be."

—Jack London

June 13, 2016.

My last full day at Danbury.

I've known my release date for several months, and have been counting down to it for the past five days, but I can't believe the day is finally here. It's surreal. I do what's called the merry-go-round, getting signatures on my release paperwork from every department head. It's a joyful pain in the ass.

It's a mildly warm day, and I play handball with my friend George. I give away my things to the few people I'm close to, including John Willis, who came here from Cumberland and who gets a gold chain Viviane brought me from Brazil. I'm going to walk out of here with only a couple of keepsakes, like a pair of prison-issue khakis I've turned into cutoff shorts, and my journals, and the white Chucks I first wore at Lewisburg. They've been to hell and back and look like it, and I cherish them.

The next morning, around eight, I hear the words I've been waiting to hear for nearly eight years: "Cameron Douglas to R&D." I've already packed. I say my goodbyes to friends, and then I walk to Receiving & Discharge, where I sign some paperwork.

I step through a little door in the side of the prison, wearing prison sweats and a T-shirt and clutching my little bag of belongings, and I'm outside the walls. It's an amazing feeling. I'm still inside a couple of layers of security fencing, and can't see beyond them, but I let out a primal scream. The cop walking the perimeter looks at me warily, like I might be a threat. Then I walk through a gate, and I'm in the parking lot.

The blue sky is cloudless. Mom is running toward me. Hawk, Hudson, and Imara are running behind her, and Viviane behind them. Mom reaches me first, and we hug, rocking from side to side. The kids join us. Then Viviane. We all just hold each other, crying and laughing. It's very emotional.

They arrived in town last night, stayed at a motel, woke up at five this morning, and got to the prison at six, the earliest they were told I might be released. It's now 11:30 a.m. When we reach Mom's and Viviane's cars, they show me the huge banners they made: WELCOME HOME CAMERON.

I ride with Viviane, as we all go back to the motel for what Mom calls the Freedom Breakfast. I ask the kids if they remember me before I went to prison, and they say no. They were so young then. I try on some outfits Mom and Viv have bought for me. It feels awkward to be wearing clothes picked out by someone else. Then Viviane and I have an hour and a half at the motel to ourselves. After fantasizing about this moment for so long, there's a little awkwardness at first, but we laugh about it. I'm also a bit nervous about how I'll be able to perform in the flesh, but I surprise myself and her. And with the touch of her skin, everything else melts away. There's an underlying tenseness to our reunion, because I'm on the clock. I have to report to a halfway house in the Bronx within four hours of my release, so Viv drives me there.

———

The Bronx Community Reentry Center, off of Fordham Road, is known among the BOP suits I've talked to as the worst halfway house in the country, and the loosest, and occupies a run-down brownstone apartment building. It will soon be gutted and its administrators replaced.

It feels bittersweet to have had a few hours of freedom with people I love, only to return so soon to a version of prison. The people here are the same people as there: convicts and BOP staff. The vibe is the same, and you interact with people the same way. Right away, I'm under pressure. I have to get a New York State Identification Card, which is a catch-22, since you need identification to get identification, and all I have is my prison I.D.

Shortly before my release from Danbury, I received $90,000 from the government from my negligence lawsuit over the BOP's mishandling of my knee injury at Loretto. I have the check, but I can't cash it without a bank account, and I can't get a bank account without identification. You have to get special passes to leave the halfway house, like a half-hour pass to go and buy snacks or clothes, or a forty-five-minute pass to go and do your laundry. It takes me a couple of trips to the DMV, and a lot of waiting around, to get a new I.D. Every time I leave the halfway house, I have a fixed amount of time before I have to return, and it's very stressful. I've just gotten out of prison, and I'm scared of getting back late.

I'm one of the lucky ones, since I have a job lined up—reading scripts for Dad's production company, Furthur Films—which I have to start within forty-eight hours of my release from prison. The scripts come in by the dozens—screenplays for his consideration as an actor and as a producer, as well as new drafts of scripts he already has in production. I've read scripts before, during my years of making a half-assed effort to be an actor. Now, though, I read them with a new vigor, and as I jot my notations in the margins, I soak them in in a different way. I'm reacclimatizing to the business.

I have other BOP-mandated obligations. Any night, a halfway-house staffer might tell me I need to take a urine test before I leave the building the next morning. I attend weekly, one-and-a-half-hour group counseling sessions for reintegration into society. At the same place, I meet for an hour each week with a social worker. And, for the first time in my life, I give psychotherapy a shot.

When I was younger, I thought that that's what friends were for. Or I dealt with issues internally. But where did that approach get me? Now I want so badly to succeed that I'm ready to use any possible tool to achieve that and to help me live the life I've envisioned all these years. People I respect tell me therapy has helped them. And I have a lot of stuff to get off my chest. I start seeing a psychiatrist, Rami Kaminski, once a week.

With everything else that I have to do, if I have an hour to burn I'm seeing Viviane or Mom or Dad. Everyone asks me questions about prison, but I don't think any of them can really imagine how dark my life was—and I'm happy about that. Mom gets an audience with a visiting healer from Brazil named John of God, who's credited with performing psychic surgeries, and tells him her story. He gives her a crystal bracelet he has prayed over to give to me, and I start wearing it. My attitude about the supernatural boils down to what I call my Big Bang theory: If scientists agree that in one one-thousandth of a second, a point smaller than a grain of sand became an infinitely large universe, then it's hard for someone to tell me that *anything* isn't possible. So whenever I'm confronted with something that is both interesting and preposterous at the same time, I think: *Okay, maybe it's full of shit, but maybe it isn't.* If someone has put as much energy into an object as I'm told John of God did into this one, then I'm willing to hope that maybe it does have some sort of positive vibrational energy.

After a couple of weeks at the halfway house, I get my first home pass, to spend the weekend at Mom's. Her town house, on the Upper East Side, is as different from prison as I can imagine. When I walk in, I'm greeted by Pasha and Blanca, Mom's pair of albino Dobermans, and by Namaste, her Italian greyhound. In the foyer, I see the 6′ x 4′ birthday card on canvas, "to Dia," painted for Mom when she was a child by Joan Miró, who also lived on Mallorca. I sleep in the room where Viviane has been living for the past couple of months. It's beautifully

On Mom's patio after my release.

decorated, and has a huge, comfortable bed with a padded headboard and a comforter and lots of pillows.

I take a shower. It's so opulent. The floor is marble. After years of wearing shower shoes, this is the first time I've touched a bathroom floor with my bare feet since I can't remember when, and it's such a nice feeling. The shower has a rain showerhead, and I let the spray flow down over me. After years of showers that were too hot or too cold, and which shot out a stinging jet or an ineffectual mist, the biggest luxury is just having some control over the experience.

There's a full-length mirror. It's the first I've seen in years and also, because prisons have only polished metal versions, the first clear one I've seen my reflection in. It's weird to see my entire body at once—naked, cut, tattooed. It's a map of the damage done. The scarred finger from the bone-deep cut I got in Idaho when I was a teenager. The faint, bowl-shaped line on my brow, from driving my car into a tree next to the highway in Santa Barbara. The hairline crack along my jaw, made by Amanda's mini–morning star, which has never fully healed: I can still feel the break with my finger, I can only open my jaw so wide, and it sometimes locks open. The red puncture mark on my elbow from being stabbed in Las Vegas. The ugly bump on the finger I broke playing football at Loretto. The surgical scar from the base of my thigh to the top of my calf bone, from my knee injury at Loretto, and another scar on my hip, where they put some more screws in.

I'm still working out five days a week, and I'm as fit as I've ever been. I feel lucky not to have track marks or scarring or abscesses from my years of addiction. Especially the cocaine years. That year and a half of shooting coke—typically trash product from delivery dealers that had been stepped on who knows how many times—was

In Mom's kitchen after my release.

far more damaging to me than my half-decade on heroin. Amazingly, I have no obvious long-term health issues from those years of using. I do worry about less visible impacts. Can I still get a woman pregnant? What have I done to my memory? I don't know how my overdoses affected me, what exactly that loss of oxygen did to my brain. I'm unsure of the toll of sleep deprivation during my benders, or of the years of stress and burnout and paranoia.

When I'm at Mom's, the halfway house calls her landline every three and a half hours, day and night. When I answer the phone, a recorded voice says "Contact," and I respond with my register number: 70707-054. No one in the house gets a full night's sleep.

In prison, people used to say things to me like "It will be hard getting out" and "It's a hell of an adjustment." I'd laugh at them. I'd say, "This isn't my life, that's my life," and "I'll fit back in like I didn't skip a beat." I was sure of that.

But it is difficult. Sometimes, at the halfway house, marshals take someone away in chains, and I get a small shiver, aware of how precarious my freedom is. Prison bars have given way to a straitjacket of restrictions and obligations. While I have more family support than most, I have to contend with many of the same workaday challenges all inmates reentering society face, like building credit, and I open a card with a tiny limit to begin the process.

As I reacclimate to the normal world, I feel the same queasiness that comes from surfacing too quickly when you scuba dive. Riding the subway is jarring. I watch everyone with their heads lowered, staring at their phones like zombies, and feel like I'm in the Twilight Zone. Having become programmed to be on high alert around people, I have trouble with the crush of bodies, the jostling, the lack of personal space. A few times, I start sweating so profusely that I ask Dr. Kaminski about it. He says I'm having panic attacks.

It's a lot, and it's hard on Viviane and me. We're both fiery, and our relationship has its ups and downs. Everyone else is getting the best I have to offer. She's getting the excess steam I have to blow off. After a few months, when I start settling in and finding my routine and relaxing a bit, I realize just how stressed I've been.

It's hard not to have one foot back in prison. I'm still in the convict mindset of *I do for you, you do for me; you fuck me, I fuck you.* I'm grateful for the loyalty of old friends who stuck by me through my seven-year ordeal, writing and calling and visiting, and I remember those who didn't. I remember people I wrote to who didn't write back. People who say, "I didn't know where to reach you" must not have tried very hard. The BOP's Inmate Locator makes it very easy, or that's what I tell myself anyway.

Out on the street, if you have an hour with someone, you get the best version of that person. It takes a long time to see what they're really about, how they act in different situations, what they're capable of and what they aren't. In the joint, that stuff comes out in a matter of weeks. When you spend three months with someone, you really get the measure of that person, so the bonds come quickly and feel more solid.

Apart from the other residents of the halfway house, I'm prohibited from having contact with any current or former prisoners, but I hear from friends from time to time. I learn that Mike Bridge got his last offensive tattoo, the outsize swastika on his chest, covered up and that his mother is really happy about it. I run into a few guys just while I'm going about my business. In Tribeca, I see Jerry, an Italian guy I liked who was Jackie D'Amico's sidekick at MCC. On the subway, I run into Peter, a bunkie from MCC, and Black, a friend from Lewisburg. I see Dimitri, from Loretto, and he says, "Holy shit, dude, what the fuck?" I'm 190 pounds, as bulked up as possible, and look ridiculous; my head looks small on top of my body. It will take me a few months to get back to a more natural weight.

One day, Dad invites me to have lunch with him and Dylan. Dad wasn't around when I was released from Danbury, and he hasn't made much effort to see me since then. Maybe he doesn't trust my sobriety, or my relationships with other cons and ex-cons, or my resolve to stay on the right side of the law. I don't want to say no to his lunch invitation, but my halfway-house restrictions make the logistics tough for me. I start thinking out loud how I could make it work.

"Forget about it," he says.

"What do you mean, I want to come."

"Nah, don't worry about it, it doesn't make sense."

He hangs up. My feelings are really hurt. He can't send a car for me, so I can spend the day with him? If he did, I'd be able to get back to the halfway house in time, and I know it's an option he would consider, so the fact that he doesn't suggest it feels intentional. Like he doesn't really want to see me. I'm angry.

A week later, I go over to his apartment to see him, and I mention our last conversation. He says, "Nah, I didn't say 'Forget about it.'" I say, "You did say 'Forget about it,' and you know you did, so don't sit there and tell me you didn't." I think he feels bad about it, and when I sense my anger getting the better of me, my eyes are opened: for an instant, on his face, I glimpse the effect of my outburst on him. I know I'm not going to do anything to escalate this. I know that I'm of sound mind. But given where I've been, and how recently I've come home, I can't expect other people to know that. He's starting to get to know me again, and I'm starting to present myself to him again. He's visibly unsettled. I don't want to make people feel that way. I'm still relearning how to express my feelings appropriately in my new reality. Clearly, I need to learn to temper my emotions.

After a few months, Dad starts warming up to me. We talk a few days a week and get together two or three times a month. I think he's seeing that I'm on the right track, and he feels safer exposing himself to me. One day, we're hanging out and he says, "I don't know how you did it. How you went through the things you did." It's the first time he's ever acknowledged it quite like that. I say, "Well, I'm home now."

We never really became friends, as many fathers and sons do at a certain point, but now we're starting to do that. We're forming the relationship I've always wanted. Someone tells me there's a tabloid story suggesting that Dad's closeness to me is causing tensions between him and Catherine, but the truth, as far as I can tell, is the opposite: I credit Catherine with pushing him to extend his paternal love to me.

He becomes more generous. On my birthday, I show up at a restaurant in the West Village for what I think is dinner with Mom and Viviane and my brothers and sister but turns out to be a surprise party with some of my oldest friends, including Serebe and Eyal, from DJing. Dad is in L.A. for Pappy's birthday, but he had reached out to Viviane to suggest this party, and has paid for it and helped to organize it. For a gift, he's gotten me tickets to *Hamilton*. It's a great evening, though I have to rush out of there, like Cinderella, to be back at the halfway house by my 9 p.m. curfew.

I have to live at the halfway house for six months. Then I can move into my own place. I've been looking forward to this, after so many years without privacy or solitude or quiet or any control over my environment. Dad feels strongly that after being in prison for so long, I should have my freedom. But I love Viviane, and we decide to move in together.

Finding a landlord willing to rent to an ex-con is a major problem for inmates reentering society. Even with all of my advantages, including parents willing to cosign my lease, several buildings reject me before I find an unfurnished one-bedroom rental in a building in Tribeca. While we're waiting to move in, I live at Mom's house for a month. Finally, Viviane and I move into our apartment with Phoenix, her white Maltese.

It's incredible to be in my own place. Dad gives me a framed cartoon by Jules Feiffer of Dalton Trumbo soaking in his bathtub, which I hang on the wall. From our small balcony, I can see across Lower Manhattan to the gold figure that caps the Municipal Building, right next to the federal courthouse where I was sentenced and the jail where I lived for nearly a year. Every day, taking the 4 or 5 train to the halfway house or the Furthur Films offices or Mom's, I glide beneath those buildings.

Dog-breeding history has passed me by. There are now Mastadors, which are pretty much like the Boerbadors I envisioned. Instead, I get a chocolate Lab puppy, a solid little ball I name Truck. I get a kick out of simple novelties, like using emojis in my text messages. Shopping feels new. I can't believe the array of breakfast cereals now, and I buy several. Kashi Vanilla Pepita? In prison, I saw ads for all these amazing new video games that I wanted to try, so I go to Best Buy and get a PlayStation 3 and a bunch of games. The gameplay could be better, but the graphics are amazing. I don't play much. I have too much else to do.

You forget what a luxury dentists are until you don't have access to them. Now that I have six-month checkups, I really appreciate them. I also have a near-religious experience at my first post-release teeth cleaning. My mind is so pure and clear and chemical-free. They put the nitrous gas on me, and keep it on the whole time they're cleaning my teeth, and I go into a celestial realm with angels.

Then I come back down to earth. In prison, it was easy to imagine that when I got out, everything would be beautiful. And that's not always the case. I'm so conscious about time lost and don't want to waste any more of it. I want to act. I want to vindicate Granny's belief in me and her steadfast encouragement. I meet with an agent and go on an audition and am convinced I'm going to get the part. Of course, I don't. I want to see Pappy before it's too late, and when the rest of the family celebrates his 100th birthday in California, I hope to join them, only to be denied permission by my case manager.

My impatience and frustration and overall stress affect my relationship with Viviane. I know when things are off between us. I don't doubt that Dad and Mom loved each other, but they didn't like each other. Because of their example, I'm hyper-attuned to interpersonal conflict. If there are any issues in my relationship, I go immediately to: *Wait, I can't do this.* But I'm trying to let myself go with the flow this time. I'm happy to find that I'm able to keep things in perspective. When I'm getting carried away or letting something affect me negatively, I can keep the feeling in check.

Viviane is a huge part of why I'm on the right track and focused. She teaches yoga at Jivamukti, and she really does have a Zen personality, most of the time. She's been a rock, and so loving and support-ive and attentive. If I weren't with her, I might be out on the prowl, staying out late, sleeping late, hanging in nightclubs, living a lifestyle not conducive to what I'm trying to accomplish. I want to grind and focus. As Dad sees her effect on me, and her devotion to our relation-ship, he starts to come around a bit on our cohabitation.

I'm taking a longer view of my acting goals. Dad asked if I was plan-ning to take any acting classes, and I realized that if this is some-thing I'm really serious about, I need to put in the work and time. I've joined a class that meets for five hours twice a week, on West Fifty-Fourth Street in the Theater District. The teacher is Wynn Handman, a legend who taught Dad as well as Denzel Washington, Christopher Walken, Mia Farrow, and many others. Wynn is ninety-four and still teaches four of these five-hour classes every week, and is present for all of them. The class is limited to professional actors, and Wynn can be blunt and critical. If I'm going to be exposed as a fraud, this is where it will happen.

The roles Wynn assigns me tend to be poetic soldiers or troubled artists. After all my concerns about frying my brain, I'm heartened to find that I can memorize lines well. My vocabulary is there for me when I need it. And though I haven't been making TV or movies for the past seven years, to survive prison I was acting day in and day out. This feels like a natural fit for me, like it's what I'm meant to do, and I get generally positive feedback.

At a class in May, I'm reading a scene from Tennessee Williams's *Orpheus Descending,* in which I play a drifter from New Orleans who's had a lonely life and isn't welcome in his new community. We've been working on the scene for two months, and I've been playing the part with a *N'awlins* accent. This time, Wynn says: "Let's leave the accent out of it." I'm embarrassed, because I know he's right. I've been focus-ing more on nailing the accent than on the text and subtext.

Running the lines without the accent is hard. It keeps wanting to come back. I feel my face burning and am really self-conscious. All I want to do is take off and leave the class. I hate when people feel bad for me. It makes me feel weak. I cut out five minutes early to avoid having to talk to anyone. The next day, I have to run the scene again. It's humbling, but I know that as an actor you have to have a thick skin. I think what I can do is dig really deep and offer a certain level of genuine emotion, of less-is-more naturalism.

I appreciate the art form in a much less superficial way than I did before. Now I understand what a rare and great thing it is to be able to use your persona and your body and your experiences as if they were an instrument to tell a story that inspires and touches people. When it's done right, that's what happens. There are different approaches, but the one that makes the most sense to me, and informs the techniques I work on, has to do with understanding a character and putting myself in their shoes. And what gives it authenticity is drawing from a real place inside you. The performances by other actors that I appreciate most have that quality.

I spend a lot of my time outside of class rehearsing. I'm hungry. I want to be fully immersed in this, pushing and working to make something happen. It feels really good to see, four or five months after my release, that the drive and determination and discipline I nurtured in prison are still with me. I'm going to keep plugging away until I get a break, until someone's willing to take a risk on me. My plan is to move to L.A.—that's where the work is—when Judge Berman permits it.

I'm also looking into getting some of my tattoos removed. The whole process is long and painful: as many as nine sessions for a single tattoo, over as long as two years. But I'm concerned some of my tats could deter directors from hiring me for certain roles. The ugliest ones I have I got before I went to prison. Tick and Tock, which run the length of my forearms, definitely have to go. They're eyesores and don't mean anything to me anymore, and with tats in such a visible place, it's going to be hard not to get typecast. I also like the idea of being able to wear short-sleeve shirts without any ink showing.

The acting classes have an unexpected effect on me. For the past seven years—and really for a much longer time—I've been perplexed by my failure to grieve over what's happened to me and what I've done to myself. After being numb and closed off for so long, acting is forcing me to access long-buried experiences and emotions. It's really cathartic and also exciting, because I'm realizing how much I have to draw from as an actor and finding that I can access it readily. I knew the emotions were there, because I know myself and I knew they had to be, so it makes perfect sense, but I was nervous I'd never be able to access them, that I was permanently numbed out. For years, in fact, thinking about what impact those buried, unacknowledged feelings and experiences and memories might have, I worried about what outlet they would find, and exactly how I might let them breathe and not just rot and die somewhere deep inside me.

I have a lifetime of deflected emotion to catch up on. I think about those years when I would run into people in New York and be unable to recall anything about our relationship, other than that it had been significant at some point. I think about everything I missed, like seeing Granny before she died. One day in late May, I'm walking Truck when for some reason my childhood friend Paul comes strongly into my mind. Paul is the friend who overdosed when we were in our early twenties. I was sinking into my cocaine addiction then, and I never really felt anything. Now I see Paul's face, and I get choked up. I stop where I am on the sidewalk to gather myself. All these moments with Paul, buried inside me, start bubbling up. When I get back to my building and into the elevator, I let myself cry. I mourn the loss of my friend, feeling what I should have felt seventeen years ago.

In retrospect, I feel that during all those years I was too angry to cry, too deeply infuriated by how my life was shaping up to make room for any other emotion. Now, increasingly, when I speak about anything from the heart, like telling Dad or Mom or Viviane or friends how much I love them, I get a knot in my throat. It starts happening so often that I think I'm going to need to learn to control this and rein it in, or else I'm going to make a lot of people uncomfortable. I'm touched, watching the Olympics, seeing people giving their all to be the best. I weep while watching the animated film *Coco*, especially the last thirty minutes, about a family's reconciliation.

I'd thought that my sessions with Dr. Kaminski might become a regular Noah's flood of snot and tears too, and sometimes, digging around my history with him, I do get emotional. But we actually don't talk that much about my past. Dr. Kaminski, who speaks with a heavy Israeli accent, is very smart and has lots of accolades and is very expensive. He's well worth it, but he does most of the talking.

35

2017: Planning for the Past

In March, I switch to supervised release, which is parole for federal inmates. It will last for five years. I've had six months in a halfway house (and another three months under halfway house supervision) without incident, and two and a half years in prison before that without a major shot. I've been expecting that now I'll just have to check in from time to time, but otherwise be able to live like a free man.

I'm in for a bucket of cold water. In addition to my continued weekly sessions with Dr. Kaminski, several stipulations made by Judge Berman in my original sentence eight years ago kick in. It's an invasive regimen. Every night after eight o'clock, I call a number and punch in a code to hear a recording that tells me whether or not I have to report to the probation office the next day. If I do, then I have to go there, give a urine sample, and meet with my probation officer, or P.O. Sometimes she shows up unannounced at my apartment building with another officer and calls from downstairs to say they're here for a spot visit. They come up in the elevator wearing bulletproof vests and carrying handguns.

But the rigidity is in line with my intentions. I like to be out and about, and someday I will be again, but right now isn't the time for that. I don't want to be partying or catching up with casual acquaintances. I want to focus on building a new life. I'm reading less but am watching a lot of documentaries. I still meditate every day. I work out. I work.

Every time I report to the probation office, which is in the same building as the courthouse where I was sentenced, I see the MCC next door. When I was in there, I'd look out the one non-frosted exterior window on my unit and see people down on the street, going about their lives, and think that one day that would be me, and how nice it would be then to look up at this building from outside. It is nice. I'm back where the nightmare began, but now things are going well. Sometimes I'm hit with a wave of euphoria. I stop whatever I'm doing and think: *I made it. I'm here.* It's an amazing feeling.

I'm still readjusting to civilian life. The day I left prison, I weighed 190. More than a year later, the scale says 161. I think it must be broken. I've been trying to stick to a gluten-free diet, and sometimes that has meant not eating when the right food wasn't ready-to-hand. But I don't want to be less than 175. Up in Westchester County, where Dad lives, I get my learner's permit to drive a car; my license had lapsed before I went to prison. I still need to take a five-hour course on defensive driving, and then take a test, to get my license.

My sobriety feels strong. I was able to kick heroin for good in an environment where it was easily available and most people could and would do it from time to time. I generally no longer feel the acute lack of something that long-term opioid dependence caused me to feel even as recently as a couple of years ago. It was a constant discomfort in my own skin, a feeling of anxiety and discontentment, of a roughness in my life that could only be smoothed by one thing. Now I'm finally coming to terms with not having heroin to turn to, with letting go of that security blanket.

I do smoke pot sometimes. It's not allowed under the terms of my probation, and Dr. Kaminski wants to get me a prescription for medical marijuana. It has been found to help people with opioid dependence, and an increasing number of states are legalizing its use for

PTSD, which Dr. Kaminski also thinks I have. But it's not currently prescribable for either diagnosis in New York.

During a surprise spot urine check in April, I go into the testing room, which has mirrors everywhere, including the floor and ceiling, and do my business under the gaze of a technician whose job it is to watch me piss. I test positive for THC.

This is a big setback. Ben Brafman, who's now my lawyer, is worried that Judge Berman will revoke my probation and send me back to prison. We have a hearing, where Dr. Kaminski explains to the judge that my pot use was deliberate and moderate and not indicative of a relapse. My P.O., Ms. Josephs, whom I have developed a mutual respect with, is supportive too, saying, essentially: These things happen. Ben is so worried about Judge Berman's possible reaction that we're voluntarily proposing an even more rigorous package of requirements for me. I'll attend ninety AA or NA meetings in ninety days, and be escorted to them by a sober companion who'll vouch for my attendance. I'll also attend a weekly hour-and-a-half group therapy session focused on substance abuse.

I haven't been in front of Judge Berman in nearly five years. At the hearing, he has a chance to see me, and I have a chance to speak my piece. I become emotional. I tell him it's been a long road, that I've spent a lot of time in high-security prisons and two years in a cement box, and that I kept using heroin for a few years into prison. I tell him I've done everything I can to get my life back together, and now I spend all of my free time either working on building a career or being with my family. I think he hears me. He says he knows it's been difficult, and that he's confident I'm on my way to a promising life. I feel like the hearing has turned a negative into a positive.

After my violation, I have to wear an adhesive sweat-absorbing patch on my shoulder. It's designed to be tamper-proof, and the probation office will switch it out for drug testing once a week. I hate leaving the office with something of theirs attached to my body. At first, I have an allergic reaction to the patch: my eyes itch badly and my hands swell, and I have to go to an urgent care center to get an epinephrine shot. The patch, which has a serial number on it, is also

Family portraits with Pappy and Oma.

embarrassing. It's summer, and it pains me that when my shirt is off at Mom's house, my brothers and sister can see it. Sometimes I tell people the patch is a homeopathic screener for toxins. My P.O. agrees to at least move it to my back.

I'm ambivalent about my other obligations. I like my sober companion, whose name is, of all things, Mescal; and AA and NA are great programs that have given hope to a lot of people who were hopeless. I find it inspiring to hear other addicts' stories. But I happened to overcome my addiction in a weird and painful way that I'd never recommend to anyone else. I'm not sure the Twelve Steps are for me. And in my group therapy session, every Wednesday evening and way uptown, I feel miscast. The rest of the group are kids between twenty and twenty-eight, from very wealthy families, who are currently running wild with drugs and booze. I kind of become the big brother in the group, dispensing advice, which is something I'd like to do more of in the future.

In the spring of 2017, Viviane and I get wonderful news. She is pregnant. We'd been trying. *Phew.* I guess my sperm wasn't eradicated by my drug use. And I'm going to have a child, which is something I very much want.

When I tell Mom, she's really excited, even gleeful. "I can't wait for you to have your own kid," she says. "Now you're going to see what I went through." She says she hopes I won't unconsciously perpetuate my own family dynamics, which she calls "the invisible cross."

I don't tell Dad the news right away. I know him. I'm pretty sure that he'll think I'm not in the best place to be having a kid. That a child could be a financial millstone, for one thing. Sometimes I worry that Dad sees me as a burden and doesn't entirely trust that I will stay on the path I'm on.

When I call Dad to tell him the news, he's quiet. Then he says, "Okay." He's quiet again. I say, "All right, okay, Dad." I hang up. My feelings are hurt. Two days later, he starts calling my phone, and I don't return the calls. When I get home that evening, there's a message on the answering machine for Viviane: it's Dad and Catherine and the kids congratulating us and saying how excited they are, and how Catherine wants to be called "Zeze" and Dad wants to be called "Bubba." It's nice. I call Dad. "I just needed a little time to digest the news, Cam." He invites me up to Bedford.

When I go there for the weekend, Carys and Dylan are excited about the baby on the way, and Dad already seems to have come around on the subject. He says he thinks I'm ready for it, and that it's going to be a good thing. He knows I'm planning on moving to L.A. as soon as the judge permits it, but thinks it might be a better idea for me to stay on the East Coast, where I'll have family around. I don't really envision him or Mom doing much baby duty, but in time I'll find that I'm mistaken.

Viviane and I go in for an ultrasound and see the baby moving all over the place. It's a girl. I'm glad. Somehow it seems simpler, for me anyway. Viviane suggests a name, Lua, the Portuguese word for moon, which I like. For a middle name, I suggest Izzy, as Pappy was known before he became Kirk. Lua Izzy Douglas.

My relationship with Viviane is extremely different from my past ones. I'm approaching life in a very different way, with a functioning moral compass. I saw Amanda a few times after I got out of prison, but the old bitterness quickly rose to the surface, and we don't talk anymore. I've spoken with Erin on the phone, but I really have no business being in touch with her, given my relationship with Viviane.

June 14, 2017, is the one-year anniversary of my release from prison. Since I got out, whenever I've seen people I haven't seen in a long time, they've all had the same reaction: surprise. I think they assumed I'd emerge from prison a mess, and they see that I'm in the best place I've ever been.

Their surprise is understandable. Most people in prison, in my experience, are slowly degraded over time. The longer they're in there, the more diminished they become as people. Someone who made a mistake spends years in that element, surrounded by those people, making those ties, and now you have a real criminal on your hands. The time breeds anger, resentment, and prejudice. You carry these things with you, and you try to keep them at bay, but they're there; and the longer you're in there, the more they stack up. It's all you can do to hang on to whatever positive changes you've made.

I was a hard case, and it seems like I needed to learn my lesson the hard way. It was only in the depths of bleakness, when all my hope was gone and I could barely get out of my rack each morning, that I started to turn things around and try to make each day mean something. And it was a couple of years after that that I finally saw that heroin didn't fit with my new priorities, and finally stopped doing it.

In July, I learn that my childhood friend Hans died two years ago. I was at Danbury then, and we'd spoken on the phone just months earlier. I'm surprised I didn't hear about it from our mutual friends.

When I get the news, I rub my head and shake it. My voice gets husky. What a fucking shame. Hans had wanted to come and visit. I'd told him it didn't make sense at that point, but I'd see him after my release.

I find a couple of articles about him online. One, which describes Hans as a "transient," says he choked his girlfriend unconscious with a cord at the Premier Inn in Thousand Oaks, California, and left her for dead. After he fled, she came to and called 911. Police arrested Hans in Venice Beach and charged him with attempted murder. While he was being held in a jail in Ventura, he hung himself in his cell. He was thirty-eight.

Hans and his girlfriend had been on their way to Orange County. It probably had something to do with meth; Hans was in a meth cycle. God, you just turn into such a fiend. That's what the lifestyle has in store for you. Either you change, or you go to prison for the rest of your life, or you die, or you, I don't know, squirm through life. There comes a time when the party's over and . . . what do you want to do with your life? You had your days of being a wild stallion, and there was an appeal to it, and it was cute to some, and you were tough and doing all these crazy things. Then that ends, and what remains is just wreckage. It's not cute anymore. It's not cool. It's not crazy. It's just disgusting. Unfortunately, when you get to that point, you're so roped in that for some people, like me, nothing short of a monumental, life-changing bomb exploding has even a chance of changing things.

I think about what my life would look like if I'd never been arrested and gone to prison, if I was still out there, just living that borderline existence that I'd always told myself I never would—barely making it, far from living at the level I'd been aiming for. Is there a chance I'd be a successful, extremely rich, worldwide drug dealer? A small one, I guess. But more likely than not, I'd be in some fucking hotel room, acting like a fool.

So many moments, when I look back on them, could have ended differently, and so much worse, than they did. Fuck, I don't even know where to begin. More friends dying. Me being killed. Me killing someone. All these terrible things were very real possibilities that didn't materialize. What did materialize was my doing a lengthy prison sentence. So when I went to prison, and even when I got my time doubled, part of me felt like: *This is fair.*

I can almost say I feel blessed by my prison experience. Not in every way, but it was in prison that I began to get my life together. I got my priorities together. I answered questions about myself that I'd always had. When I went in I was thirty, but mentally I was seventeen. Right up until my arrest, I wore my pants sagging all the way down, like I had my whole life. I'd always wondered: *At what point do you pull up your pants?* Then I got to thirty, and it still hadn't happened, and I was like: *I guess never.* I kept doing it through my entire time in prison. But when I was released, I found that I rarely did it anymore. I'd gone into prison a boy, and I came out a man.

One afternoon in New York, Viviane and I go to a party on the roof of a hotel. Back in the day, I'd have rolled up with five guys, cut to the front of the line, received comped drink tickets, and generally been lavished with VIP treatment. Now I wait in line like everyone else.

I'm wearing white pants, a blue collared shirt, and red boat shoes. It's a beautiful evening, and we listen to music and take in the sunset while I catch up with old friends. But I also find myself wondering: *What am I doing here?* It's a struggle to make small talk. We have to yell to hear each other. Nightlife isn't that appealing to me right now.

Viviane and I leave, and as we walk downstairs a good-looking guy on the way up, a little taller and younger than me, gives me a once-over and says: "Fucking clown." I've never, even in prison, been so blatantly disrespected. Without thinking, I jump on him, grab him, and start hitting him. He instantly wilts and folds. Viviane is hitting me and biting me, and I snap out of it. A couple of security guys pull me off the kid. I say, "I'm here with my girlfriend, she's pregnant, I didn't come here looking for trouble."

The security guys escort me out to the street. I don't know if the kid recognized me, but I get really lucky. No one took out a phone and snapped a picture. No one Instagrams it. The kid could have called the police, and he would have just gotten kicked out of the party; I would have had to go before Judge Berman, and very possibly could have been sent back to prison.

Viviane is angry that she had to get in the middle of it, and scared by my reactiveness. So am I. The next day, when I have time to reflect on what happened, I feel a deep shiver of fear at how easily that one moment could have led me back down a terrible path.

For so long, I was seeking confirmation of my toughness. From my early teenage years, no matter what I did, it was never quite enough. I always needed more. Now, for the first time in maybe twenty-five years, I'm not looking for more confirmation. But prison made me very sensitive about establishing my space and boundaries. It ingrained in me how important it is not to give anyone the idea that you're a pushover. I avoided a lot of problems that way. But I'm the last person who can afford to get in a fight now. And fighting is hardly the only way to show toughness or command respect outside of prison. I try to stay away from crowded situations. It's hard, since I ride the subway all over the place.

Dr. Kaminski talks about planning for the past, instead of planning for the future. He means making decisions based on how you'll look back on them. I want to look back on this time and have good memories. I'm trying to enjoy the moment.

I'm continuously adjusting to a different, non-prison way of thinking. My initial spite toward people I didn't feel had been in touch enough while I was in prison melts away, and I reach out to some of them, like my old friend Taylor. Now I see, being out here myself, that life is going on. It's a little more complicated out here, and the tit-for-tat prison mentality doesn't really apply. I recalibrate my expectations for people.

I'm still capable of feeling hope, but now, instead of using it to rationalize terrible things, I apply it to realistic, healthy goals. I still value the thrill of adrenaline, but where I used to get it by sticking up liquor stores or getting in fights, I now know that I can get it by landing jobs, finding success, competing healthily, traveling, trying new things, being inspired. It's a good feeling: I'm doing what I said I was going to do. I'm reaping what I sowed during those dark, difficult years in prison.

There's that old saying: *When the student is ready, the teacher will appear.* My teacher just had to be razor wire, hardened felons, and the loss of my liberty. How else would I ever have found myself in a situation where I was alone, surrounded by enemies, and had to come to terms with that? After a lifetime of cocooning myself in groups of people, unable to be comfortable by myself and needing everybody to like me, I learned to truly be on my own and be okay with that. It gave me confidence. It taught me something about myself. Having to push forward alone through adversity was the missing piece that I desperately needed in order to have a fulfilling, productive life. It's also an essential quality for an actor, and I don't know how else I would have achieved it. I was such a stubborn person, so stuck in my ways.

That's something I'm trying to make up for now. I wasn't around a lot for my family during those years. I didn't feel guilty then, but I do now. I'm sorry I wasn't a more productive and involved family member for all that time. Now I'm trying to be as present as possible.

I feel overdue gratitude. Mom and Dad have supported me long after their parental obligations required them to do so. I've caused both of them a lot of pain, and they've never turned away from me. When I was in solitary, Mom's daily letter writing to me verged on heroic. Because of the regular long drives she made to visit me, bringing my siblings with her each time, I have close bonds with each of them, which I cherish. Now that I'm out, I see them and Mom every week.

Dad, too, wrote and visited consistently, and he has spent a lot of money over the years getting me out of jams of my own creation. He still bounces around a lot, but when he's in town we make a point of seeing each other. I've always enjoyed watching sports with Dad, but I want to find another activity we can do together. He's been playing golf for twenty years and is obsessed with it. I used to go with Granny to her country club, where she played, and I'd hit the ball every now and then. Now I take my first lesson, an hour with a pro at Chelsea

Piers. Even wearing gloves, I get serious blisters. The pro says I'm sort of a gorilla: I hold the club too tight and try to hit the ball too hard. But I connect with it, and think there's some potential.

On a Saturday in early July, I fly out to L.A. to visit Pappy for a week. As the plane lifts off from Newark Airport, I become emotional. For eight years, the planes I saw flying over me, and made up stories about, symbolized freedom. Finally, I'm on one of them.

I arrive at Pappy's house in Beverly Hills in the afternoon, put my bags in the guesthouse, and go right into the main house to say hello. Seeing Pappy after so much time, I feel like I can let out a breath I've been holding for too long. Right away, he checks out my muscles. The next morning, we have breakfast, and it lasts three hours. He's one hundred years old, and his stamina is so impressive. He has so much curiosity, asking endless questions about prison life. "Were you in a gang? Did you fight a lot? Did you kill anyone?" Oma is here too. She's ninety-eight and also completely lucid, with an amazing memory. In the evening, we have a family dinner with Dad and Catherine and Dylan and Carys, who are in town, as well as Peter, Pappy's son with Oma, and his kids.

Over the next week, Pappy and I have breakfast together every morning and dinner most evenings. I feel grateful to have the chance to spend all this time with him, and soon we're over the hump of me being an awkward guest and us getting reacquainted. Pappy proudly shows me the pastel drawing of me and him that I'd commissioned from an inmate artist at Loretto as a gift, and which Pappy has framed and hung on his bedroom wall. I show him my tattoo of him and Dad. I'm not sure how he'll react, given Dad's seeming discomfort, but Pappy is really taken with it. Every time a guest comes over, Pappy calls me over and has me show off my abs.

And actually, Dad says something nice about it too. He and I have lunch most days while I'm here. One day, he says to Pappy, "Hey, Dad, did you see the tattoo Cameron got of us?" Pappy says, "Yeah, it's amazing. What do you think, Michael?" Dad says, in front of me, that he feels honored and that it's really good work. The men in my family have notoriously thin legs, and Dad also makes a point of showing off my muscular legs to Pappy. It's nice to watch them interact; they have a lot of love and respect for each other. There are also traces of the rivalry that has always been part of their relationship. Pappy keeps bringing up how much Dad was recently paid for one week's work in China, which he can't get over.

I'm itching to work, but I'm trying to be discerning. I turn down an offer from *American Idol*'s producers to be the subject of a reality show. I've read a lot of scripts over the past year, and so many of them are bad. Finally Dechen Thurman, one of Viviane's mentors at Jivamukti, brings me something interesting, a short film a friend of his is making called *Dead Layer*. I've been hired to play a graffiti artist who's trying to make it as a gallery artist when he gets caught up in a murder. I also recently completed my first paid, post-prison acting gig. Pappy's putting out an audiobook version of a collection of letters between him and Oma, and I did his voice for the letters, going to the publisher's offices in Manhattan to record it.

While I'm in L.A., I have a good meeting with agents at United Talent Agency, who've agreed to represent me. A year ago, I met with one of them in New York and got the distinct sense that he was there only as a favor to someone. This meeting, the feeling is very different, and I don't question their sincerity. If agents feel like you can help them further their careers, they're all in, so their enthusiasm is reassuring. But when they ask if I can come back out to L.A. for auditions in the near future, I have to say no, not yet. My pot violation has slowed down the timeline for a move. It's frustrating.

While I'm here, though, they've booked a couple of auditions for me. One is for the part of a religious leader in a sci-fi trilogy, *Chaos Walking*, cowritten by Charlie Kaufman, with Doug Liman set to direct. It's a video audition, as an increasing number of auditions are these days, and I film a bunch of takes on my iPhone. I go over them with Dad. He tells me which ones he thinks are best and what to do differently next time. He says not to push so hard, because I have a strong presence naturally. Dad, talking about the acting lifestyle, has told me, "Hopefully the good things outweigh the bad things." He has also said it takes "ninety percent hard work, ten percent talent."

The other audition is with a major casting director. On the way to meet her, I take the same street I used to drive to get to Granny's house in Sherman Oaks. I think about Granny often, and really wish that I could see her and she could see me now. For today's audition I've memorized the text, and the casting director feeds me my first line. Then I freeze, my mind blank. The words come back, but when I leave I don't feel great about my performance. Later, my agent says the casting director is notoriously prickly and cold and I shouldn't be offended. That's my first inkling that maybe things went okay, because actually she was really warm and enthusiastic about my acting; and then my agents get positive feedback from her too.

I'm hoping to move here in the next few months, and, optimistically, I spend a fair amount of my time in L.A. looking for a house to rent. Driving around the city, I can't get over how much it has changed since I was last here. It's weird to see all these stores selling marijuana legally. The development is nonstop. It feels like every third car is a Tesla. I'm struck anew by the size of the freeways—five, six lanes in each direction. The traffic is still terrible, maybe worse. Now it's bad even during off-peak hours. I wonder if Uber has something to do with that. Even the Hills are now crawling with cars following Waze-suggested shortcuts. It seems like there are a lot more people everywhere than there used to be.

I drive around the flats of West Hollywood, down Sunset and Franklin, places where I spent a lot of time in the years before my arrest. I pass storage places, UPS stores, gas stations I pulled into a million times. When I see my dear old friend Isaac, who I used to break dance with, and his family, we end up eating lunch at Swingers, a restaurant on the ground floor of the Beverly Laurel, my old hideout. I look up through the hotel sign to the corner room behind it where I used to stay all the time. These are the same places as before, but they feel a world apart. My life was so different then, and it seems like a lifetime ago.

I'd love to live near the beach, but you get less for your dollar there, and, what with the traffic, I also don't want to be so far from the studios. I move my house hunt to the Hollywood Hills, which I know and like. I think I nail down a place, but the owner decides to go with another family, which is a bummer. I imagine that my legal status may have something to do with it.

Back in New York, Judge Berman gives me the go-ahead to move to L.A., but in the meantime my apartment lease is expiring, so I fill out a bunch of applications for places to move into as a stopgap. I'm in a much better position than most other ex-cons, but I keep getting turned down. My broker says that the landlords get prickly right after they do a background check on me. Finally, Viviane and I move into an Airbnb in Hell's Kitchen, which Viv can book in her name. It's me and Viv and two dogs and, soon, a baby in a 650-square-foot space. My huge houseplant, George, takes up literally 5 percent of the apartment.

It's funny: Dad is starting to get really involved in my plans. We talk for an hour on the phone, and he says, "Cam, you have to realize, I'm the grandfather of this child, I want to make sure your priorities are in the right order." It's nice. For my birthday, as I turn thirty-nine, Dad takes me out for a sushi lunch at Zuma. We talk and laugh, and he gives me fatherly advice about money and relationships, which I appreciate, as well as his old car, which is still pretty sharp. When I get his and Catherine's Christmas card, I see that it says it's from them and Dylan and Carys and me, with a photo of us all. It feels good to be included.

On the night of December 17, when Viviane is scheduled to be induced, there's a big football game between Pittsburgh and New England, and Viviane is such a good sport, seeing how much I'm enjoying the game, that she puts off our trip to the hospital until it's over. At NewYork–Presbyterian, on the East River, a nurse and I take turns supporting Viviane as she goes through labor. Viviane really wants to have a natural childbirth, but after hours of pushing, the ob-gyn convinces her that she should have a C-section. I scrub up and join her in the operating room, peeking over the curtain to make sure everything's going smoothly. Finally, Lua is born. She's 7 pounds, 9.3 ounces. A nurse hands her to me, and while the doctors sew Viviane up, I sit in the other room, holding my new daughter as we look into each other's eyes. She's so beautiful.

Last Christmas, I was at the halfway house. This is my first Christmas with my family, and I spend it at Mom's house. She does a beautiful job. My relationship with her is really good. When the twins are done with high school, she wants to follow me to California with Imara. Her years of drama, which took a real toll on her, are well behind her. To pave the way for a West Coast move, she has already put her farm on the market and is looking to downsize her city home. Having a child does change how I see Mom and Dad. I already have more respect for them, a glimpse of insight into what they were going through with each other and with me, and a new appreciation for them. I also now have another thing—parenting—in common with them.

"Alexa, change your location to California. What's the weather forecast?"

"The forecast in New York City is partly cloudy, with a forty percent chance of rain."

"*Alexa,* recalibrate your system to California. What's the weather going to be like today?"

"The weather in New York City is partly cloudy, with a forty percent chance of rain."

Jesus fucking Christ.

Anyway, we've moved into a beautiful house in the Hills, and the weather here has been predictably amazing.

Truck loves it. Every morning I put on shorts, no shirt, and Chucks, and walk him to some vacant land next door to us, where we play fetch with a tennis ball and Truck takes dips in the swimming pool of a neighbor who, kindly, doesn't seem to mind. It feels like people are nicer out here, which takes some getting used to. In New York, you keep your eyes down. Here, people are chatty and have no hesitation about asking a lot of questions.

My new P.O. is a straitlaced, thorough, by-the-book guy, with a big office downtown. The first time I meet him, he tells me I need to register with the LAPD.

"What, like I'm a pedophile?"

"Yeah," he says. There are three crimes that require it: arson, sex offenses, and drug offenses.

The ghosts of my past keep showing up. On my drive back from a looping session for *Dead Layer* in Burbank, I pass the Chevron where I used to meet with Gabriel, and the Carl's Jr. parking lot where I'd meet my heroin dealer. I've found an NA meeting I like, in Venice Beach, and every time I drive there I pass the building on Sawtelle where I was living when I was arrested with a gun and sent to county jail for six months.

Ideally, I'd like to land a part in one of the flood of great new TV shows coming out. A bunch of auditions, including one for a part opposite Elizabeth Banks in an indie film, come and go without callbacks. I want so much for myself, and from myself. I struggle to be patient.

Because there was a time when everything did come to me—and I took it for granted and blew it—I have to catch myself when I'm feeling that everything *should* come to me. It's an attitude, unconscious if I'm not vigilant, that before I went to prison made me feel like: *I'm important, people should come to me with offers. What do you have for me?* Even when I came home from prison, I probably still had it. I need to get over it. It just takes away from me going out and doing the legwork and pushing to succeed. One day, after moving to L.A., I meet with Jeremy Barber, a partner at UTA, and he's up-front and honest with me: I have a hole to dig myself out of, and I need to take acting seriously if I want to be taken seriously. There are a lot of talented people out here working their asses off. It's been a learning curve. Finally, I feel open and not defensive, and ready to see and understand my sense of entitlement and how it gets in my way.

Everything takes time. I try to be satisfied with steady, incremental progress. These are the ups and downs of life, which I insulated myself from during all those years of addiction. I'm giving it my best shot, understanding that it's not always going to go my way. I'm more accepting of uncertainty now. I don't need instant gratification the way I used to. For better or worse, I'm optimistic. I've always been my own worst enemy, but I've never doubted I could be an actor.

Looking back on it, I feel like I've been acting for most of my life in one sense or another, and doing a pretty good job of it. Now I'm trying to do something worthwhile and make a career out of it. I hope that one day people will look at me and my past and find hope and inspiration.

My time in prison is never far from my thoughts. I think about my friends; about Talib. He's up for parole again, in the next six months. It will be so tragic if he's turned down again. He was convicted of violent crimes, but he was a juvenile, and he's done everything imaginable to merit release. I pray he'll get it. (And, in August, he will!)

Flipping through channels on TV one night, I stumble on *Intervention*, the drug rehab show that Candy Finnigan, my old interventionist, is on. I've never actually seen the show before, and I watch the episode. It brings up so many memories about the stranglehold of addiction, and I'm really moved.

Viviane is a great mother, and we're a good team. She had some professional goals moving out here, which she's already beginning to accomplish. I feel like we're doing a really good job, between us, in raising Lua. She's a happy little girl, developing so quickly. Viviane and I both like it out here.

One morning, I drive up to Santa Barbara. I haven't been there in nearly ten years. It's nice to be back behind the wheel of a car. I like the tranquility of driving on the open road. I've spent so much of my life around groups of people—in cities, nightclubs, prisons—and now I feel a sense of peace and quiet in my chest.

I start out on 101, the inland route. I used to make this drive all the time. There are fewer cops here than on the Pacific Coast Highway,

With Lua Izzy Douglas.

and this was the way I'd come when I was driving with kilos of meth or coke in my trunk. I didn't have a driver's license, other than a Bermudan one I kept on me just in case. Especially if I was high, it would be easy to mindlessly start speeding, which could create a problem, so I'd always use cruise control and try to stay with the flow of traffic. One less thing to worry about. Now I use cruise control for the hell of it. It's a good feeling to not worry, to know that I'm not doing anything I could get in trouble for.

I cut over to the PCH. Driving through the canyons near Topanga, I'm struck by the beauty. I don't believe in an interventionist God, but the nature here is proof to me of a grand intelligence behind it. In Malibu, I pass Neptune's Net, a restaurant where Dad took me when I was young. I remember him almost getting into a fight with a pair of hippies there who were arguing and cursing in front of me. I see a bunch of surfers out on the water, and I muse about their simple, idyllic lives.

But everyone's life is complex, if not complicated. I know people look at me and assume I have it easy. I pass some steep dunes. Once, when I was a kid, and Pappy was bringing me home after Cirque du Soleil, we pulled over here, and I climbed to the top of them and slid down. Driving through Oxnard, I pass the bar where I tried to kidnap Kevin, the high school friend who stole $11,000 from me. If I were to see him now, I know that any anger I might still feel wouldn't overtake me.

The drive becomes a montage of my childhood. Golf N' Stuff, which had my favorite arcade. Rincon, a surf spot I loved. The Golden Nugget, where I'd go with my friend John for breakfast. The Spot, for burgers. Stacky's Seaside. Big Yellow House. Summerland. In Santa Barbara, I drive down State Street, past the Dolphin Fountain where I once crashed with a Secret Service agent hanging off my car. Out onto the Santa Barbara pier, which has been rebuilt after burning down a year after my crash there.

In Montecito, I see news vans and the aftermath of the recent mudslides. There was so much destruction. I pass the house Mom and Todd were going to move into. I pull into the driveway of the house on Hot Springs Road where I grew up. There's major construction underway. I get out of the car and pick some jasmine, my favorite-smelling flower, and rub it between my fingers, bringing it to my nose and inhaling.

In July, I get permission to make a short trip back to Spain, where Mom is spending the summer with Imara and Hawk and Hudson. I haven't been back in a decade, and returning to S'Estaca, my favorite place on earth, is a healing experience. I feel lighter and refreshed, like some of the darkness that has clung to me has been washed away.

My first night here, Mom takes me to dinner at a little restaurant on the Cala Deià where we always used to go. At S'Estaca, Juán makes red wines, including one called Cameron Reserva, which he has made for years. The restaurant, which is only open during the busy season, and whose owners have known Mom since she was a child, has kept a bottle of it since I went to prison, setting it out on the bar at the start of each season and packing it back up at the end. We take a boat to get to the restaurant. I have a happy reunion with the restaurant owners, who've known me since I was a kid. They suggest that we open the bottle, but we decide it might not taste the best, so we may as well leave it up there. Forty-five minutes into the meal, a handful of my childhood friends who I haven't seen in years arrive. Oro, who now has a wife and two teenagers. Sam. Eva and her cousin Maria.

That night, there's a near-eclipse of the moon, and it gets super red. After dinner, we pack into a boat to go look at it. On our way out to sea, I witness the most amazing shooting star of my life, with a long tail and appearing very close. When we're out a ways, Sam, who's always been wild, says he's going to swim back to shore. That sounds pretty amazing to me, and I jump in first. The phosphorescence is active, and we trail glowing streamers behind us as we swim. I flip onto my back and just float there, looking up at the stars. The sky is so clear, and we're so far from a city, that it feels like we're in a planetarium. After all the years in prison when I fantasized about the future, now I close my eyes and imagine I'm back behind bars, then open them, taking in the sea and the sky and the stars and letting my appreciation for my freedom fill me.

Without forgiveness, our species would've annihilated itself in endless retributions. Without forgiveness, there would be no history. Without that hope, there would be no art, for every work of art is in some way an act of forgiveness. Without that dream, there would be no love, for every act of love is in some way a promise to forgive. We live on because we can love, and we love because we can forgive.

—Gregory David Roberts, *Shantaram*

Out of the night that covers me,
　　Black as the Pit from pole to pole,
I thank whatever gods may be
　　For my unconquerable soul.

In the fell clutch of circumstance
　　I have not winced nor cried aloud.
Under the bludgeonings of chance
　　My head is bloody, but unbowed.

Beyond this place of wrath and tears
　　Looms but the Horror of the shade.
And yet the menace of the years
　　Finds, and shall find, me unafraid.

It matters not how strait the gate,
　　How charged with punishments the scroll,
I am the master of my fate:
　　I am the captain of my soul.

—William Ernest Henley, "Invictus"

Acknowledgments

I'd like to acknowledge all those who have contributed to my journey thus far, both positively and negatively. You have my gratitude for helping to shape the man I am today.

Also to those special few whose direct contributions to the making of this book have been invaluable:

Benjamin Wallace, in particular. Thank you, my friend, for your guidance and your gift.

Janis Donnaud and Peter Gethers. Each of you is an integral piece of this work.

And: Brett Rapkin, for your keen insight and honesty.

The quote on page 280 is from "Dirge" by Stevie Smith, which appeared in *Mother, What Is Man?* (Jonathan Cape, 1942), and the quote on page 301 is from *Shantaram* by Gregory David Roberts (Scribe, 2003).

Illustration Credits

Pages 2–6: Courtesy of the author

Page 11: Judie Burstein/Zuma

Page 18: Courtesy of the author

Page 21: Courtesy of the Michael Douglas Collection, Howard Gotlieb Archival Research Center at Boston University

Page 24: Courtesy of Annie Leibovitz and Jann Wenner

Page 29: Courtesy of the Michael Douglas Collection, Howard Gotlieb Archival Research Center at Boston University

Page 30: Courtesy of the author

Page 36: © Maddy Miller

Pages 46–78: Courtesy of the Michael Douglas Collection, Howard Gotlieb Archival Research Center at Boston University

Page 89: Michael Montfort

Page 97: WENN

Pages 105–158: Courtesy of the Michael Douglas Collection, Howard Gotlieb Archival Research Center at Boston University

Page 172: Courtesy of the author

Page 184: Courtesy of the Michael Douglas Collection, Howard Gotlieb Archival Research Center at Boston University

Page 188: Adam Nemser/PhotoLink

Page 196: Jim Henderson

Page 204: Courtesy of the Michael Douglas Collection, Howard Gotlieb Archival Research Center at Boston University

Page 227: Ben Marsh

Page 242: Courtesy of the Michael Douglas Collection, Howard Gotlieb Archival Research Center at Boston University

Page 244: Courtesy of the author

Page 249: Courtesy of the Michael Douglas Collection, Howard Gotlieb Archival Research Center at Boston University

Page 252: Courtesy of the author

Page 295: BOP website

Pages 302–334: Courtesy of the author

Page 342: Courtesy of the Michael Douglas Collection, Howard Gotlieb Archival Research Center at Boston University

Pages 351–379: Courtesy of the author